SACRED LANGUAGES AND SACRED TEXTS

Sacred Languages and Sacred Texts is the first comprehensive study of the role of languages and texts in the religions of the Greco-Roman world, including Judaism and Christianity.

It explores bilingualism, language learning, literacy, book production and translation, as well as more explicitly religious factors, including beliefs about language, missionary zeal, ritual, unintelligibility, conservatism and the power of the priestly establishment.

Sacred Languages and Sacred Texts sheds new light on the role of the power of words, spoken and written, in religion.

Professor John Sawyer, formerly Head of Religious Studies at Newcastle University, is now Senior Research Fellow in Hebrew and Biblical Interpretation at Lancaster University. He is the author of *The Fifth Gospel. Isaiah in the History of Christianity* (1996) and the Religion Editor of the ten-volume *Encyclopaedia of Language and Linguistics* (1994).

RELIGION IN THE FIRST CHRISTIAN CENTURIES
Edited by Deborah Sawyer and John Sawyer, Lancaster University

Too often the religious traditions of antiquity are studies in isolation, without any real consideration of how they interacted. What made someone with a free choice become an adherent of one faith rather than another? Why might a former pagan choose to become a 'Godfearer' and attend synagogue services? Why might a Jew become a Christian? How did the mysteries of Mithras differ from the worship of the Unconquered Sun, or the status of the Virgin Mary from that of Isis, and how many gods could an ancient worshipper have? These questions are hard to answer without a synoptic view of what the different religions offered.

The aim of the books in this series is to survey particular themes in the history of religion across the different religions of antiquity and to set up comparisons and contrasts, resonances and discontinuities, and thus reach a profounder understanding of the religious experience in the ancient world. Topics to be covered will include: women, conversion, language, death, magic, sacrifice and purity.

Also available in this series:

WOMEN AND RELIGION IN THE FIRST CHRISTIAN CENTURIES
Deborah F. Sawyer

THE CRUCIBLE OF CHRISTIAN MORALITY
J. Ian H. McDonald

SACRED LANGUAGES AND SACRED TEXTS

John F.A. Sawyer

London and New York

First published 1999
by Routledge
11 New Fetter Lane, London EC4P 4EE
Simultaneously published in the USA and Canada
by Routledge
29 West 35th Street, New York, NY 10001

Routledge Ltd is a Taylor & Francis Group company

© 1999 John F.A. Sawyer

The right of John F.A. Sawyer to be identified as the author of this
work has been asserted by him in accordance with the Copyright,
Designs and Patents Act 1988

Typeset in Garamond by Routledge
Printed and bound in Great Britain by MPG Books Ltd, Bodmin

British Library Cataloguing in Publication Data
A catalogue record for this book is available from the British Library

Library of Congress Cataloging in Publication Data
Sacred languages and sacred texts/John F.A. Sawyer.
Includes bibliographical references and index.
1. Language and languages – Religious aspects –
History. 2. Rome – Languages – Religious aspects
– History. 3. Sacred books – History and criticism.
4. Bible – Language, Style. I. Title. II. Series.
BL65.L2S25   1999   98–54120
291.8'2–dc21   CIP

ISBN   0–415–12546–4 (hbk)
ISBN   0–415–12547–2 (pbk)

IN MEMORY
OF
JIM, NAN AND MARGARET

"IT MAY BE WE SHALL TOUCH
THE HAPPY ISLES, AND SEE THE
GREAT ACHILLES, WHOM WE
KNEW."

CONTENTS

Acknowledgements   *viii*
Abbreviations   *ix*

1 Introduction   1

2 The language situation   9

3 Sacred languages   23

4 Literacy   44

5 Canonization   59

6 Translation   76

7 Beliefs and controls   96

8 Names and numbers   112

9 Styles and strategies   129

10 Interpretation   143

11 Conclusion   162

Bibliography   *171*
Index   *183*

ACKNOWLEDGEMENTS

I am extremely grateful to many people for their expert advice on specific matters: of these I would single out James Russell, Max Sussman, Anthony Bryer, Sebastian Brock, Alan Millard and the late Michael Weitzman. I also benefited enormously from my work with the authors and editors of the magnificent *Encyclopedia of Language and Linguistics* (Pergamon, 1994) of which I was privileged to be Religion Editor, and currently with Seumas Simpson as co-editor of the forthcoming *Concise Encyclopedia of Language and Religion* (Elsevier, 2000). In addition to the University Libraries of Newcastle upon Tyne and Lancaster where much of my recent research has been based, I gladly acknowledge my debt to the John Rylands Library in Manchester and the Library of the Pontifical Biblical Institute in Rome.

For general advice and encouragement during all stages in the production process, I must mention the editorial staff at Routledge, especially Richard Stoneman, Coco Stevenson, Wendy Lees and Ceri Prenter, and for help with this little monograph, as with other projects, past, present and future, the series co-editor, Deborah Sawyer.

John F.A. Sawyer
Rome

ABBREVIATIONS

ABD	Anchor Bible Dictionary (ed.) D.N. Freedman, 6 volumes (1982) New York: Doubleday
ANEP	Pritchard, J.B. (ed.) (1969b) *Ancient Near Eastern Pictures Relating to the Old Testament*
ANET	Pritchard, J.B. (ed.) (1969a) *Ancient Near Eastern Texts Relating to the Old Testament*
BT	Babylonian Talmud (tractate titles abbreviated as in Danby (1933) Cant. R. Midrash Rabbah, Song of Songs)
CHB	Ackroyd, P.R. and Evans, C.E. (eds) (1970) *Cambridge History of the Bible*, vol. 1
DBI	Coggins, R.J. and Houlden, J.L. (eds) (1990) *Dictionary of Biblical Interpretation*
DSST	Martinez, F. Garcia (ed.) (1994) *The Dead Sea Scrolls Translated: The Qumran Texts in English*
EH	Eusebius, *Ecclesiastical History*
ELL	Asher, R.E. (ed.) (1994) *Encyclopedia of Language and Linguistics,* 10 vols.
Exod. R.	Midrash Rabbah, Exodus
Gen. R.	Midrash Rabbah, Genesis
IDBS	Crim, K.R. (ed.) (1976) *Interpreter's Dictionary of the Bible, Supplementary Volume*
JE	(1903) *Jewish Encyclopedia*, 10 vols
JSS	*Journal of Semitic Studies*
JT	Jerusalem Talmud (tractate titles abbreviated as in Danby (1933))
LPAW	Bowman, A.K. and Woolf, G. (eds) (1994) *Literacy and Power in the Ancient World*
M	Mishnah (tractate titles abbreviated as in Danby (1933))

NTA	Hennecke, E., Schneemelcher, W. and Wilson, R. Mcl, (eds) (1963–5) *New Testament Apocrypha*, 2 vols
OCD	Hornblower, S. and Spawforth, A. (eds) (1996) *Oxford Classical Dictionary*, 3rd edn
OTP	Charlesworth, J.H. (ed.) (1983–85) *The Old Testament Pseudepigrapha*, 2 vols
POTT	Wiseman, D.J. (ed.) (1973) *Peoples of Old Testament Times*
RA	Montefiore, C.G. and Loewe, H. (eds) (1963) *A Rabbinic Anthology*
VT	*Vetus Testamentum*

1

INTRODUCTION

Until comparatively recently scholars working on Jewish and Christian scripture in antiquity, and the primary biblical languages, Hebrew, Aramaic and Greek, have often tended to work in isolation. Jewish Studies specialists concentrated on the Hebrew and Aramaic sources, frequently neglecting relevant Greek, Latin and Syriac data. Old Testament experts were rarely interested in what happened to the Hebrew text after the end of the 'Old Testament period' (second century BCE) and after it was translated into other languages. New Testament scholars often knew little or no Hebrew and Aramaic. A whole field of study, known by the bizarre and tendentious title 'Intertestamental Studies', had to be invented to deal with all the other parts of Jewish and Christian scripture traditionally (and no less tendentiously) known as 'apocryphal' or 'pseudepigraphical'. This involved the specialist study of Ethiopic, Arabic, Armenian and other languages in which some of the texts survive, and yet another discrete compartment in the field was created.

As we approach the end of the twentieth century, however, the fragmentation of the study of the first Christian centuries into confessional, canonical compartments has begun to be a thing of the past. The Jewishness of Christian scripture, and of Christian origins generally, is now acknowledged. Students at all levels are much more aware of the need to have some knowledge of rabbinic Judaism if they want to appreciate the nuances of the Gospels and Paul. The enormous significance of works like D. Daube (1984) *The New Testament and Rabbinic Judaism*, W.D. Davies (1948) *Paul and Rabbinic Judaism*, G. Vermes (1973) *Jesus the Jew* and E.P. Sanders (1985) *Jesus and Judaism*, as well as the work of historians like Fergus Miller and Martin Goodman, who are both classicists and Jewish Studies experts, is being increasingly appreciated. Even the

1

traditional gulf separating 'patristics' from 'rabbinics' has been bridged by scholars like Peter Brown and Daniel Boyarin.

Another characteristic of recent scholarship is a fresh interest in the ancient versions of the Bible, no longer merely of marginal interest to biblical scholars who had previously consulted them merely as aids to reconstructing the original text, but as important witnesses to early religious developments in Judaism and Christianity. The Greek Septuagint, the Aramaic Targumim, the Syriac Peshitta, the Latin Vulgate and other ancient versions of the Bible are increasingly being studied as 'sacred texts' in their own right. Expensive new critical editions have been published or are in the process of being published. The same is true of all the many Jewish and Christian texts written around the same time as the later books of the Bible, though not included in the canon of the Western Church. Under the titles 'Old Testament Pseudepigrapha' and 'New Testament Apocrypha' these too are currently the subject of much research and have been published in magisterial new editions (Charlesworth 1985; Hennecke, Schneemelcher and Wilson 1963–1965; Elliott 1993) as further evidence of a change of emphasis in biblical teaching and research. Of course the discovery of the Nag Hammadi texts in Egypt and the Dead Sea Scrolls played a very important role in sparking off new interest in sectarian texts and alternative canons.

There is also a growing number of monographs on what Gadamer called Wirkungsgeschichte, that is, the 'impact-history' of the texts: the history of how a text has influenced communities and cultures down the centuries (Beuken, Freyne and Weiler 1991; Jeffreys 1992). There are now many studies in the history of interpretation, from general studies like Michael Fishbane (1985) *Biblical Interpretation in Ancient Israel* and J.F.A. Sawyer (1996) *The Fifth Gospel. Isaiah in the History of Christianity* to those devoted to one particular passage such as C.A. Evans (1989) *To See and Not Perceive. Isaiah 6:9–10 in Early Jewish and Christian Interpretation* and Jeremy Cohen (1989) *'Be Fertile and Increase, Fill the Earth and Master It.' The Ancient and Mediaeval Career of a Biblical Text.* Reception-history is now taken seriously by many biblical scholars, and the forthcoming one-volume *International Catholic Bible Commentary* (Farmer 1998) has separate sections dealing with the reception-history of selected texts; and a major new Bible commentary series in which the main focus will be on the reception-history of the text is to be published by Blackwells in the coming years. There is plenty of evidence that the compartmentalization that has for so long bedevilled the study of the Bible has begun to break down, and that the time is ripe for a fresh, interdisciplinary look at the processes involved in the writing, canonization and interpretation of the sacred texts of which it is composed.

Mention must also be made of the recent application to biblical texts of what are often loosely referred to as the new literary approaches, which are in many ways revolutionizing the study of the Bible (Alter and Kermode 1987; Carroll and Prickett 1997; cf. *The Postmodern Bible* 1995). By focusing on such concepts as reader-response (Tompkins 1980; Fowler 1991), for example, attention switches from questions of who originally wrote these texts and what they originally meant to how have they been interpreted or used in other contexts, such as liturgy, preaching and education in the early Church or ancient Judaism. The notion that a text may have many meanings, not just one, opens the way for a relatively new form of descriptive literary analysis, and one which echoes in a quite remarkable way some of the exegetical insights of the ancient Jewish and Christian commentators. The same applies to the literary critics' concept of intertextuality, which has enabled biblical scholars to handle larger texts, such as the Pentateuch and the Book of Isaiah, not to mention the Hebrew Bible (Genesis to 2 Chronicles) of Judaism and the Greek Bible (Genesis to Revelation) of Christianity, as single units as the rabbis and church fathers once did (Alter 1992).

The contribution of the social sciences to the study of sacred texts in recent years likewise cannot be overestimated. Contributions to J.N. Bremmer and F.G. Martinez (eds) (1992) *Sacred History and Sacred Texts in Early Judaism*, J.G. Davies and I. Wollaston (eds) (1993), *The Sociology of Sacred Texts*, *The Encyclopedia of Language and Linguistics* (10 volumes, 1994) and other recent publications have heightened our awareness of some of the anthropological, sociological, political, economic and sociolinguistic issues involved in the study of sacred languages and sacred texts. These include new articles by social scientists on such topics as 'myths about language', 'ritual', 'war memorials', 'blessing', 'ecstatic religion', 'taboo', 'preaching' and 'meditation'. Recent work by the anthropologist, Mary Douglas, on Leviticus and Numbers, raising entirely new questions about the origin and function of sacred language, is also relevant (Douglas 1999).

The biblical texts constitute only one part of our subject, however. The role of language and sacred texts in the religions of the Hellenistic world and late antiquity, including the cults of Isis and

Serapis, Zoroastrianism and Roman state religion, raises important issues for us to consider as well, both in their own right and as data for comparative study. Relevant questions include the use of Homer as a 'sacred text' and the translation and interpretation of Semitic religious texts into Greek, the role of Egyptian and Greek in the mystery religions, the function of Virgil's *Aeneid* and the Sibylline Books' (a collection of oracles kept by the Roman State), and the interaction between Christian Latin and Roman paganism. A thematic approach to the issues involved in these cases, alongside roughly contemporary developments in Judaism and Christianity, is likely to throw new light on both.

For the purposes of our wide-ranging study we shall treat the terms 'sacred languages' and 'sacred texts' as shorthand for languages and texts known to have had various special functions or roles within a religious context. The terms themselves are used most frequently and paradigmatically in the context of Judaism and Christianity. The Jews called Hebrew their 'sacred language', or *leshon ha-qodesh*, almost before it was called Hebrew (Weitzman 1994: 1829). The terms themselves are not used with equal regularity in all religious traditions, but very similar phenomena can be observed elsewhere. Popular beliefs about Greek, in a class by itself and distinct from all other 'barbarian' languages, and Syriac, the language of eastern Christian literature, come very close even though the actual term 'sacred language' is not used.

The term 'sacred script' has its most obvious use in relation to ancient Egypt where the terms *hieroglyphika* (*grammata*), literally 'sacred carved letters', and *hieratika* were coined by Greek observers to describe the mysterious writing systems of the Egyptian priests. The Egyptians themselves claimed that their script had been invented by Thoth, the ibis-headed god of wisdom and scholarship. They described it as 'the writing of the language of the gods', and treated it with exceptional awe and reverence. Even if the term 'sacred script' is less prominent in the Jewish sources, the relationship between Hebrew, 'the sacred language' par excellence, and the Hebrew script was also an extremely close one. Respect for it as well as beliefs about the magical powers of the Hebrew alphabet, its role in creation and the like, gave it a status not dissimilar to that of Egyptian hieroglyphics.

From the earliest times, both Jews and Christians spoke of their scriptures as 'sacred' (1 Macc. 12:9; Rom. 1:2). Rabbi Akiba is reputed to have said: 'All the scriptures are holy, but this [the Song of Songs] is the holiest of the holy' (Cant. R. 1:1). According to one of the first Bishops of Rome, the words of Jesus were 'sacred' too (1 Clem. 13:3). The importance of the written word in these two religions is unparalleled and the term 'sacred literacy' has been coined to epitomize the special relationship that existed in both religions between religion and literacy (Lane Fox 1994: 128). But once again the role of sacred texts in other traditions, for example, the Avesta in Zoroastrianism and the Sibylline Oracles in ancient Rome, offers plenty of parallels even if the term 'sacred text' is not actually used.

Similar considerations apply to the word 'canon'. Because of the unique role of scripture in Jewish and Christian tradition, discussions of canon often tend to focus exclusively on the complex and well-documented processes of canonization whereby, during the first Christian centuries, decisions were taken on which texts were canonical in which parts of the Church, which were deutero-canonical and which were excluded as extra-canonical or non-canonical. In fact similar factors also operated in other schools and libraries of late antiquity, where canons of the Orphic Hymns, the works of Pythagoras and classical writers from Homer to Virgil were established and debated, and the possibility of interaction at all levels has to be considered. Parallel developments in relation to the 'collection' of the Qur'an, the Sanskrit texts of Hinduism and the Pali canon of Buddhist scripture may also be relevant. We may also mention the use of 'canon' in modern parlance with relation to popular or scholarly perceptions of literary works. In recent years, for example, women writers have proposed an alternative canon of texts which 'explore the absences and silences in recorded history' especially as they relate to the experience of women, slaves and other marginalized groups of men and women. These would include 'cult-texts' like *The Colour Purple* by the black woman writer Alice Walker and the novel *Beloved* (1987) by Toni Morrison which, in a recent paper entitled 'Haunting the margins of history', can arguably be considered 'a sacred text' (Anderson 1993).

Our terms of reference are thus fairly wide, but I hope that despite this it will be possible to survey, within one small volume, a variety of topics normally shared out among specialists in Biblical Studies, Religious Studies, Jewish Studies, Patristics, Classics and Oriental Studies. When we come to define the chronological and geographical limits of our study, the problem is somewhat simpler. The period covered begins with the late Hellenistic age when the tradition of Greek literary scholarship had been established in Alexandria and elsewhere, the main oriental religions were spreading westwards, and the Hebrew Bible was more or less complete. It ends with the crystallization of Western orthodoxy in the creeds and councils of the fourth and fifth centuries CE, the establishment of vernacular Christianity in Egypt, Syria, Armenia, Ethiopia and elsewhere, and the compilation of the Babylonian Talmud and the Zand Avesta.

Our geographical region is roughly coterminous with, in the East, the extent of Hellenistic influence after the campaigns of Alexander the Great, and, in the West, the boundaries and influence of the Roman Empire: from Britain in the west to Armenia and Persia in the east, from southern Germany in the north to Upper Egypt and Ethiopia in the south. The region is a vast one, covering many languages, cultures and religions, but during most of this period it was sufficiently unified, on the surface at any rate, by a common language and excellent communications for us to be able to discuss the interaction between languages and religions there as a discrete object of inquiry.

In the interests of clarity we shall have two focal points around which much of the discussion will revolve: Jerusalem and Rome. No religious group has ever had such respect for its scriptures and the language in which they were written as the Jews. The story of how that came about and how it has influenced the rest of the world provides us with an ideal case study. No religious institution in the ancient world wielded as much power as the Church did once it had been established under Constantine the Great as the official religion of the Roman Empire. The major participants in our discussion will thus be Judaism and Christianity, both of which will always be seen in the wider context of the world in which they evolved towards self-definition in the first centuries CE.

Our evidence for the sacred languages and sacred texts of antiquity varies enormously, from vast numbers of clay-tablets or papyri that have lain untouched under the ground for thousands of years, more or less in their original form, to copies made by scribes in mediaeval monasteries centuries after they were first written. We have the originals of many documents from the ancient Near East, like the Egyptian 'Book of the Dead' (on papyrus), the code of the great Babylonian king, Hammurabi (on stone), and the Dead Sea Scrolls (on parchment). In other cases we have to rely entirely on written records from many hundreds of years after the native speakers of the language in which they were written had died. This is true of most of the documents we will be looking at – biblical, rabbinic, classical and Zoroastrian. The latter are in Avestan, a dialect of Old Persian which was not written down till over a thousand years after it had died out. Even then most of the resulting written texts of the Avesta were destroyed in the Islamic invasions of Iran in the seventh century, and we have to rely on summaries, quotations and copies from a much later time.

We also have to allow for the accident of archaeological discovery. We possess almost no originals from ancient Palestine apart from short inscriptions. However, we cannot assume that this means writing was a rare accomplishment and libraries non-existent, let alone that the 'people of the book' were largely illiterate and dependent on oral tradition for most of the biblical period (Niditch 1996). It is almost certainly due to chance that the earliest substantial collection of Hebrew documents, in jars hidden in caves at Qumran in the Judaean desert, come from the second century BCE and later. Allowances have to be made for the fact that even this rare find does not provide direct, contemporary evidence for the mainstream of Jewish history, but only for a small eccentric community, albeit thrown by a happy accident into the blaze of twentieth-century publicity. We have to remember that only a fraction of the literature written during the period has survived, and that in turn represents only a fraction of what was said and thought. So generalizations about the 'Hebrew mind', 'Greek thought-forms' and the like must be treated with the utmost caution.

On the other hand, written documents, whether originals or later copies, are for the most part all we have to go on. For languages and language groups without a script we have to rely on passing comments by contemporaries, which are rare and inadequate, and on place-names. Our knowledge of Gothic, Armenian, Slavonic and other languages before Christian missionaries invented scripts for them is limited. Classical writers sometimes refer to the spoken languages of 'barbarians' and their attempts at writing them down. The Druids according to Julius Caesar, for example, did not write down their religious traditions, partly to keep them secret and partly because they valued the faculty of memory so highly. That same priority given to orality for hundreds of years by the first Zoroastrian priests was probably a characteristic of many societies in the ancient world. We must not forget that there is an inevitable bias built into any approach to the study of antiquity which is entirely dependent on the chance survival of written or literary remains. With that caution, however, we cannot help but place the emphasis in this study of sacred languages on the written evidence available.

After an overview of the language situation in general, which will at the same time introduce some of the issues to be discussed in detail later (Chapter 2), our first task will be to define and describe the main sacred languages documented in antiquity and the process that led to their 'canonization' in particular religious communities (Chapter 3). Hebrew, Greek and Latin are the main ones, but there will be some discussion of the role of other languages in religious contexts, including Jewish Aramaic, Christian Syriac and Avestan. The phenomenon of glossolalia belongs to this part of our survey as well. Religious conservatism, nationalism, bilingualism and literacy are some of the factors of particular importance here. This leads to an examination of the role of writing and literacy in religion (Chapter 4). The flowering of literary scholarship in the Hellenistic world, epitomized by the great schools and libraries established in Alexandria and elsewhere, followed by an explosion in the book trade and a relatively high literacy rate in the early Roman Empire, provide the background for our discussion of the writing down of religious literature.

The canonization and translation of sacred texts provide the subjects of Chapter 5 and Chapter 6, and then we look at the elaborate system of beliefs and rules set up to protect their sacredness in Chapter 7. These include, on the one hand, notions of divine authorship and inspiration, beliefs about the role of human authors, pseudonymity, false attribution, and, in particular, the special case of the words of Jesus, and, on the other, systems of rules and regulations governing the copying and transmission of scripture. Chapter 8 is devoted to the intriguing subject of personal names, popular etymologies, wordplays, gematria and the like. Chapters 9 and 10 take a brief look at how texts interact with their audiences and what happens to them after they have become accepted as in some sense sacred, in the hands of patristic, rabbinic and pagan interpreters. The final chapter attempts to draw together a few conclusions on the relation between language and religion in general.

2

THE LANGUAGE
SITUATION

A brief look at the language situation in the first few centuries of
the Roman Empire will not only provide us with a general socio-
political and cultural background for the subject, but also introduce
us to some of the issues to be examined in detail in later chapters.
Which were the international languages of commerce and trade?
Which languages were official, state-supported languages and
which remained local or minority languages? What led to the
isolation of some languages as 'sacred'? How do political and
economic factors affect such things as education, literacy, book
production, translation and the like? What specifically religious
factors, such as missionary zeal, conservatism and the power of a
priestly hierarchy, have to be taken into account? What effect did
the translation of a sacred text from one language into another have,
if any, on the religion of those who believed it to be sacred? Does
translation from a Semitic language to an Indo-European language
(Hebrew to Greek, for example) raise particular problems? What
languages became associated with particular religions, and why?

By about 200 CE the Roman Empire appeared, on the surface at
any rate, to be characterized by a remarkable linguistic unity. The
educated classes in the Greek world wrote and spoke the same
language, known as koine Greek, as far as Persia in the east and
Arabia in the south, while in the west Latin was the common
language of government and the land-owning classes from Britain,
Gaul and Germany in the north to Spain and North Africa in the
south. Many were bilingual, switching effortlessly between Latin
and Greek as they travelled from one part of the Empire to another.
This cultural elite probably felt they had more in common with
each other than with the native population of the countries where
they lived. A Latin-speaking African landowner, for example, could

find himself quite at home in a literary salon of well-to-do Greeks at Smyrna in Asia Minor (Brown 1971: 14).

The mother-tongue of by far the greatest majority of people living in the Roman Empire, however, was their own regional vernacular: Aramaic in Palestine, Coptic in Egypt, Berber and Punic in North Africa, varieties of Celtic in Britain and Gaul, varieties of Gothic in Germany, a bewildering range of languages and dialects in Asia Minor including Lycian, Carian, Pisidian, Lycaonian (Acts 14:11) and Phrygian, and farther east the languages of Syria, Armenia, Persia and Arabia. Some of these languages were never literary languages and are known to us almost entirely from a few inscriptions and passing references in Greek and Latin literature, while others such as Aramaic, Syriac, Middle Persian and Coptic are the languages in which sizeable bodies of literature were written. Educated people, politicians and the international business community were normally able to communicate in Greek or Latin, or both, as well as speaking their mother tongue. But these were the languages people spoke at home, the languages that gave people some kind of regional or national identity, the languages that emerged in their own right as soon as the centralizing authority lost control. These are the languages that we shall be surveying.

Our main centres of attention will be Jerusalem and Rome. Semitic Jerusalem as the earliest capital, both real and symbolic, of Judaism and Christianity, and Indo-European Rome as the political force which brought together these two and other religious traditions in one society, and eventually in 324 CE, under Constantine the Great, gave unique imperial authority to one of them. The Semitic language group derives its name from the Book of Genesis, according to which the peoples of the world and their languages are said to belong to three families descended from the three sons of Noah, Shem, Ham and Japheth (Gen. 10). The organization of this family tree is clearly motivated, not by a concern for scientific truth, but by the desire to draw a clear distinction between the author and his people, on the one hand, descended like the Aramaeans and the Arabs from Shem (Greek *Sem*), and the Egyptians, Canaanites, Babylonians, Assyrians and Philistines who are descended from Ham, and the Persians, Greeks and Romans (as *kittim* in verse 4 was interpreted) who are descended from Japheth, on the other. But it does bear some resemblance to linguistic reality and modern scholars from the eighteenth century (Gesenius–Kautzsch 1910: 1) applied the term 'Semitic' to a clearly defined language group consisting of the following: a western group including Canaanite, Hebrew, Aramaic and probably Arabic; an eastern group including Babylonian and Assyrian; and a southern group including Ethiopic and a language known exclusively from south Arabian inscriptions from the eighth century BCE to 1000 CE (Moscati 1964: 3–17).

The term 'Hamitic' came to be applied to a group of African languages, including Egyptian, Coptic, Berber and Hausa. The term 'Hamito-Semitic' was coined to denote a larger grouping, which comprises what is nowadays more often known as the 'Afro-Asiatic' language group. The term 'Japhetic' has also occasionally been applied to the Indo-European languages of Western Asia and Europe.

Like most large cosmopolitan cities, Jerusalem and Rome were multilingual societies, but for very different reasons – one religious the other political. Jerusalem was the site of the Jewish Temple and at the major festivals attracted huge crowds of pilgrims from all over the world. According to a first-century tradition recounted in Chapter 2 of the Book of Acts, Jews in Jerusalem during the feast of Pentecost spoke a dozen languages or more. Probably Jews from many of the places mentioned there spoke Aramaic or Greek. However, the allusions to place-names in Asia Minor, North Africa, Arabia and the East, as well as the phrase 'each in our own native language' (*te idia dialekto* v. 8), must in this context have been intended to suggest some of the exotic languages still current there in the first century CE.

Parthians, Medes and Elamites (v. 9) probably all spoke varieties of Persian. The large Jewish community in Mesopotamia, especially Babylonia, spoke Aramaic, while the Jews in Judaea spoke both Aramaic and Hebrew, as well as Greek (v. 9). In Cappadocia, Pontus, Phrygia, Pamphylia and the rest of Asia Minor (vv. 9–10) Jews were probably speakers of Greek too, although the names may also be intended to refer to some of the local languages of Asia Minor, such as Phrygian, Armenian and the Celtic language spoken in Galatia. Greek was the language of educated Egyptian Jews at that time too, like Philo of Alexandria, and the same probably goes for those in Libya, Crete and Rome as well. However, the references may be intended to add Coptic, Punic and Latin to the list, that is to say, the vernacular languages spoken by ordinary people in these countries as well (vv. 10–11). Finally, the inclusion of Arabia reflects a situation in which a significant number of Jews, including St Paul (Gal. 1:17), had contacts with the kingdom of King Aretas and his capital Petra. Jews there probably spoke a dialect of Aramaic known as Nabataean.

Even allowing for religious and rhetorical hyperbole, this gives what must have been a fairly accurate picture of festival time in first-century CE Jerusalem. The 'miracle' of Pentecost was that all these people could understand one another's languages. Without wishing to explain it away altogether, it is important to remember that the languages spoken by co-religionists in a restricted context, limited in vocabulary and subject matter and probably peppered with Hebraisms, Aramaisms and other religious loanwords common to many of the languages, were probably more mutually intelligible than might appear at first sight (Blanc 1994: 355). However that may be, we have no reason to doubt the general observation that first-century CE Jerusalem was a place where many languages were spoken and understood, especially during the major pilgrim festivals.

Until its destruction at the hands of the Roman army in 70 CE, Jerusalem had been the capital of a Jewish state in which two Semitic languages were widely used, namely Hebrew and Aramaic. Hebrew was one of the main languages of ancient Israel and Canaan (cf. Isa. 19:18), related to Ugaritic, a language spoken on the Mediterranean coast of what is now Syria and Lebanon from the fifteenth to the thirteenth century BCE, and thanks to the spectacular discoveries at Ras Shamra in 1929, the best-documented Canaanite dialect next to Hebrew.

Throughout most of the biblical period, several languages and a variety of religious factors vied with one another for supremacy in Israel and Judah. In Jerusalem the spread of Aramaic can be traced back to the end of the eighth century BCE and is reflected in an intriguing incident recorded in the Bible. According to the biblical account of Sennacherib's siege of Jerusalem in 701 BCE, the leaders of the city pleaded with the Assyrians to conduct negotiations in Aramaic, the language of international diplomacy, rather than Hebrew, 'the language of Judah' (Hebrew *yehudit*), so that the ordinary people sitting on the city wall would not be able to understand (2 Kings 18:26–8). From the fifth century, Jewish documents written in Aramaic become increasingly common. They include the Elephantine texts from Upper Egypt (*ANET* 491–2; Driver 1957) and the extracts from Persian government records preserved in the Book of Ezra (4:8–6:18; 7:12–26).

From the time of Alexander the Great, Greek posed a further threat to the survival of Hebrew. By the time of Christ a significant proportion of the Jews living in Palestine spoke Greek and Aramaic, and there is evidence that there were some who spoke Latin as well (Millard 1995b: 451–8). Archaeological evidence confirms this polyglot picture of Judaism. From over 1,500 Jewish epitaphs, most of them from Rome and Palestine, the largest proportion is in Greek, but many are in Hebrew, Aramaic and Latin (Horst 1991: 22–39). A single Jewish family archive discovered in the Judaean desert, dated to the first part of the second century CE, contains documents in Hebrew, Aramaic, Greek and Nabataean (Yadin 1971: 229). Yet it was still spoken by ordinary people in parts of Palestine after 70 CE, and used as the language of religious discourse by scholars in Tiberias, Sepphoris and the other centres of Palestinian Judaism down to the fifth century CE. There are references in the Talmud to the fact that the maids in the house of Judah the Prince (c.200 CE) in Galilee spoke beautiful Hebrew, although this is presented as somewhat exceptional (BT Megillah 18a; RH 26b; Naz. 3a; Erub. 53a). By that time the Jews all over the world spoke other languages. Hebrew had become exclusively the language of worship and religious discourse. Biblical Hebrew survives to this day as the sacred language (*leshon ha-qodesh*) of Judaism, a remarkable success story – the reasons for which will be discussed in the next chapter.

Two other Canaanite languages, closely related to Hebrew, are Phoenician, the language of the ancient coastal cities north of Palestine such as Tyre and Sidon, and Punic (or 'neo-Punic'), the language of their Mediterranean colonies in Spain, the Balearic islands, Corsica, Sardinia, North Africa and elsewhere. Place-names like Cadiz, Ibiza, Malta and Carthage, personal names like Hannibal, Hamilcar and Dido, and the names of Punic deities like Melkart and Tanit, are all of Canaanite origin. The use of the term *barbaroi* in Acts 28:2 for the native inhabitants of Malta when Paul landed there, indicates that they spoke a language other than Greek or Latin – probably Punic. Vernacular language and religion survived longer in North Africa than in some other parts of the Empire. When the city of Carthage was destroyed by the Romans in 146 BCE, its libraries were carefully preserved and given to the neighbouring Numidian peoples, who like most of the other peoples of North Africa adopted Punic, the language of Carthage, as their official language. In Carthage the highest local official was still known as a *sufet* (cf. biblical Hebrew *shophet* 'judge') in the first century CE, and relics of the ancient Phoenician language survived in official documents and religious rites. The Emperor Septimius

Severus (193–211 CE), who was born in Tripolitania, spoke Latin very badly we are told, while the writer Apuleius' stepson, in the middle of the second century CE, claims he neither knew nor wanted to know Latin. Christian converts later adopted ancient Carthaginian names, now translated into Latin, such as Donatus from Punic *Muttumbaal* 'gift of Baal'. A comment by St Augustine proves that Punic, which he recognized as a language closely connected to Hebrew, was still spoken alongside Latin in North Africa at the beginning of the fifth century CE (Warmington 1964: 255–7).

Aramaic, the language of ancient Syria (Hebrew *aram*), became the language of international communication throughout the Assyrian, Babylonian and Persian empires from about the eighth century BCE down to the time of Alexander the Great when Greek rapidly superseded it. Early evidence for the use of Aramaic in official documents has been found in Egypt, Turkey, Syria, Iraq, Arabia, Persia, Western India and elsewhere. The Buddhist king, Ashoka, in the third century BCE erected inscriptions in Aramaic (and Greek) in Kandahar. The success of Aramaic was undoubtedly due in the main to the fact that it was written in a relatively easy alphabetical script (Widengren 1973: 341). There are frequent references to Aramaean scribes and Aramaic letters in cuneiform documents from the ninth century BCE onwards (Malamat 1973: 147–8).

By the time of Christ, it had superseded Hebrew as the everyday language of most of the Jews in Palestine and Babylonia. It was written in the same 'square' script as Hebrew, also known as the new Aramaic or Assyrian script (M Meg. 1:8). Outsiders, like the author of the Acts of the Apostles, often confused them (Acts 21:40; 22:2), but they are quite distinct languages. The two major Jewish varieties of Aramaic, Palestinian and Babylonian, are known mainly from the Palestinian and Babylonian Talmuds, which record sayings and conversations of the rabbis down to *c.*500 CE, and from the Targums, Aramaic translations or paraphrases of Hebrew scripture, freely produced from the time of Ezra (fifth century BCE) to early mediaeval times.

In addition to these two Jewish varieties of Aramaic, the isolated Samaritan community based at Samaria 50 km north of Jerusalem also spoke a dialect of Aramaic, although like the Jews they preserved their most sacred text, known as the Samaritan Pentateuch, in Hebrew. In a remarkable example of religious conservatism, which distinguishes the Samaritans from the Jews and everyone else, they did not adopt the new Aramaic script but continue to this day to use a distinctive form of the Old Hebrew script. Other dialects of Western Aramaic were used by two important Arab states which flourished on the eastern borders of Judaea from the first century BCE to the third century CE, the Palmyrenes in Syria to the north, remembered mainly for their greatest monarch Queen Zenobia, and the Nabataean Arabs with their renowned capital at Petra in the south.

Farther east, alongside Jewish Babylonian Aramaic, there were two other important varieties of Aramaic: Syriac and Mandaean. Syriac, originally the local dialect of Edessa (Urfa) in south-east Turkey, which was the main centre of eastern Christianity from the second century, became the literary language of most Aramaic-speaking Christians in Syria and Mesopotamia from where it spread as far as South India. A rich literature written in Syriac from the third to the thirteenth centuries has come down to us, including an important ancient version of the Bible known as the Peshitta. Syriac remains the liturgical language of the Assyrian Church and the Syrian Orthodox Church, and dialects of Syriac are spoken in Christian communities in Turkey, Syria, Iraq and elsewhere. Mandaean was the language of a Gnostic sect that flourished in Mesopotamia between c.200 and 800 CE.

The ancient Semitic languages of Mesopotamia, Assyrian and Babylonian, written on clay tablets in a form of the old Sumerian script, had all but disappeared by the time of Christ, having been officially superseded by Aramaic and Greek as the language of trade and commerce. Only a few priests and professional scribes could still handle the difficult cuneiform writing system, and only a few hundred texts from our period, mainly of an astronomical or astrological nature, survive (the latest is dated 74 CE). Even where the worship of ancient gods like Nergal, Shamash, Asshur, Ishtar and Nabu survived down to the third and fourth centuries CE alongside Greek, Iranian, Aramaean and Arabian cults, as at Hatra, Uruk, Ashur, Borsippa and elsewhere, there are no traces of any of the ancient languages (Ghirshman 1954: 382–4).

South of Palestine, the spoken language of the tribes of northern Arabia, including probably the Nabataeans, was an ancient (pre-classical) variety of Arabic known from a series of inscriptions dating from the fifth century BCE to the fourth century CE. The ancient city states of south-west Arabia, such as the Sabaean kingdom of the legendary Queen of Sheba, spoke varieties of a south Semitic language also known almost entirely from inscriptions and referred to as Epigraphic South Arabian. Ancient Ethiopic (Ge'ez), another south Semitic language, is first attested in epigraphic material from the first few centuries CE, and in particular from the great fourth-century Aksum inscriptions. Christianity reached Ethiopia in the fourth century and the Bible was translated into Ethiopic over the next few centuries. Ge'ez remains the sacred language of the Amharic-speaking Ethiopian Church to this day.

Moving west from Jerusalem there was the accumulation of 3,000 years of the Egyptian hieroglyphic tradition, still visible in stone monuments like the pyramids and the great temples at Luxor. Egyptian is a Hamitic language, like Berber, Hausa and other African languages which are probably distantly related to the Semitic languages we have been surveying in the large 'Hamito-Semitic' or 'Afro-Asiatic' language grouping which I mentioned earlier. It survived in various forms down to the Roman period. The appearance of ancient Egyptian hieroglyphic writing on the famous Rosetta Stone, discovered during Napoleon's Egyptian campaign in the Nile Delta in 1799, and other documents, proves that ancient Egyptian was still in use in the second century BCE – at least for official documents.

While both hieroglyphic Egyptian and cursive forms of writing known as hieratic and demotic continued to be used, alongside Greek, in letters, contracts, religious texts and scientific writings down to the time of Constantine, the language of the peasant population of Egypt was a variety of Late Egyptian, known as Coptic, written in a script derived from Greek and containing numerous Greek loanwords. Most Jewish and Christian scholars in Hellenistic Egypt wrote in Greek, but Coptic was the language of the mass of Egyptian Christians from the second century CE. Some very important Christian documents in Coptic have survived, including ancient versions of scripture and many Gnostic and apocryphal texts like those discovered in 1945 at Nag Hammadi. Otherwise, knowledge of the ancient Egyptian language and the hieroglyphic script in which it was written had been totally forgotten by the time of Constantine, even in the Egyptian mystery cults where Greek was the language used in ritual. Only a few symbolic hieroglyphs like the *ankh*-sign, the 'eye of Horus' and the 'knot of Isis', continued to appear on amulets and in other magical or mystical texts.

Although originating in a predominantly Semitic, Aramaic-speaking world, Second Temple Period Judaism was strongly influenced by non-Semitic languages and cultures, especially the Indo-European languages, Persian and Greek. For two centuries following the victories of Cyrus the Great (died 529 BCE), Jews lived under Persian authority and were much influenced by the language and religious beliefs of the Persians. Jewish angelology and eschatology show signs of Zoroastrian influence, for example, and it is significant that it was from the Medes and Persians that the Hebrew word *dat* 'law, religion' was borrowed via Aramaic (Ezra 7:21; Dan. 6:8). The most ancient sacred texts of Zoroastrianism, the Gathas, were composed originally by the prophet Zarathustra in Old Iranian or Avestan (*c.*1000 BCE), an Indo-Aryan language similar in many ways to the language of the Indian Vedas. Writing played no significant role in the transmission of these texts until the third century CE when they were written down for the first time in a form of the Aramaic script designed to write Middle Persian or Pahlavi, the official language of Iran under the Sassanians. The language of the Parthians, who threatened the stability of the eastern frontiers of the empire on more than one occasion, and exported Mithraism to the West, was another variety of Middle Iranian. Elamite, another ancient Persian dialect known from third-millennium BCE inscriptions, is listed among the languages spoken in Jerusalem in the first century CE (Acts 2:9), but whether or not Elamites still spoke their own distinct dialect at that time is not known.

The Armenian language, at one time thought to belong to the Iranian group, is now considered a separate branch of the Indo-European family. It was spoken by a group of fiercely independent people living in an area east of the Black Sea and conquered, like the Jews, first by the Persians and then by the Romans. They were the first nation to embrace Christianity after the baptism of their king, Tiridates III, towards the end of the third century CE, and it was a Christian bishop, Mesrop, who invented the distinctive Armenian script in the fifth century. Among the great variety of Indo-European languages of Asia Minor, Phrygian, which may possibly be related to Armenian, survived in the Greek script down into the second century CE, as did the Celtic language spoken in Galatia (see p. 19). Others are survivals of ancient Hittite, an early Indo-European language known from numerous cuneiform texts from the middle of the second millennium BCE. These include Lydian, Lycian, Pisidian and Lycaonian, a language encountered by Paul at Lystra (Acts 14:11).

Much more significant, however, was the influence on Judaism and early Christianity of Greek which steadily began to replace Aramaic as the lingua franca from the time of Alexander the Great (356–323 BCE). The earliest evidence of the Greek language comes from the Linear B texts found in the Mycenaean palaces of fourteenth- to thirteenth-century Greece and Crete. From the eighth century when the Greek alphabet was invented, the use of Greek is documented not only throughout mainland Greece and the Aegean islands, but in all the many Greek colonies which spanned the ancient Mediterranean world from Spain and Italy in the west to the Black Sea, Syria and Egypt in the east. Various ancient dialects can be distinguished in the literature of Asia Minor (e.g. Homer, Hesiod, Sappho, Herodotus), Athens (e.g. Sophocles, Thucydides, Plato, Aristotle) and elsewhere. But with the collapse of independent city states and the political unification of Greece in the fourth century, a new common language based mainly on the literary language of Athens (Attic) emerged, known as the 'koine'. The much travelled historian, Xenophon (c.430–354 BCE), is often regarded as the first writer of koine Greek.

Following the military successes of Alexander the Great of Macedon, koine Greek spread far beyond the shores of Greece as the language not only of commerce, trade and politics, but also of education, literature and religion. In Persia, for example, it soon replaced Aramaic and continued in use both as a spoken language and in official documents down to the fourth century CE (Ghirshman 1954: 229–30). During the third and second centuries BCE, Alexandria in Egypt was the literary capital of the Greek world, and many important authors including the Sicilian, Diodorus, Strabo from Pontus on the Black Sea and Appian of Alexandria, wrote in Greek. The earliest Roman historians, Fabius Pictor and Cincius Alimentus, wrote in Greek mainly because in the third century BCE it did not occur to them that they could write such works in Latin. The large number of Greek loanwords in Hebrew and Latin is a very good indication of the dominant position of Greek over a long period.

Greek was an important language in Judaism, in some areas competing successfully with Hebrew. There are Greek synagogue inscriptions in Egypt from the third century BCE. Coins minted in Jerusalem by the Hasmonaean dynasty in the second century are bilingual – in Greek and Hebrew. Two famous inscriptions prohibiting gentiles from entering the inner precincts of Herod's Temple in Jerusalem are also in Greek. Greek loanwords appear in the later books of the Bible (e.g. Dan. 3:7), and by the end of the Talmudic period (c.500 CE) there are hundreds of Greek loanwords in everyday Jewish Aramaic (Kutscher 1982: 138–41). Greek personal names became increasingly prominent. Even the high priest, Jeshua, preferred to be known as Jason (Josephus, *Ant.* 12.5.1), and of Jesus' twelve disciples, almost half have Greek names: Peter, Andrew, Philip, Thaddaeus (probably an aramaized form of Theodotus) and Bartholomew (from *Bar-Ptolemaeus*, meaning 'son of Ptolemy'). Evidence from Jewish ossuaries found in or around Jerusalem indicates that a minimum of 10–20 per cent of the total population must have spoken Greek, although their knowledge of Greek grammar and literature was poor (Hengel 1989: 10; Horst 1991: 32). Jewish epitaphs and synagogue inscriptions prove that Greek was spoken by the Jews in most of the other cities of Palestine as well. Seventy-five per cent of the epitaphs in the famous rabbinic cemetery at Beth Shearim in the north, for example, where Jewish leaders of the second to fourth century CE were buried, show that even the rabbis and their families spoke Greek (Hengel 1989: 15–16), despite the fact that the debates attributed to them in the Mishnah and Talmud are of course always in Hebrew or Aramaic. The evidence from epitaphs proves that the Jews in Rome, unlike other orientals, continued to speak Greek well into the Christian era (Horst 1991: 22–3).

This brings us to our other focus, Rome and the language situation in the West. Latin was originally the language of Latium (modern Italian *Lazio*) in central Italy and of its main city Rome. By the beginning of our period it had almost totally taken over as the language of Italy. Most of the other Italic languages had disappeared completely, while a few such as Ligurian, Oscan and Umbrian survived only as spoken regional languages in shrinking local communities. Etruscan, the non-Indo-European language of Rome's powerful neighbours in Tuscany to the north, had died out by the time of Christ, although not without leaving its mark on Latin in the form of numerous loanwords, including *histrio* 'actor', *persona* 'mask' and *atrium* 'entrance hall'. The Romans had also learnt the art of writing from the Etruscans.

Various Celtic languages, especially Gaulish, were spoken in parts of northern Italy and France (*Gallia* 'Gaul' as the Romans called it) until the fifth century CE, by which time Latin had superseded them. In his description of Gaul, Julius Caesar refers to the languages of the Druids and Helvetii, as well as their use of the Greek alphabet in writing. Other ancient Celtic languages survived in isolated regions of northern Spain, Germany, Austria, Poland and even Asia Minor, where the language of the Galatians was in ancient times a dialect of Gaulish. The 'neo-Celtic' languages of France (Breton), Britain (Scots Gaelic, Welsh, Manx, Cornish) and Ireland (Irish) are not attested before the fifth century CE when the earliest examples of Old Irish, written in the Ogam script, first appear. Little is known of the languages spoken in the Roman provinces of Dacia, Pannonia and Dalmatia in the region covered by modern Romania, Bulgaria and the former Yugoslavia. Although much influenced by Celtic and Gothic languages, a distinct Dacian language, which is probably the ancestor of Albanian, is known mainly from Balkan place-names.

The Germanic peoples, whose various languages and dialects, including ancient Gothic as well as modern German, Dutch, Yiddish and the Scandinavian languages, form another branch of Indo-European, came into contact with Rome in the first century BCE. They are described in some detail by the Roman historian, Tacitus, in a work dated 98 CE, although the earliest textual evidence comes from numerous inscriptions, written in the runic alphabet, found in northern and eastern Europe from the third century on. In the fourth century, the Bible was translated into Gothic, an East Germanic language spoken in what is now Bulgaria, by the Ostrogoth Ulfilas (c.311–83), who devised a special writing system based on the Greek, Latin and possibly runic alphabets for the purpose. The Vandals, who invaded Spain and North Africa in the time of Augustine (354–430), spoke another east Germanic language, as did the Burgundians whose kingdom in the Rhône valley flourished on a smaller scale at about the same time.

In Italy, Latin had to compete with Greek, especially in the context of philosophy and religion, right down into the Christian era. The influence of the Greeks on Italy goes back to their eighth-century BCE colonies, especially strong in the southern region, which known for many centuries as *Magna Graecia* ('Greater Greece'). From the third century BCE, senior officials were able to address Greek-speaking audiences in their own language. Greek was given a massive boost in the second century BCE when the Romans conquered Greece. Roman soldiers serving overseas picked up sufficient Greek to enrich their vernacular. Aemilius Paulus, a hardened military man, insisted that his two sons be given a Greek education as well as the traditional Roman education, and chose to keep for himself the library of King Perseus when under his leadership the Roman army finally conquered the Macedonians in 168 BCE. According to the historian, Polybius (c.200–118 BCE), there were many Greek nationals teaching in Rome. Even Cato the Censor (234–149 BCE), known for his opposition to all things foreign, knew Greek well, and by about 150 BCE virtually every educated Roman was bilingual. In the first century BCE, Greek remained an important language of culture and power in Rome. The Roman general, Sulla, brought Aristotle's library to Rome. Greek was still considered an essential element in every Roman boy's education. Both Julius Caesar and Cicero studied in Greece.

Latin was the official language of the Roman administration, however, and eventually superseded all other languages in Italy and the West, including Greek. Monumental inscriptions in the famous Roman lettering appear throughout the empire from the first century BCE on. The *Res Gestae* of Augustus, his official version of the main events of his reign, is inscribed in Latin and Greek on the marble walls of his temple at Ancyra in Galatia. The Roman military conquest of Judaea in 70 CE is epitomized by a column found in Jerusalem with a Latin inscription mentioning the emperors Vespasian and Titus, as well as the commander of the Tenth Legion – the one that destroyed Jerusalem – and bricks from the beginning of the second century CE stamped with the Romans' name for Jerusalem: *C(olonia) AEL(ia) C(apitolina)*. Latin is one of the three languages in which the inscription above Jesus' cross was written (John 19:19–20) and the influence of Latin, albeit indirect, can also be seen in the many Latin words in Hebrew, Aramaic and Greek documents from first-century Palestine and elsewhere (Millard 1995b). Religious texts in Latin, including early Jewish ossuary inscriptions and dedicatory inscriptions addressed to the Iranian God, Mithras (*Sol invictus*), become increasingly frequent throughout the Roman Empire.

Roman literature in our period, both prose and poetry, to a very large extent consciously imitated Greek models. The serious study of language was introduced to Rome in 159 BCE by Crates of Mallus in Asia Minor, who on a visit as envoy to Rome stimulated a great deal of interest among the Roman intelligentsia with a series of lectures. But nowhere was the presence of the Greek language in Rome more evident than in religion and philosophy. The Sibylline Books, a collection of oracles kept by the Roman state and consulted from time to time, were in Greek. The language in which the rituals of some of the popular oriental religions practised in Rome, the Egyptian Isis cult for example, was also Greek. The Jews in Rome used Hebrew in religious contexts, but, as we have seen, their spoken language was Greek.

Under the enthusiastic philhellene, Hadrian, and his successors, in particular Antoninus Pius and Marcus Aurelius, the Latin and Greek languages and literatures flourished everywhere, promoted in virtually every educational and cultural institution throughout the peaceful empire (Grant 1994). But towards the end of our period, from the middle of the third century on, the imperial frontiers were threatened and in some cases breached by the Goths in the north and the Persians in the east. Imposed Greco-Roman uniformity was broken wide open by the exploits of the dynamic little kingdoms of Armenia and Palmyra. The exclusive supremacy of Latin and Greek began to recede as the churches in Egypt and the east chose to adopt their own vernacular languages for their liturgy in preference to Greek, providing a stimulus for the creation of the rich and extensive Coptic, Syriac and Armenian literatures. Regional differences assert themselves even in the Latin-speaking West where, alongside the official language of the ruling class, the beginnings of the various Romance languages can be identified in the vernaculars of Gaul and the Iberian peninsula. By the time of Constantine, Latin became the language of the state religion as well, and succeeded in imposing itself as the lingua franca on Spain, Portugal, France, Italy and the rest of 'Romance Europe'. But it remained in most cases the second language of the learned classes whose mother tongue was a regional variety of spoken vernacular Latin, now clearly distinguished from official Latin and closer to French, Spanish, Portuguese or Italian than to what eventually evolved into Church Latin.

3

SACRED LANGUAGES

From a wide-angled view of the language situation in general, we move now to the issue of the special languages and language varieties used in particular religious contexts. Common to many religions is the tradition that rituals must be performed in a particular language, frequently a language clearly distinguished from the language of everyday use. In some cases it is a special variety of the participants' own language, perhaps an obsolete, forgotten dialect, while in others it is a completely different language which is totally unintelligible to the worshippers. At one end of the spectrum, Greek represents a language widely used and understood to a greater or lesser extent by almost everyone, but given special status in some religious contexts. At the other end of the spectrum, Avestan, the language in which the sacred texts of Zoroastrianism were transmitted, was a variety of Old Iranian known only from those texts and, for most of its history, unintelligible to all but a few experts. Between these two extremes, Hebrew was the spoken language of a small community which withstood the pressures from other stronger language groups and was eventually canonized as the sacred language of the Jews. There is an interesting contrast between Judaism and Christianity here. Jews successfully learnt the language of the country they found themselves in, but preserved their scripture and their liturgy almost entirely in ancient Hebrew. Christians on the other hand, in those first centuries, appear to have made a special effort to communicate their religious teaching, including their sacred texts, in the language of ordinary people. Although Jewish scripture was of crucial importance in Christianity, the original languages in which it was written, Hebrew and Aramaic, never had the same significance for them.

Early Christianity was exceptional, however. There are many familiar examples of this phenomenon still evident today, such as the special religious use of Arabic by Muslims, Sanskrit by Hindus, Latin by pre-Vatican 2 Catholics, and Avestan by Parsees. Less well-known examples from the Greco-Roman world which we shall be considering are the survival of ancient Phoenician in the rituals of Carthage, the use of Greek in Roman state religion and the recitation of the 'Carmen Arvale' sung each year in May by the Arval Brethren in an almost unintelligible variety of archaic Latin. Glossolalia or 'speaking in tongues' (Acts 10:46; 1 Cor. 14) is a special case in which a language unknown to humans has an important function in worship. In some traditions, including Islam, the translation of a sacred language or text into the vernacular or the use of such translations in worship is forbidden. In other traditions, particular translations like the Greek Septuagint, the Latin Vulgate and the King James' Authorized Version of the Bible, themselves come to be treated almost as though they were as sacred as the original text.

The retention of such sacred languages has some far-reaching sociolinguistic and religious consequences. In many cases it means that there arises a class of priests or other experts who are the only people who can translate and interpret, and this gives them a unique status and power over the rest of their community. Unintelligibility plays an important role in binding the disciple to the master (Gellner 1957: 34; Gordon 1990: 189). Alternatively, where the people are permitted or encouraged to learn the sacred language and participate more fully in the religion, education is inevitably dominated from an early age by language-learning. Mnemonics are devised to make the learning and memorizing of language easier. Techniques were invented to help scribes in their painstaking task of reproducing accurate copies of the sacred text. New writing systems were developed. Where oral transmission was preferred to written, the emphasis was naturally on the faultless pronunciation of every syllable. In the case of the Sanskrit tradition in ancient India, the science of phonology actually evolved, thanks to the great grammarian Panini (around fourth century BCE), to protect the oral transmission of the Vedic literature. There are sometimes restrictions on such matters for example, what writing materials must be used in the production of a sacred text, who can handle it, who can recite it in the liturgy and is it permitted to translate it into another language. Cautionary tales are created to protect the special status of such languages, for example the Jewish tradition that pronouncing the divine name in the wrong way or at the wrong time leads to disaster. A sacred language is often surrounded by a variety of other myths and traditions: it is the language of the angels or the language by which the world was created or the original language from which all other languages are derived.

We begin with the question of what makes a language sacred. Many factors, sociolinguistic as well as theological, are involved in this canonization of a language, and its consequences for the development of religion are no less varied or significant. It is not a characteristic of every religion, at least to the same degree, and the question of how it arose is an interesting one for us to consider. Relations between a religious community and other speech communities with which it comes into contact, play a crucial role in some cases. A group may be forced into isolating itself from the rest of the world, and that isolation is then expressed in the preservation of its own language. The incidence of bilingualism may also affect the survival of a particular language. Nationalism or ethnocentricity may also be significant as it shapes attitudes towards other languages and communities. Literacy is another important issue to take into account when we are considering how written texts are transmitted, in what language they are preserved and who is responsible for their transmission. The role of a priestly hierarchy or other dominant political authority at some crucial point in the canonization process is often another factor in determining which language becomes a sacred language.

Respect for the original sources, especially when these are believed to have been composed by a much revered prophet or teacher, if not by the actual deity himself or herself, is a major factor in many cases. To recite or hear the actual words of Moses or Zoroaster or even the words of Allah, which Muslims believe are contained in the Qur'an, in the very language in which they were originally uttered or written clearly means a great deal to many religious groups. Christianity is prima facie a notable exception (to be discussed more fully later), in which there was apparently no interest in preserving the words of Jesus in their original language, although the words of Jesus are already described by one of the first bishops of Rome as sacred (*hagia logia*).

Religious conservatism is another important factor related to this concern for getting back to the original. A fierce reluctance to accept innovation is common to many religious groups, despite pressures from many directions to evolve or move with the times. It is partly due to a desire to maintain continuity with the past, or even, somehow, an attempt to bring the past into the present during the experience of worship: to 'stand again before Sinai' (cf. Deut. 5:3) or, in the words of the well-known native American spiritual, 'Were you there when they crucified my Lord?' There is also the fact that language often has a dynamic of its own: words, phrases, even sounds hallowed by centuries of use in the highly charged context of religious ritual, can have a hold on worshippers which makes it difficult for them even to contemplate changes in language. Conservative reactions in our own day to some of the new translations of the Bible and new vernacular versions of the Church's liturgy are a case in point.

We begin with Hebrew. Because of its central role in Judaism from ancient times to the present, its history and the traditions surrounding it are better documented than most other examples. From ancient times it was designated *leshon ha-qodesh* 'the sacred language'. It is actually more often referred to by this name than by any other. Hebrew (*'ibrit*) is hardly attested before modern times (Weitzman 1994: 1829) and *yehudit* 'in the language of Judah' like the Greek term, *hebraisti*, can be ambiguous. If it was the language used by priests in the Temple, it was also the language of the angels and prayers would not be effective in any other language. The 'pure speech' (*sapha berura*) in which one day all the people of the world will call on the name of the Lord (Zeph. 3:9) is Hebrew. It was the language through which the world was created according to a tradition traceable as far back as the Talmudic period (Targum Neofyti on Gen. 11:1; Saenz-Badillos 1993: 2). It must have been the original language of the human race referred to in the Tower of Babel story (Gen. 11:1), since only in Hebrew is the wordplay possible to express the notion of Genesis 2:23 that 'woman' *isha* was created out of 'man' *ish* (Gen. R. 18).

However, not all varieties of Hebrew were considered sacred. It may be that the 'uncircumcised tongue' referred to in the Dead Sea Scrolls was post-biblical or rabbinic Hebrew. In other words, it was the Hebrew spoken and written by the Jewish scholars of the Second Temple Period associated with Jerusalem and therefore despised by the Qumran community. The authors of the sectarian documents found at Qumran clearly saw it as desirable to imitate biblical Hebrew rather than using the post-biblical variety of Hebrew known to us especially from the Mishnah. For them the sacred language presumably meant the Hebrew of the sacred scriptures. It is significant, incidentally, that none of the mediaeval grammarians, who devoted a great deal of energy to producing grammars of biblical Hebrew, thought it worthwhile to write a grammar of Mishnaic Hebrew.

Why did the language of ancient Judah, alone of all the Canaanite languages, survive for so long? In particular, why did it survive in the Jewish religion when it was superseded by Aramaic, Greek and other languages in every other aspect of Jewish life and culture? Already in the fifth century BCE, according to biblical tradition, Ezra and the Levites are described as 'helping the people to understand' at a public reading of the book of the law in Jerusalem (Neh. 8:7–8). There is an ancient rabbinic tradition that this involved translating Hebrew scripture into Aramaic (Vermes 1970: 201). In the third century BCE Jews in Egypt required a Greek translation of the Bible, and much of the Jewish literature composed in the second and first centuries BCE, including the Wisdom of Solomon and the Books of Maccabees, was in Greek. By the second century BCE, Aramaic was being used by Jews for religious purposes too, as can be seen from a large part of the Book of Daniel (2:4–7: 28), which was composed c.160 BCE, and some of the Dead Sea Scrolls, including the Genesis Apocryphon and the Targum of Job.

Yet despite these pressures from other languages, Hebrew continued to be the main language of scripture, liturgy and religious discourse of the Jews. The later books of the Hebrew Bible, Ezra, Nehemiah, 1 and 2 Chronicles, Ecclesiastes, Daniel and some of the Psalms, for example, are all in Hebrew, even if they contain a few sections in Aramaic. While some of the most famous Jewish writers of the Hellenistic period, like Philo, Josephus and the author of the Wisdom of Solomon, wrote in Greek, there was still a substantial quantity of religious literature written in Hebrew. The Mishnah, which was composed c.200 CE, but contains material going back to the time of Ezra, is in Hebrew, as are the Tosefta (c.300 CE) and most of the Midrashic literature (c.200–600 CE). Synagogue sermons were in Hebrew until the sixth or seventh century CE. Most of the sectarian literature among the Dead Sea Scrolls, composed over the last two centuries BCE and the first half of the first century CE, is also in Hebrew, although a number of interesting documents are in Aramaic and Greek. Hebrew remained the language of Jewish scholars and religious leaders, both spoken and written by them long after it had been superseded by other languages, and maintained by them in worshipping communities worldwide until the present day.

There seem to have been several factors operating initially. In the first place, from the beginning of the Second Temple Period (*c.*500–450 BCE) Hebrew was promoted in Judaea by the official establishment at Jerusalem. Whatever the language of the ordinary people, Nehemiah and Ezra insisted that Hebrew must continue to be used, at least as the language of religion. Nehemiah complains that the children of mixed marriages can no longer speak Hebrew (Neh. 13:24), and whether or not Ezra's interpretation of the Torah involved translation into the Aramaic vernacular (Neh. 8), there was no thought of preserving it, reciting it or studying it in anything other than ancient Hebrew. The occurrence of some Aramaic texts in the Bible, for example Ezra and Daniel, as well as the early translations of scripture into Aramaic and Greek, hardly affects this priority of Hebrew as the sacred language.

In subsequent centuries the ultra-conservative hierarchy at Jerusalem strictly controlled the copying of Torah scrolls, and no doubt made strenuous efforts, not unlike those of Nehemiah, to ensure that Hebrew maintained its privileged status at all levels. With the destruction of the Temple in 70 CE, their power structure collapsed and within a hundred years Hebrew had almost completely died out as a spoken language. In the period of restoration and consolidation after 70 CE, however, the new rabbinic leadership responsible for most of the Mishnah (completed *c.*200 CE) continued to ensure that ancient, biblical Hebrew was canonized as the sacred language, even without the Temple at Jerusalem and its priesthood. It was a father's duty to 'teach his son the Shema, the Torah and the sacred language as soon as he can speak: otherwise it would have been better for him if he had not come into the world' (Tos. HagRA520 1, 2).

It was laid down that while some prayers and passages of scripture must be read in the original Hebrew, others may be read in any language (M Sot. 7–9; MYeb. 12:6). Scriptural reasons are given for passages in the first category, but not for the second. The distinction seems to be primarily between public and private occasions. Texts that do not have to be recited in Hebrew include oaths sworn by individuals and frequently recited private prayers, such as the Shema and the blessing over food. Precisely why the paragraph about the suspected adulteress should be read in any language, while the one about divorce should not, is not apparent (MYeb. 12:6). The leaders of Jewish orthodoxy have always insisted on the special role of Hebrew and never given vernacular translations the same authority. Only deviant groups, like the Falashas in Ethiopia and some modern European reform communities, have produced prayer-books in their own languages.

Second, it may be that the term *leshon ha-qodesh* 'the sacred language', which from early times set biblical Hebrew apart from all other languages, contains evidence of another reason for its unique status. It has been suggested that the term was originally shorthand for *leshon bet ha-qodesh* 'the language of the (sacred) Temple', that is to say: the language used by and, as we have seen, promoted by the priestly hierarchy in Jerusalem. But there is another related term which may be even more relevant in this context, namely *admat ha-qodesh* 'the holy land'. It may be that 'the sacred language' carries the sense of 'the language of the holy land', in other words: 'the language of our homeland'. The sacred language is, as we have seen, very seldom named. The term 'in Hebrew' as often as not refers to Aramaic (for example, Acts 21:40). But it is called 'the language of Canaan' (Isa. 19:18) and 'the language of Judah' (*yehudit*: 2 Kings 18:28) as opposed to 'the language of Ashdod' (Neh. 13:24). By implication, the language of Judah is contrasted with the 'strange language' of Egypt (Ps. 114:1).

These and other texts clearly connect the sacred language with the country where it was once spoken. Maybe it was always seen as the language of Judah and Jerusalem, never wholly replacing other languages or dialects in Galilee, Samaria and other parts of the kingdom of David and Solomon. The continuing powerful Jewish nostalgia for their land and their temple with all the rich language and imagery associated with hopes for a return to an idealized 'promised land', must have played a part in the decision to keep alive the language once spoken there. It cannot be a coincidence that the term 'holy land' itself first appears in the context of prophecies about rebuilding and resettling the land of Judah immediately after the Babylonian exile, and that the prophet in question, Zechariah, the son of Iddo, was clearly a member of the priestly hierarchy (Zech. 2:12; cf. Ezra 8:17; Neh. 12:4).

By then the Samaritans had already abandoned Hebrew in favour of Aramaic, both as their spoken language and in their liturgy, so that the continuing use of Hebrew in Judaea served to highlight the differences between the two rival nations. Samaritan nationalism in turn probably also contributed to their decision not to adopt the new international Aramaic script like everyone else: even the Samaritan Pentateuch, which is in Hebrew, is still to this day written in a distinctive form of the Old Hebrew script.

Anti-Samaritan concerns may also have influenced the decision of the Jewish leadership in the early Second Temple Period to adopt the new Aramaic script in direct opposition to the Samaritans (cf. BT Sanh. 21b).

A final factor probably operating in the Jewish retention of Hebrew as their sacred language was a type of religious conservatism. From the first century CE at the latest, so much effort had been invested in teaching and preserving the language of scripture, so much mythology and theology had by then come to depend on the actual phrases, words, even letters of the sacred text, that it would seem unthinkable, both to the rabbinic leaders of the time and to the wider Jewish community, that translation into other languages could ever be substituted for the original. A similar situation also existed in regard to the canon of scripture, as we shall see in Chapter 5. Canonization was an organic process by which over the years language and religion grew together so that they became inseparable, just as the books of the Hebrew Bible had, so to speak, chosen themselves as canonical by the time of the great debates among Rabbi Akiba and his contemporaries. From the second or third century CE a class of Jewish scribes grew up, known as 'masoretes', that is to say, preservers of tradition whose task it was to devise methods of preserving every 'jot and tittle' of Hebrew scripture exactly as it always had been. Their success can be measured by comparing mediaeval manuscripts of the Bible with the Dead Sea Scrolls: although separated by 1,000 years, divergences are minimal.

Before we turn to other languages that have some degree of special status similar to Hebrew in Judaism, we shall digress briefly to consider Jewish attitudes towards foreign languages. There is ample evidence that prejudice against people who speak other languages does not ever seem to have been part of Jewish tradition in the way it certainly was in the Greco-Roman world – and later in Roman Christianity. There are references to the language problems encountered by Jews in countries where people speak 'strange' or 'hard' languages (Ps. 114:1; Jer. 5:15; Ezek. 3:5, 6), but the Jewish term *goy* 'non-Jew' never seems to have acquired the same negative linguistic implications as the term *barbaroi* has in Greek and Latin. Although they had a sacred language, surrounded by special beliefs and taboos, efforts were made by Jews to ensure that Hebrew scripture was understood by the people – the Septuagint was only the first of several Greek translations of the Hebrew Bible. There was also a series of Targums for Aramaic-speaking Jews, and probably some of the first Syriac translations were for Jews as well. According to the Mishnah (Megillah 2:1) it was legitimate to read scripture in Aramaic or any other foreign language as the occasion demanded. There is even a tradition, based on a rabbinic interpretation of Deuteronomy 33:2, that God originally introduced himself at Sinai in four languages, Hebrew, Latin, Arabic and Aramaic (*RA*: 78–9).

The story of the Tower of Babel is about the general language situation in the world and the inability of people who speak different languages to communicate with one another. However, there is no trace of animosity or disdain on the part of the author towards people who speak a different language from his own (Gen. 11:1–9). Similarly, there is little trace of ethnocentric prejudice in the table of languages derived from Noah's three sons: Ham, Shem and Japheth (Gen. 10). It was the religion and morality of the Egyptians, Philistines, Canaanites and the people of Sodom and Gomorrah that confirmed their place among the descendants of Ham, not their languages. Language never seems to have been an issue in the long story of Israel's hostility towards these foreign peoples.

Similarly, the story of the first Pentecost lists languages spoken by Jews in Jerusalem as sources of amazement and even perhaps academic interest, certainly not as evils (Acts 2). It also demonstrates an important characteristic of the Jews already apparent in the first century, namely their familiarity with and readiness to learn more than one language. It is true that, within Judaism, the Jews of first-century Jerusalem ridiculed the way Galileans spoke Aramaic, but that was an internal matter within the Jewish community and says nothing of Jewish attitudes to the language of outsiders. The prologue to the Wisdom of Jesus ben Sira (Ecclesiasticus), dated 132 BCE, gives a better idea of Jewish attitudes to outsiders and those living abroad: 'it is necessary not only that the readers themselves should acquire understanding, but also that those who love learning should be able to help the outsiders by both speaking and writing'.

Greek is our second example of a sacred language. As we have seen, the mystery religions used it. The Egyptian rituals with which Apuleius concludes his *Golden Ass* novel appear to have been carried out in Greek (Apuleius, *Metamorphoses* 11:17). The Sibylline Oracles, the most famous collection of which was entrusted to specially appointed officials in Rome and consulted in time of crisis, were in Greek poetic form. Even among the Jews Greek had a special role, comparable in some ways to that of Hebrew. A large body of Jewish literature was written in Greek during the period 300 BCE to 200 CE, including the Wisdom of Solomon, the works of Philo and Josephus, and several Greek versions of the Hebrew Bible. Simeon ben Gamaliel (mid-second century CE) singles out Greek as the only language apart from Hebrew in which scripture can be written (MMeg. 1:8). He also tells us that in his father's house, 500 children were taught Torah and 500 were taught Greek learning (BTSot. 49b). Judah the Prince studied Greek and urged Jews in Palestine to learn Greek as the language of their country rather than Aramaic (Sot. 49b). Rabbi Abbahu (early fourth century) recommended that girls should be taught Greek as it would be an adornment for them (RA: 444). The fact that the teaching of Greek had to be restricted at the beginning of Hadrian's reign, probably for security reasons (MSot. 9:14), is a clear indication of the extent to which Greek had become a popular alternative to Hebrew for Jews in Palestine. The significance of this, incidentally, for our understanding of the use of Greek by the first Christians and the extent of intellectual trafficking between what we nowadays compartmentalize as rabbinic and patristic literatures, cannot be overestimated.

A number of factors appear to have made Greek particularly appropriate for elevation to some kind of special status in those religious communities in which it had a religious function. In the first place there is the fact that after the campaigns of Alexander the Great, koine Greek soon had more influence in the Hellenistic world than any other language. Although local vernaculars continued to be spoken in rural areas, in the great cities of the Hellenistic world, and in public contexts, Greek took precedence over all competing languages. Greek was the lingua franca, the language of communication, the language of power, the language you had to learn to get on in life. This situation persisted well into the Christian era. In Rome, for example, Greek continued to be taught as an essential element in most centres of learning. Most army officers, diplomats and businessmen could handle Greek as well as their own vernacular. This situation was given a final boost in the second century CE, when there was something of a Greek renaissance initiated by the Emperor Hadrian whose special fondness for Greek culture earned him the nickname Graeculus ('the little Greek'). Successful state-supported efforts to collect and edit works of Greek literature were undertaken at this time. This was the heyday of the Greek sophists who led the intelligentsia in the direction of a more exclusive, elitist culture. It was in this period that the Greek upper classes began to affect an archaic Attic dialect which only they could speak, and which sharply separated them from the ordinary koine-speaking populace (Brown 1971: 64).

Related to this almost universal domination of the world by the Greek language was the attitude of Greek speakers, and their Latin imitators, towards other languages. Greeks from Homer on (*Iliad* 2.867) applied the onomatopoeic word *barbaroi* to all foreigners, because they spoke a language that sounded crude and primitive. Correct Greek was actually defined in terms of the absence, not only of 'solecisms', but of 'barbarisms' (Aristotle, *Rhet.* 1407b). The Romans took it over and carried on the Greek tradition of prejudice against foreigners. There is even an example of a Roman author calling his own language 'barbarian' against the hallowed norm of Greek. A letter from an Egyptian to his employer, written in the middle of the third century BCE, describes how he suffers from discrimination at the hands of the Greeks because he is a 'barbarian'. The fact that the letter is in Greek rather than Egyptian demotic proves just how dominant the language was. Josephus, always anxious to please his Roman friends, refers to fellow Jews in Syria as linguistic 'barbarians' (*Hist.* Preface).

The attitude of the Roman establishment towards foreigners, minority cultures and languages, in particular, is epitomized in a comment by the Roman satirist, Juvenal (*c.*55–140 CE). For him, unlike the author of Acts, the presence in Rome of Greek and Asiatic languages (for example, Persian, Armenian, Hebrew and Syriac) was a mark of decadence or barbarism. Roman campaigns in Asia Minor and Syria had resulted in an influx of Asiatics.

> *non possum ferre, Quirites,*
> *Graecam urbem. Quamvis quota portio faecis Achaei?*
> *iam pridem Syrus in Tiberim defluxit Orontes,*
> *et linguam at mores et cum tibicine chordas*
> *obliquas nec non gentilia tympana secum*
> *vexit* (Juvenal, *Sat.* 3:60–5).

(paraphrase) Fellow citizens, I cannot stand this place. It has become a Greek city. We share it with the dregs of Greece. For too long the rivers of Syria have been discharging into the Tiber, And bringing with them their language and their customs, not to mention their flutes, Their harps with slanting strings and their native tambourines.

Another example from 200 years earlier is the Roman playwright Plautus' comedy *Poenulus* ('the little Carthaginian') in which jokes at the expense of the wretched Punic-speaking North African are a recurring theme.

Both Greek and Latin were the languages of political power: both Greece and Rome aimed to impose their culture and language on other societies, and, as we have seen, to a very large extent succeeded in doing so. In such a situation there was no room for minority languages or dialects – even behind the closed doors of religious groups. Judaism and Zoroastrianism, which held on to their sacred languages through thick and thin, were conspicuous exceptions. Christianity helped to give status to vernacular languages in Egypt (Coptic), Ethiopia (Ge'ez), Syria (Syriac) and elsewhere. But among all the languages of the Hellenistic world, Greek held pride of place as the most widely used language, the only language of international communication, and the language of power.

Another factor in the canonization of the Greek language by some religious groups was the unique appeal and influence of Classical Greek literature. Great libraries were established in many of the cultural centres – notably Alexandria, Pergamum, Antioch and Pella – containing the works of Homer, Hesiod and Pindar, as well as the tragedians, historians and philosophers of Classical Greece. Some of the ancient Greek authors came to be regarded as almost on the same plane as the gods. Homer, for example, is called by Apuleius 'the divine author of ancient poetry among the Greeks' (Metamorphoses 9:13). This situation continued into the Christian era, and clearly influenced attitudes to literature written in or translated into Greek.

Finally, much of Greek literature had a religious origin or function, much of it is in the form of religious discourse and much of it has religious or philosophical content. This perhaps more than anything else made it an appropriate vehicle for expressing and communicating the teachings and beliefs of the new Hellenistic religions, as well as Judaism and Christianity. The five or six centuries of scientific and philosophical literature from the pre-Socratic philosophers to the flowering of Alexandrian scholarship made the Greek language a unique vehicle for expressing and defining religious ideas. Its suitability for precise theological discourse can be seen in the way Christian doctrine developed in the patristic period, especially in the Greek Church where the creeds were formulated. Special theological terminology was created by the early Greek-speaking Christians, for example: *apostolos, euangelion, ekklesia, charis, charisma* (Hengel 1989: 18), and it is hard to imagine the highly complicated christological controversies and definitions of the fourth and fifth centuries CE being in any other language.

Two of the most widely known and influential religious texts in the Greco-Roman world are the Orphic Hymns and the Sibylline Oracles. Both are in Greek because they purport to be by Greek-speaking prophets, namely Orpheus and the Sibyls. Greek mystery groups in many regions, in particular varieties of the Bacchic cult, were much influenced by the Orphic literature. They in turn interacted with other mystery religions, including the new oriental cults of Isis and Mithras – both of which adopted Greek as their ritual language. The Sibyls were the ten or a dozen women prophets reputed to have lived in mainland Greece (Delphi), the Greek islands (Samos), Asia Minor (Erythraea, Phrygia), Egypt, Babylon, Persia and elsewhere. The Sibyls' oracles were preserved in their original language everywhere.

The most often referred to collection of Sibylline Oracles, which were poetic texts written in Greek hexameters, was the one held in the Temple of Jupiter Optimus Maximus at Rome until that was destroyed by fire in 83 BCE. During the reign of Augustus, they were housed in the Temple of Apollo Palatinus, part of Augustus' residential complex. They remained an important part of Roman state religion, consulted by a team of 15 experts, the *Quindecimviri*, always in Greek, in times of crisis. They were influential both as prophesying weird and wonderful portents, and as political propaganda. It was under their guidance, for example, that some of the Greek cults were imported into Rome in 249 BCE, and the ludi saeculares celebrated *achivo ritu* 'according to the Greek rite' by Augustus in 17 BCE (see pp. 153f.). In the year 12 CE, the same emperor destroyed many verses because he found them dangerously subversive (Collins 1983: 317–20), while several of his successors consulted them on matters of state policy and for personal enhancement. The authority and influence of these Greek texts throughout the Greco-Roman world cannot be overestimated. Much of the language and imagery of Virgil's famous Fourth Eclogue, in which he foretells the coming of a golden age, was apparently derived from the prophecies of the Cumaean Sibyl.

The question of Aramaic's role in religious contexts, both Jewish and Christian, is also interesting, despite its continuing status among Jews as the language of common people and the absence of any reference to it as a sacred language on a par with Hebrew. Like Greek, Aramaic was for centuries the main language of commerce and communication from Egypt in the west to Persia in the east, and was widely spoken both by Jews in these areas and by the indigenous population. In Syria, Mesopotamia and Persia, Aramaic survived the inroads of Greek and, after the failure of the Roman campaigns against the Sassanian armies, emerged as the main vernacular language. Already in the Second Temple Period, Aramaic translations or paraphrases of the Hebrew Bible, known as Targums, almost certainly had a place in synagogue worship. Even if no explicit reference to Aramaic translation can be found in the much discussed biblical reference to Levites 'giving the sense so that the people could understand the reading' (Neh. 8:8; see p. 81), the Targums of Job from Qumran prove that Aramaic had been accepted into the synagogue ritual by the time of Christ at the very latest. According to a passage in the Mishnah, the Aramaic portions of the Hebrew Bible (Ezra 4:7–8; 18; Dan. 2:4–6: 28; Jer. 10:11; Gen. 31:47) were treated as no less sacred than the rest of the Bible. Indeed, if they were translated into Hebrew, they would not have the same sanctity (M Yad. 4:5). The fact that Aramaic is used in all three parts of the Hebrew Bible, the Law (Gen. 31:47), the Prophets (Jer. 10:11) and the Writings (Ezra 4:7–8; 18; Dan. 2:4–6: 28), also increased its standing in rabbinic estimation (cf. BT Meg. 71b; Gen. R. 74: Dalman 1922: 17).

Aramaic prayers were used in public worship, although, according to a completely logical tradition, angels spoke Hebrew and would not have understood Aramaic (BT Shab. 12b). Daniel is a scriptural example (2:20–3). The first words of his Aramaic prayer, which incidentally have a Hebrew parallel in Psalm 113:2, inspired the opening petitions of two of the best-known ancient Jewish prayers, namely the Lord's Prayer (Matt. 6:9–15) and the Qaddish. Although the Qaddish as we now know it from the Jewish daily prayer-book (Singer 1892: 77–8 and 86–7) is not attested before c.600 CE, references to early forms of it, always in Aramaic, are to be found in the Talmud (BT Ber. 3a; Elbogen 1993: 80–1). A fourth-century CE Babylonian rabbi claimed that what he called 'May the great name of the Aggadah' was one of the things on which the world stands (BT Sot. 49a). Its popularity, like that of the Lord's Prayer in Christian tradition, both in the liturgy and as a private prayer of individual Jews, is partly due to its eschatological content which gives it a special relevance in times of danger or bereavement, and partly due to the distinctive language in which it is always recited. Other Aramaic compositions in the liturgy, such as the Kol Nidre in the Yom Kippur service, date from mediaeval times when there was something of a renaissance in the use of Aramaic as a literary language. The Zohar, an influential kabbalistic work, written in a very difficult artificial variety of Aramaic, was composed in the thirteenth century.

Early Christian sources provide further evidence of the use of Aramaic as a liturgical language in Palestinian Jewish tradition. There are some Jewish Aramaic formulas in the Greek Gospels, which are given theological and ritual significance by the fact that they are believed to have been the actual words used by Jesus. The term *maranatha* in 1 Corinthians is a well-known example of the use of Aramaic in prayer, to which we might add the use by Paul (Rom. 8:15; Gal. 4:6) and Jesus (Mark 14:36) of *Abba* 'father' in the context of prayer. The term *talitha qumi* (Mark 5:41) is another Aramaic formula used by Jesus. The Lord's Prayer may also be cited in this context as an ancient Jewish prayer probably derived from an Aramaic source. The use of Aramaic in Jewish incantations is well documented throughout our period. In the Christian communities of Syria and Mesopotamia, both scripture and the liturgy were naturally in Syriac, an eastern dialect of Aramaic. Traditions about Syriac being the original language, the language of the angels, the language used by God when speaking to Adam and the like, although never described as 'the sacred language', developed in parallel with Jewish traditions about Hebrew.

The establishment of Latin as a sacred language in Christianity, 'Church Latin', does not properly belong to our period, but we can make a few comments on its role in the emergence and early history of the Western Church. Before the time of Cicero, Latin was to a large extent the servant of Greek, especially in matters of religion and philosophy. As we have seen, Greek was the language of several of the cults imported from the East, and the sacred texts of at least one important part of Rome's state religion, the Sibylline Oracles, were also in Greek. Jews in Rome, for the most part, did not adopt Latin till the fourth century CE. But there are some conspicuous exceptions. The first is the ancient cult of the Salii, which was practised in many towns throughout central Italy, including Rome. Twice a year they proceeded through the streets, performing elaborate dances, beating shields and staves, and singing a hymn known as the 'Carmen Saliare'. Fragments of this hymn have been preserved, but despite references to it in the ancient literature and even some commentaries on it, the archaic Latin in which it is preserved is almost totally unintelligible (Gordon 1990: 189).

The second use of Latin in an ancient sacred text is in the cult of the goddess Dea Dia, revived under the emperor Augustus. The priests, known as the Arval Brethren, preserved a hymn known as the 'Carmen Arvale', which they sang at their annual festival held in a sacred grove near Rome. The emperor himself participated as an ex-officio priest. The song is known from a reference to it in a book on the Latin language by Varro (116–27 BCE) and an inscription dated 218 CE. It is in a variety of very archaic Latin, possibly influenced by Greek, and consisting of much repetition. Both these ancient hymns were barely intelligible either to the priests or to any onlookers, and no doubt the sound of the words rather than their meaning enhanced the mystery of the occasion. A third example of a quite different kind is the introduction by Augustus into state religion of a hymn composed by Horace, the so-called 'Carmen Saeculare', a fascinating Latin interpretation of material taken from the Greek Sibylline Oracles (see pp. 153f.).

As for Christianity, Latin gradually took over from Greek in the Western Church as the lingua franca and, more important, the language of religious and theological discourse. Greek was the language of the Jews in Rome until the fourth century CE, although there is evidence of Latin-speaking Jews in Pompeii from the first century CE. St Paul's letter to the Romans and the letters of Clement, Bishop of Rome (92–101 CE), written in Greek for a Roman readership, as well as numerous inscriptions, prove that Greek was the language of Christianity there too for more than a century. It was not until the late second century that Christian writers were regularly using Latin: the theologian, Tertullian (c.160–222), a North African convert to Christianity, wrote mainly in Latin, and the first Latin translations of scripture appear to have been done in Rome round about the same time. From the third century a new type of Latin grammar, known as the 'Ars Grammatica', began to appear. Of these, the two by St Jerome's teacher, Aelius Donatus (c.310–after 363 CE), were among the most influential both in their own day and in the history of mediaeval and modern language science (*ELL* 7: 3595).

From the time of Cicero, Latin had begun to develop its own philosophical and scientific vocabulary, parallel to and often modelled on Greek. Although the great Roman encyclopedist, Pliny the Elder (c.23–79 CE), writing a century or so later, still complained about the poverty of the Latin language and apologizes for having to introduce 'rustic or foreign terms' from Celtic, Punic and Indian, as well as Greek (*Nat. Hist.* Pref.). Terms like *grammaticus* 'philologist', *philosophus* 'philosopher', *musica* 'music', *historia* 'history' and *bibliotheca* 'library' were borrowed from Greek. There are also many cases of calque (semantic borrowing) in which new Latin words and expressions like *essentia* and *qualitas* were invented on the basis of Greek parallels. For the first few centuries of the Christian era, much of the theological and liturgical vocabulary of the Western Church was translated into Latin from Greek. Some terms were imported from Greek unchanged, like *kyrie eleison*. Others were Latinized, like *evangelium* and *baptisma*. Some came from Hebrew via Greek (for example, *pascha*). New terms were invented, such as *salvare*, *trinitas* and *consubstantialis*, while existing terms were given a new Christian meaning, for example, *salus*, *fides*, *credere*, *originale peccatum* and the like. By the time of Constantine, the official language was able to cope with the needs of the official religion. By then Latin was the language of Roman power, and remained the language of the universal Church until modern times. Those who insisted on the translation of scripture into the vernacular or the use of the vernacular in worship, like Martin Luther, simply had to leave.

Our two final examples of a sacred language come right at the other end of the intelligibility spectrum from Latin and Greek. Avestan is the language in which the sacred texts of Zoroastrianism are written. It represents a third type of sacred language, one which for most of its history, and for most of those who used it, was completely unintelligible. Zoroastrianism was the religion of the Medes and Persians under Cyrus (died 530 BCE) and his successors, notably Darius and Xerxes, later of the Parthians (*c.*141 BCE–224 CE) from among whom Mithridates is probably the best-known name, and finally under the Sassanids (224–652 CE), all of which had considerable influence on the people, religions and literatures we are considering. It was under the Sassanian king, Shapur II (309–79), that the threat of competing religions, notably Christianity and Manichaeism, was finally removed. The power of the hereditary Magi priesthood established in Persia and Zoroastrianism became the state religion.

Parts of the Avesta, notably the seventeen hymns known as 'Gathas', are believed to have been composed by the founder, Zoroaster (or Zarathustra) himself, probably *c.*1000 BCE in a variety of Old Iranian similar to the language of the Indian Vedas. The 'Gathas' were believed to contain the actual words of the prophet in Old Avestan, the original language, and considered too sacred to be entrusted to any foreign writing system. They were therefore memorized and transmitted orally for well over 1,000 years, almost totally unintelligible to all but the priests or Magi. Strict rules were devised to ensure the correct pronunciation of the sacred language, for example, the recitation of it must never be interrupted by utterances in another language, even the languages normally spoken by the priests or worshippers. In some editions, the Avesta is accompanied by a Middle Persian or Pahlavi translation known as the 'Zand'. It was eventually written down in the Pahlavi script, a writing system used in Persian official documents in the Parthian and Sassanian periods. This is derived from the Aramaic consonantal script, but uses only 14 of the 22 Aramaic consonants and introduces a very awkward system of ideograms (or, more correctly, heterograms). Thus, for example, the letters YWM (Aramaic and Hebrew for 'day') would be read and pronounced as *roz* 'day' in Iranian. Therefore, even with a commentary and in written form, Avestan still remained largely unintelligible. Indeed, there were some who believed that the meaning of the Avesta was intended to be beyond human understanding, and that the effective participation in worship depended more on hearing the accurate enunciation of every sound and syllable of the text than on understanding what it was about (*ELL* 1: 290).

This brings us finally to the phenomenon of glossolalia or 'speaking in tongues', first mentioned in connection with the ecstatic behaviour of some of the first converts to Christianity. Paul acknowledges that 'speaking in a strange tongue' is an acceptable part of public worship, alongside hymns, lessons and the like (1 Cor. 14:26), but cautions that it must be accompanied by an 'interpretation', otherwise people will think Christians are mad (v. 23). If no interpreter is available, then, 'each of them must keep quiet and speak to himself and to god' (v. 28). Paul lists 'speaking various kinds of tongues' and 'the interpretation of tongues' along with healing, miracle-working, prophecy and other activities as *charismata* 'spiritual gifts or manifestations' present in the church at Corinth (1 Cor. 12:10). There is also an incident in Acts in which 'speaking in tongues and extolling God' are considered proof that new converts have received the Holy Spirit (Acts 10:44–8). Today glossolalia is widespread, especially though not exclusively in many charismatic forms of contemporary Christianity, such as Pentecostalist groups, who trace their origin back to the biblical tradition that on the day of Pentecost (seven weeks after the death and resurrection of Christ) the disciples were all filled with the Holy Spirit and began to speak in other tongues as the Spirit gave them utterance (Acts 2:4). Similar phenomena have been recorded in various forms of spirit possession, shamanism, Zulu prophetism and certain South-East Asian Buddhist rites.

There is not yet any agreement among sociologists and linguists as to the true nature of these remarkable utterances, 'dismissed as gibberish by some, while others describe it as the language of angels' (*ELL* 3: 1444). Some ancient observers were agreed that it was a foreign language, quite unknown both to the speaker and the interpreter and therefore proof of its supernatural source. Paul quotes a verse from Isaiah in his discussion of glossolalia which makes clear what he thought was going on: 'By men of strange tongues and by the lips of foreigners will I speak to this people...' (1 Cor.14:21; cf. Isa. 28:11). Similarly, the story of the miracle at Pentecost tells how many of the bystanders, who were visitors to Jerusalem from many foreign lands, could understand the mysterious language spoken by the disciples as if it was their own native language. Others, more sceptical and obviously without the gift of interpretation, recognized no natural language in the utterances and concluded that the disciples were drunk.

Comparison with some aspects of biblical prophecy has been made by scholars (Trevett 1996: 89–91). There are plenty of references to ecstatic behaviour in the Bible, including stammering exclamations (Isa. 28:11), various forms of trembling and shaking (Isa. 21:3–4; Dan. 10:10, 11), staring (Ezek. 3:15) and falling to the ground (Ezek. 1:28; 3:23; Dan. 10:9). Bystanders, like those just referred to in Acts, express amazement when someone like Saul 'behaves like a prophet' (Heb. *hitnabbe*'; 1 Sam. 10:10–12), and Jeremiah compares his experience to that of a drunken man: 'My heart is broken within me and all my bones are shaking. I am become like a drunkard, someone overcome by wine, because of the Lord and because of his holy words' (Jer. 23:9). Philo, in his description of the physical effects of divine inspiration, uses a word associated with the physical intoxication of worshippers of Bacchus or Dionysus, and notes that to the unenlightened it may seem like the behaviour of drunks or madmen. He does maintain, however, that these are only superficial resemblances since divine intoxication (*theia methe*) is 'more sober than sobriety itself' (Philo, Leg. Alleg. 3, 83). Objections have been raised to such comparisons on the grounds that the biblical references are lacking in precise detail, and also in the light of the fact that modern glossolalic speakers often claim they do not in fact experience such physical and psychological symptoms.

Modern cross-cultural studies of glossolalic speech among pentecostal groups in Wales, the United States, Mexico and elsewhere show that it is characterized by rapid rhythmic sounds often progressing to word-like or even sentence-like structures before dying away into silence. Every pulse begins with a single consonant; there are no initial consonantal clusters. Stress is always on the first pulse of each phrase. Phrases are of equal length. Even though occasional recognizable words may occur, 'tongues' are unintelligible both to the speaker and the listener, and the interpretation or translation, which often employs familiar phrases from the biblical Prophets and Psalms, rarely corresponds in length to the original utterance. The interpreter is himself or herself believed to be charismatic, and the function of the 'interpretation of tongues' is more to contribute another independent, divinely inspired proclamation, than to provide anything like a translation. Occasionally an interpreter claims to be able to identify the meaning of recurring syllables or words, for example: 'le le' which occurs at the end of many 'sentences' was interpreted as 'Praise God!', related perhaps in his mind in some way to Hebrew 'Hallelujah' or 'El' or Arabic 'Allah'. But such instances of rationality in the process are exceptional and probably artificial. Usually the power and effectiveness of the phenomenon depends on the fact that the glossolalic speaker and the interpreter do not share the same linguistic code (Samarin 1972).

No reliable evidence has yet been produced for the traditional view that the language of glossolalic utterances and their interpretation is ever a natural language unknown to the speaker, a phenomeon known as 'xenoglossy' and 'responsive xenoglossy'. Pentecostal writers often refer to this. In a school in Houston, Texas, it was claimed that twenty Chinese dialects were spoken at pentecostal worship, while at Mukbi in India over a period of three years from 1905 to 1908 illiterate girls at an orphanage are said to have spoken and prayed in English, Greek, Hebrew and Sanskrit – all languages which they had never learnt (Williams 1981). Such claims, like the notion that it is often Aramaic, the language of Jesus, no doubt arise from the understandable awe of believers in the presence of what is a truly remarkable feature of public worship.

If it is not a known language, what is it? There are two opposing views. According to one it is a pseudolanguage, sharing phonological and structural features with natural languages, but, what is more significant, capable of evolving and developing into a kind of idiolect on the lips of a particular speaker. This would imply a degree of skill or aptitude, learned or instinctive, on the part of the speaker, and more evidence would be needed before this could be established. The other view focuses more on the trance-like state of the speaker, and suggests that glossolalia is a 'speech automatism produced in an altered state of consciousness' (Samarin 1972: 22–34). It cannot be called a language since speakers have no control over what they are saying. Again, more research is needed, especially comparative research involving the study of other types of ecstatic utterance, the use of mantras in Indian religious traditions, meditation techniques in various contexts and other similar phenomena. This might establish whether, for example, there are recurring vocalization patterns in such utterances, whether there is any correlation between bilingualism and glossolalia, and whether clarifying the social function of this type of behaviour might shed any light on its nature.

4

LITERACY

The spread of literacy in the Hellenistic world and the Roman Empire is one of the most important features of the early part of our period. It is evident to the archaeologist not only in the masses of surviving inscriptions, carved by professional writing experts in bronze and stone, but also in the numerous scrawls on the walls and pavements of buildings excavated all over the Empire. By 100 CE even the handwriting in Latin documents from outposts of the Empire as far apart as Upper Egypt and the north of England is astonishingly uniform (Bowman and Woolf 1994: 12). A recent estimate reckons a maximum of 20–30 per cent literacy was achieved in the Roman Empire (Harris 1989; *OCD*: 869; cf. Gamble 1995: 1–10) as opposed to estimates of between 2 and 7 per cent for pre-Hellenistic Egypt (Ray 1994: 64–5). This was due in part to the enormous number of schools, many of them like the one endowed by the Younger Pliny at Comum, established by private investors. There were also an increasing number of institutions of higher education in which rhetoric was central – there were eleven such centres in Gaul alone (Cary 1980: 691).

Books at moderate prices became widely available. Small libraries became commonplace even in the smaller country villas, and books newly published in Rome quickly became known throughout Spain, Gaul and North Africa. Rome was an even more book- and library-orientated society than Greece had been. You could read books on almost every conceivable topic. Writing was an essential accompaniment to life at almost all levels to an extent without parallel in living memory (Roberts 1970: 48). Metaphors about reading and writing were common. Paul provides us with an extended example:

Do we need, as some do, letters of recommendation...?
You are yourselves our letter of recommendation, written
on your hearts, to be known and read by all; and you show
that you are a letter from Christ delivered by us, written
not with ink but with the Spirit of the living God, not on
tablets of stone but on tablets of human hearts.

(2 Cor. 3:1–3)

Even if this picture is exaggerated and refers to the literacy of only a
fraction of the population, excluding women and the uneducated;
for example (Harris 1989: 281–2), it does reflect a general situation
where an unusually receptive market for Christian publications
existed.

Talmudic teaching on lending books provides an interesting
indication of how books were regarded in ancient Jewish circles.
According to Rab Hisda (died 309 CE) anyone who writes the Law,
the Prophets and the Writings and lends them to others will have
'wealth and riches in his house, and his righteousness will endure
for ever' (Ps. 112:3; BT Ket. 50b). In a midrashic comment on
another verse from scripture, Rabbi Tarfon says that the one 'who
acts charitably at all times' in Psalm 106:3 refers to people who
write books and lend them to others. Later commentators discussed
whether the recommendation was intended to include books in
general and whether lending books to others actually amounted to a
halakhic 'obligation' (Ya'ari 1958: 179–97). Respect for writing and
shared learning has been a characteristic of Judaism from ancient
times.

In the Hellenistic world, institutional libraries modelled on the
peripatos library at Athens, which originated in Aristotle's private
collection, were established in many cities (Gamble 1995: 144–
202). Alexandria's library was the most famous containing nearly
500,000 rolls, equivalent to perhaps around 100,000 modern
books, but there were many others such as those at Pella, Antioch
and Pergamum. The situation in Rome was different. The earliest
texts of treaties, ritual laws and other official documents like the
Acta Populi, written on bronze tablets, were lodged in the Temple
of Saturn, which functioned as sanctuary, treasury and record office.
The Annales Maximi, a kind of annual priestly chronicle containing
a calendar of religious festivals for the ensuing year as well as
references to other events involving religious ceremonies, such as
dedications of temples, triumphs, famines and prodigies, were

originally exhibited on tablets in public places, but in 125 BCE were published in book form.

Earlier in the same century, the library of King Perseus of Macedonia found its way to Rome (167 BCE) and that of Aristotle in 86 BCE (see pp. 20–21). Private libraries became increasingly common throughout the Greek and Roman world. Cicero had a large personal collection, and visited several others in Rome. Magnificent libraries were built in Rome by Augustus, Vespasian, Trajan, Marcus Aurelius and others. By the second century CE there was an official, known as the 'procurator bibliothecarum', to oversee the libraries of Rome, and according to a fourth-century source, there were twenty-eight libraries in Rome at the time. Substantial libraries from other parts of the Empire have been excavated at Ephesus (the library of Celsus) in Asia Minor and Timgad in North Africa, while Origen's library at Caesarea is another well-known example.

Latin literature was in many areas closely modelled on Greek originals known through the Hellenistic writings. Horace's *Odes* are based on Hellenistic lyric poetry, for example, and Virgil's *Aeneid* is a Roman version of Homer's *Odyssey*, much influenced by Apollonius' *Argonautica*. The emperor Vespasian, despite his military upbringing and obscure origins, could quote Homer fluently. As we have seen, the second century CE saw a revival of Greek culture under the emperors Hadrian, Antoninus Pius and Marcus Aurelius. The great cultural centres like Smyrna, Pergamum and Ephesus in Asia Minor owe many of their magnificent temples and libraries to this period. There was a proliferation of manuals of astrology, dream books, books of sorcery (Brown 1971: 63). There was renewed interest in Greek history, science, philosophy and culture. Historians of the period include Plutarch, Arrian, Appian and, a little later, Dio Cassius (*c.*164–230 CE). Their works became later generations' main sources for the classical tradition, as did the medical encyclopaedia of Galen (*c.*130–200 CE) and the treatises on geography and astronomy composed by the Alexandrian scholar, Ptolemy, between *c.*146 and 170 CE. These were the works consulted and studied by every educated person, both in Christendom and the Islamic world, for the next 1,500 years (Brown 1971: 17).

Alongside the reverence for the written word of scripture there existed, both in the Greco-Roman world and within Judaism, a distrust of books. Plato argues persuasively for the priority of the spoken word – in particular the cut and thrust of spoken dialogue –

and even states that the profoundest truths cannot be written down at all (*Phaedrus* 274f.). We shall see later how the same reverence for living debate characterizes the literary form of rabbinic literature, known collectively as the 'Oral Torah', even though it now occupies thirty or forty substantial volumes of printed text. The Book of Ecclesiastes ends with an invidious comparison between the spoken words of the wise, which operate like goads or 'nails firmly fixed', and the wearisome nature of bookish learning (Eccles. 12:11–12). Paul's warning that 'the letter killeth, the spirit maketh alive' (2 Cor. 3:6) also places the emphasis on oral tradition. The continuing reverence for the sound of the text is also evident in the fact that the word *qara* 'to read' in ancient Hebrew meant 'to read aloud, recite', and it is from that verb that one of the Hebrew words for Bible, *Miqra*, and, incidentally, the Arabic word *Qur'an* are derived.

Oral tradition often has an important role to play in the transmission of religious texts. Julius Caesar tells us that the Druids did not commit their religious tradition to writing, partly because they did not want outsiders to have access to it, and partly because they valued the faculty of memory very highly (*Gallic War* 6:14). In ancient Persia the Zoroastrian priests taught that their sacred text, the Avesta, which was believed to contain the actual words of their founder, had never to be written down. For many centuries, their sacred text was an oral text. This was because they believed, as did the ancient Hindu priests, that the sounds of the text, which were known only to them, were in some special way sacred.

Another reason was probably that they considered no human writing system worthy of the task. Writing was fit for secular uses only. Unlike Jews and Muslims, the Persians never had a beautiful script designed for their own language. The earliest Old Persian documents were written in one of the cuneiform writing systems that were current throughout the Near East from before 3000 BCE to the time of Christ. From the eighth century BCE, when Aramaic became the language of trade and commerce, the much easier alphabetical script, known as the Aramaic or Square script, was also used for writing Persian. An Assyrian bas-relief shows two scribes together, one writing in cuneiform with a stylus on a clay tablet, the other writing in Aramaic with pen and ink on papyrus (Ghirshman 1954: 163–4). Much later, Persian scribes modified the Aramaic script in various ways, for instance, using only some of the twenty-two letters of the alphabet and devising a bizarre system of ideograms to create their own unique Pahlavi writing system. This was the medium in which the Avesta and other religious texts were eventually written down in the fifth century CE. The very bizarreness of it may have contributed to the change of policy on the part of the Magi, although, as we shall see, there were other important factors operating as well in the eventual decision to write down their sacred text.

Other religious traditions, by contrast, place special emphasis on the writing down of their sacred texts and on the special power and sanctity of their script. An early rabbinic ruling states that 'only if scripture is written in ink, on leather, in the original language and in the original script, is it deemed sacred' (MYad. 4:5). The painstaking efforts of the Masoretes to transmit the Hebrew text as perfectly as possible are another indication of the importance placed in Jewish tradition on the written text. The Jewish and Christian use of the term for 'the writings' in Hebrew (*ha-ketubim*), Greek (*hai graphai*) and Latin (*scriptura*) without the adjective 'sacred, holy' to mean 'the sacred writing(s), holy scripture' (e.g. John 19:37) shows just how much emphasis was put on the uniqueness of these sacred writings. The same applies to Christian uses of the Greek term *ta biblia* 'the books (sacred books, scripture)' (2 Clem. 14:2) from which the word 'Bible' is derived, to which we might compare Muslim uses of Arabic *al-kitab* 'the book' in expressions like *umm al-kitab* 'the people of the book'. Studying Judaism and studying the Torah were virtually synonymous. Jewish scholars and Torah-teachers were known as 'scribes'. The respect in which scribes were held (cf. Sir. 38:24–39:11) and the power they wielded can be seen as another indication of the centrality of the written word in Judaism (Goodman 1994: 99–108).

It is no coincidence that both in Judaism and in Islam the art of calligraphy was so highly developed. This was a natural conse-quence of the reverence in which the written words of holy scripture were held. But it was also due to the fact that in both religions representational art was forbidden (cf. Deut. 5:8). We shall look later in more detail at Jewish mystical speculation regarding the precise forms of the letters, the role of the Hebrew alphabet in the creation story, the pseudo-science of gematria and other beliefs about the writing system in which the Hebrew Bible is written. For the moment let us simply note these two totally different attitudes to sacred text, one written and one oral, and consider the relation-ship between written and oral tradition in these two and other religious traditions, and the factors leading to the writing down of sacred texts.

Exactly when and for what reason Hebrew scripture was first written down is not known. There is of course no external evidence that Moses actually wrote the five books of the Torah that tradition attributes to him. Someone, like Moses, brought up in ancient Egyptian society (Exod. 2), would certainly have been able to read and write in at least one of the three main writing systems most widely used in Egypt and Palestine during the second half of the second millennium BCE. These were Egyptian hieroglyphics, Assyro-Babylonian cuneiform and the Canaanite alphabetic script. Moreover, a vast body of Egyptian literature, including myths, legends, travellers' tales, hymns, prayers, oracles, prophecies and didactic texts written in Egyptian hieroglyphics on papyrus, is known to have been in existence by then and was much used in schools, royal courts and elsewhere. So biblical references to Moses and his contemporaries' writing are not anachronisms (e.g. Exod. 17:14; 24:4; Num. 17:27; Deut. 24:1–3). But that is quite different from saying that the 'Five Books of Moses' existed in writing at such an early date in the history of Hebrew literature. There are in them many indications of multiple authorship, and modern scholarship is virtually unanimous in dating the finished product to a period at least seven or eight centuries after any proposed date for the death of Moses.

On the other hand, recent research suggests that the knowledge of writing was considerably more widespread in ancient Israel than used to be thought. Attention has been drawn to the sheer variety and distribution of epigraphic material in Palestine from the tenth century BCE on, and to the fact that the Canaanite alphabetical system of writing was far easier to learn and use than any of the systems employed in Egypt and Mesopotamia. All three systems, alphabetical, hieroglyphic and cuneiform, were known in Palestine. However, let us concentrate our attention on Hebrew writing. There are numerous examples of the routine writing of ephemeral administrative notes, which would not have required any specialist expertise. Many of the inscribed potsherds (*ostraka*) from eighth-century BCE Samaria in the north and Arad in the south belong to this category. Large numbers of seals and clay bullae originally attached to papyrus documents that have long since perished prove that such documents did once exist in Palestine. The accidental discovery of a few stone inscriptions, like the Mesha inscription from Moab (cf. 2 Kings 3) and the fragment of a similar one from Tel Dan in the north, both dated to the ninth century BCE, and the famous Siloam inscription in Hezekiah's tunnel at Jerusalem

(2 Kings 20:20) from the eighth century BCE suggests that many more may have been destroyed or reused in later buildings (Millard 1995a).

The famous Gezer Calendar from the tenth century proves that writing was in use by then for other purposes than purely administrative, as do the many ancient graffiti from a variety of places, including Jerusalem. A chance find in the Jordan valley shows that someone in the ninth to eighth century BCE was able to write a copy of a story about the prophet Balaam (Num. 22–4) on the plastered wall of a building at Tel Deir Alla. There was clearly far more writing in everyday use than the accident of archaeological discovery might prima facie suggest. One reason for this is the relative simplicity of the Hebrew alphabet. No expensive equipment or writing material was required: no special stylus or pen and ink, and no clay tablet, expensive papyrus or vellum was necessary. Anyone with a knowledge of the Hebrew alphabet can scratch graffiti onto a piece of stone or a potsherd with almost any sharp instrument.

Another characteristic of the Hebrew alphabet is that it has far fewer signs than the alternative systems: twenty-two in Hebrew as against over 300 cuneiform signs and over 700 hieroglyphs. Not that a simple comparison like this is entirely helpful, since obviously the function of the signs differs greatly between systems, and the more signs there are in a system may actually make it easier to read. Political, commercial and religious factors also affected the spread of literacy. But there can be no doubt that the mechanics of writing Hebrew were far simpler than for any of the other systems, and the fact is that in the ancient Near East (though not in China) all the competing systems eventually gave way to an alphabet (Coulmas 1992).

However that may be, there is now enough evidence from ancient Israel to conclude that literacy was more widespread than used to be thought. When we remember that our main finds come from small places, we can only imagine how much there must have been in the large political and religious centres, which so far have provided the archaeologists with so little. Therefore, we must take passing biblical references to written records seriously, like the 'Book of the Chronicles of the Kings of Israel' (e.g. 1 Kings 14:19; 15:31; 16:14) and the 'Book of the Law' (2 Kings 22:8). We should also take seriously the literary activity of people like 'the men of Hezekiah' (Prov. 25:1) and the person who claims to have written 'the thirty sayings of admonition and knowledge' (Prov. 22:20) –

even if it is extremely unlikely to have been Solomon himself as tradition claims (Prov. 1:1; 10:1).

All this, however, does not give us a date for the writing down of the Torah. Even if the reference to finding the 'Book of the Law' in the Temple at Jerusalem during Josiah's reign (639–609 BCE) (2 Kings 22:8) is to be taken at face value, the identity of it is by no means certain. Indeed, the indications are that whatever it was – possibly part of Deuteronomy – it was not the Torah or the 'Five Books of Moses' in their present form. It may be significant that, within a few generations of that first reference to the existence of a sacred text in the Temple at Jerusalem, we have our first sizeable collection of written documents from a Jewish source. These are the Elephantine papyri, a collection of letters and other material written in Aramaic by Jews living in Egypt between c.495 and 400 BCE, including written correspondence with the temple at Jerusalem. There may also be some truth in the statement in 2 Maccabees that Nehemiah (fifth century BCE) founded a library in which he made a collection of 'the books about the kings and the prophets, the books of David and letters of kings about sacred gifts' (2 Macc. 2:13).

There are other indications that at least the first part of the Hebrew Bible, the Torah, was in existence in written form by about that time. First, there are the repeated references to the 'Book of the Law' (Neh. 8:8) or 'The Book of Moses' (Ezra 6:18; Neh. 13:1) in the account of the restoration under Ezra and Nehemiah in the fifth century BCE. Second, there is the fact that the Samaritan community, which had split off decisively from Jerusalem by the end of the fifth century BCE at the latest, had a complete Hebrew Pentateuch of their own which is almost identical to that of the Jews. This proves that a common text must have existed in Judah and Samaria before that time. Third, there are persistent traditions about the role of Ezra in establishing the 'Book of the Law' as authoritative for his community (Neh. 8:8). What purports to be an official letter from 'Artaxerxes king of kings', which is included in the biblical account of Ezra's reforms, confirms that he was given powerful support for his reforms by the mighty Persian government (Ezra 7:11–26). Rabbinic tradition is unanimous about the role of Ezra. The Torah had been forgotten in Israel and Ezra restored it to its rightful place (BT Sukk. 20a). He was reckoned to be the model Torah scholar (Gen. R. 36, 8). He restored the correct text of the Torah and was also credited with introducing the new Aramaic or

Square script (BT Sanh. 21b) in which all copies of the Torah have subsequently been written (MYad. 4:5).

We can be fairly confident that the first part of Hebrew scripture, the Torah, had reached more or less its present written form by the end of the fifth century BCE. Traditions about a Greek translation of the Torah in the third century BCE confirm that conclusion. The next firm date is *c.*180 BCE when a reference to the 'Law, the Prophets and the other books of our fathers' in the prologue to the Book of Ecclesiasticus (or the Wisdom of Jesus ben Sira) provides clear evidence that the second part of the Hebrew Bible was in existence by then, along with some indication that the third part was already taking shape, if not yet in its final form. There is an interesting tradition, in which there may be some historical truth, that Judas Maccabaeus, like Nehemiah two centuries earlier, was responsible for making a collection of religious writings after the crisis of 167–164 BCE was over (2 Macc. 2:4f.). The Dead Sea Scrolls (*c.*150 BCE–70 CE) provide ample written evidence for the existence of most of the books of the Hebrew Bible, only the Book of Esther being conspicuous by its absence. The formula, 'the Law and the Prophets', occurs with great frequency in the New Testament and other Jewish literature of the period, sometimes 'the Law, the Prophets and the Psalms', while references to the Psalms and other parts of the Hebrew Bible as scripture become increasingly common. By the second century CE, the written form of Hebrew scripture was complete, and became known by the acronym TaNaK, 'the Bible', from the initial letters of its three parts: Torah, Nebi'im and Ketubim.

Why was the written form of the sacred text so important in Judaism, and subsequently in Christianity and Islam? There is an ancient tradition that the first words of scripture were actually written down by God at Sinai on stone tablets: 'the tablets were the work of God and the writing was the writing of God, graven on the tablets' (Exod. 32:16). In a passage immortalized in Cecil B. de Mille's literal interpretation of it in his film, *The Ten Commandments,* divine authority for the written form of scripture is even given a physical dimension: 'And he gave to Moses...the two tablets of stone, written with the finger of God' (Exod. 31:18; cf. John 8:6). In fact, writing is a recurring theme throughout the legends about the origins of Hebrew scripture (cf. Exod. 24:4; 32:32–3; 34:27–8; Deut. 10:4; 27:3, 8; 29:20, 21, 27; 30:10; 31:19, 22). The king is to write out for himself a copy of the law (Deut. 17:18). Joshua wrote a copy of the law of Moses in stone (Josh. 8:32; cf. 24:26).

David apparently received in advance a plan of Solomon's Temple 'written by the hand of the Lord' (1 Chron. 28:19). There are a good many references to writing in the prophets as well, although none of them amounts to unambiguous evidence that their words were ever written down as a matter of course: 'Now go, write it before them on a tablet, and inscribe it in a book' (Isa. 30:8; cf. 8:16; 29:11–12; 1 Sam. 10:25; Jer. 30:2; Ezek. 2:9–3:3; Dan. 12:4; Nah. 1:1; Hab. 2:2; Zech. 5:1–2). Only Jeremiah has a scribe beside him with instructions to write down what he says, and that was only on one specific occasion (Jer. 36).

There are repeated references in the Bible to 'the book of the covenant', 'the book of the law' and the like. In Talmudic times scripture is referred to as *ha-katub* 'the written (sc. word, verse, passage)' and the third part of the Hebrew Bible is called the 'Writings' (*Ketubim*) (BT Ket. 50a), presumably shorthand for the 'other writings' (cf. Sir. Prologue) (Beckwith 1985: 166f.). In Greek, Jewish writers applied the corresponding terms *graphe* and *graphai* to scripture, often with the adjective *hiera* or *hagia* 'sacred' (e.g. 4 Macc. 18:14; Matt. 21:42), which was represented in Latin by the word *scriptura* and eventually English 'scripture'. Reading is also repeatedly referred to: 'Moses took the book of the covenant and read it in the hearing of the people...' (Exod. 24:7; Deut. 31:11; Josh. 8:34). The reaction of the hearers to the words of scripture read out to them is another familiar theme: 'All that the Lord has spoken we will do, and we will be obedient' (Exod. 24:7); 'and when the king heard the words of the book of the law, he rent his clothes' (2 Kings 22:11); 'for all the people wept when they heard the words of the law' (Neh. 8:9); 'and he rolled up the scroll and gave it to the attendant and sat down: the eyes of all the synagogue were upon him' (Luke 4:20).

There are several possible reasons for the importance of writing in Jewish tradition. One may be the simple fact that the sacred language and the sacred script are inseparable in a way that does not apply to many other languages and scripts. The Hebrew consonantal script represents the twenty-two consonants of the alphabet exactly, and is perfectly designed for writing Hebrew. A second factor, which may have been crucial, arises out of the unique centrality in the biblical tradition of the notion of a covenant made between Yahweh and his people. Modern research has drawn attention to a number of striking parallels between the language used in ancient near eastern vassal treaties and the language of covenant making in the Hebrew Bible. These include the stipulation that, to be legally binding, the terms of the covenant must be written down (cf. Exod. 24:4; 31:18; 34:1, 27–8; Deut. 10:2; 31:9; Josh. 8:32; 24:26). The written document or 'book' (Exod. 24:7) must then be treated as sacred, kept in a special place, guarded by the priests and ritually read aloud to the people. Whether this familiar metaphor from international law goes back to the origins of Yahwism or to the time of Moses, as some have argued, or whether, as is more likely, it was adopted much later in the history of Israel, it certainly provides a compelling explanation for why the written form of at least part of the text had such authority. The same authority was extended to cover the words of the historiographers, prophets, psalmists and wisdom writers of the biblical period, and, by the time of Christ, the whole Tanak constituted the very heart of Judaism.

Reading and writing Hebrew were high on the educational agenda, especially when Hebrew was no longer the language of everyday conversation. There was plenty of scriptural authority for this, particularly in Deuteronomy (6:7; 11:19) and Proverbs (1:8; 2:1; 3:1; 4:1). Rabbinic tradition is unanimous in stressing the need to study the text. It is said that R. Hiyya did not have breakfast until he had taught a boy some scripture, going over with him what he had learnt the day before and teaching him a new piece (BT Qidd. 30a). We are told that youngsters were encouraged to start their Hebrew reading lessons on the Book of Leviticus (BT Men. 110a), partly no doubt because they enjoyed learning ordinary, everyday words like 'griddle' (Lev. 2:5) and 'hoopoe' (11:19), which are rarely found elsewhere in the Bible, rather than 'sin', 'righteousness', 'salvation' and the like, and partly because the constant repetition of words and phrases, which is a characteristic of ritual legislation, is pedagogically helpful.

Teachers were known as 'rabbis', but there also had to be experts in interpretation and translation as well, scholars known as 'scribes' (*sopherim*) like Ezra (Neh. 8) or sages (*hakhamim*) as the rabbis were later referred to. Tradition credits Ezra (c.400 BCE) with the beginning of this process, identifying in Neh. 8:8 the first reference to the Targum, a free interpretative Aramaic translation of the Torah. Two hundred years later, Ben Sira contains an early eulogy of a scholar: 'devoted to the study of the law of the Most High...who delights in penetrating the "subtleties" and "obscurities" of parables and the "hidden meanings" of proverbs, and meditating on the secrets of scripture...his memory will never disappear, and his name will live through all generations,

(Sir. 39:1–3, 7–9). Philo describes how the text was handled by the experts in an Essene community: 'one takes the books and reads them aloud, another more learned comes forward and instructs them in what they do not know' (*Quod omn. prob.* 81–2).

By that time, too, the importance alongside the written Torah of an oral tradition, known as the *torah she-be'al peh*, was firmly established and by the beginning of the third century CE, an authoritative selection of this oral tradition had been written down in the Mishnah. The process culminated in the fifth century with the compilation of the Babylonian Talmud, a vast collection of the sayings, disputes and anecdotes of the rabbis, arranged as a rambling verse-by-verse commentary on the Mishnah. It was in this period, too, that the Persian priests finally committed their sacred text, the Avesta, to writing, probably partly under the influence of the religions of the book, Judaism and Christianity in the West (Ghirshman 1954: 318). This was also a crucial stage in the history of official Christian literature, following the conversion of Constantine and the establishment of Christianity as the state religion of the Roman Empire.

The influence of Christianity on the spread of literacy and the consequent survival of vernaculars, especially in the East, was considerable. The success of Syriac, the language of the countryside and of ordinary people, in withstanding the pressure of first Greek and then Arabic was due to its role in Eastern Christianity. It has survived in parts of Turkey, Syria and elsewhere down to the present day. The Armenian patriarch, St Mesrop (*c.*345–440), invented the distinctive Armenian alphabetic script, which was soon adopted by the Georgians. Later, a Greek Orthodox missionary to the Slav peoples, St Cyril (ninth century), invented the Cyrillic script. In the West the situation was rather different. In Germany the Goths were given a specially designed script by Bishop Ulfilas in which to write their own language, but elsewhere literacy accompanied the spread of Latin, both before Constantine and after. In Gaul, for example, although there is some evidence before the Roman conquest of Gallo-Greek and Gallo-Latin, that is to say, Gaulish written in Greek and Latin letters, it was not long before Latin became the official and dominant language.

At this time, momentous decisions were taken by the great Ecumenical Councils at Nicaea (325 CE), Constantinople (381 CE), Ephesus (431 CE), and Chalcedon (451 CE), not least those affecting the language and literature of the Church. Individual or regional factors may have been operating in some of the contemporaneous developments as well, especially nationalism and the consequences of a centralized definition of orthodoxy, but for a few centuries they were all occurring within the same vast international context, aware of one another and reacting to one another: the canonization of Christian scripture, the formulation of the Christian creeds, the compilation of the Talmud and the writing down of the Avesta. This was also the time when the earliest and most complete surviving manuscripts of the Greek Bible were written: *Codex Sinaiticus, Codex Alexandrinus, Codex Vaticanus* and *Codex Bezae*. It was no doubt due to a large extent to the new power of the Church that such beautiful manuscripts could be produced and have survived down to the present. This was the culmination of a process of literary and scholarly enterprise which we can trace back to its roots in the Hellenistic world.

Jewish scripture has always been written on scrolls from biblical times to the present day (cf. Jer. 36; Ezek. 3:1–3; Zech. 5:1). One of the best-known icons of recent biblical archaeology is that of the Dead Sea Scrolls, which date from 150 BCE to 70 CE. Of these the largest and most perfect is the beautiful Isaiah Scroll A, familiar to visitors to the Shrine of the Book in Jerusalem. It is made of seventeen strips of leather stitched together into an enormous scroll almost seven and a half metres long. The Torah scroll, written on the finest parchment according to the strictest regulations, with its embroidered velvet mantle and its silver casing, finials, crown and breastplate, is still the central symbol of synagogue worship, and the little Book of Esther is always known simply as the *Megillah* 'the Scroll'.

By contrast, Christians from the earliest times seem to have preferred for canonical works the codex, a relatively new type of book with pages that turn like modern printed books. All the Chester Beatty papyri found in Egypt in the 1930s, of which the earliest were written in the early part of the second century CE, are codices. The codex was a distinctively Roman invention: the Greeks did not even have a word for it until the third century. It was invented and popularized in Rome from the first century CE. The Christian predilection for the codex may have been to distinguish themselves from Jews, or perhaps because codices were easier to carry around than scrolls (Roberts 1970: 58f.). Alternatively, it may have had something to do with the fact that Christians from the beginning saw themselves as innovators rather than preservers of tradition. The new codex, like the languages and scripts used and occasionally invented by them, pointed nicely in this direction (Gamble 1995: 63–6).

One further development in the history of Hebrew scripture was the invention of 'pointing', a system designed to represent vowel sounds, accents and musical notation. Although Hebrew scripture had been preserved for centuries in written form, the script in which it was written down was a consonantal script, which can be pronounced only by people who already know the language. As fewer and fewer people knew Hebrew, there was a need for a new writing system in which vowels and musical notation could be represented. The first attempts to do this were probably in the fourth or fifth centuries CE, roughly contemporary with the invention of a similar system for Syriac, as well as the creation of the Pahlavi writing system by the Persians, and the Armenian and Gothic scripts mentioned earlier, and is known collectively as 'Masoretic pointing', that is to say, the pointing system invented by the Masoretes. Masoretes were the scholars entrusted with the task of protecting the sacred text of the Bible with the *masora* 'the tradition'. In Rabbi Aqiba's famous words, 'The masora is a hedge round the Law' (MAboth 3:14).

These scholars were at first known as *sopherim* 'scribes', ingeniously explained in the Talmud as 'those who count' (Heb. *saphar* 'to count'). One of the methods they employed to ensure that the text was always copied perfectly was to count letters and words, and indicate, for example, that the word *darosh* in Lev. 10:16 is the middle word of the Torah. Later, they came to be known as the 'Masoretes' to whom we owe all our manuscripts of the Hebrew Bible, apart from the Dead Sea Scrolls and a few other fragments from the ancient world. Various different Masoretic systems of vocalization can be identified from the surviving manuscripts, which are all mediaeval. They include the Babylonian system, which is supralinear and probably derived from Syriac, and the Tiberian system, which is the one used in most modern printed editions of the Hebrew Bible.

The consonantal text, however, continued to have an independent existence of its own and was always considered more sacred than the pointing. Officially produced Torah scrolls were written without the points, and as every one had to be copied by hand from a standard copy held in the Temple at Jerusalem, according to the strictest rules, they were virtually identical. But the independence of the consonantal text from the vocalization system led to an important distinction noted by scribes from ancient times, between the written, consonantal text (Aramaic *Ketib*), which was considered especially sacred, and how it was pronounced (*Qere*), which could vary considerably from one region to another. It was forbidden to alter a single letter of the *Ketib*, but if for any reason the scribes wished to emend the text, they could do this by writing the consonants of the original word and the vowels of their emendation. The best-known example of this convention is the name of Israel's god, which was written in the consonantal text with the four letters (tetragrammaton) as YHWH. Rabbinic law prohibited the actual pronunciation of this sacred name except on a few special occasions, and by writing it with the vowels of the word *Adonai* 'the Lord' or sometimes *Elohim* 'God', the scribes sought to ensure that readers never broke that prohibition.

Another example of how scribes could exploit this two-pronged writing system is polemical. Several times in the Hebrew Bible they have written the consonants of the name of a foreign deity with the vowels of a word for 'abomination'. The Moabite god, Moloch, is regularly written as *molek*, that is, with the vowels of the word *boshet* 'abomination' known from the polemical forms Ishbosheth, Mephibosheth and the 'abomination of desolation' *boshet shomem* (Dan. 8:13 AV). Similarly, two Assyrian astral deities, Sakkuth and Kaiwan, are pointed *sikkut* and *kiyyun* in a way that associates them immediately with *shiqqutz* 'abomination' (Zech. 9:7), *gillul* 'idol' (or ball of dung) (Deut. 29:17) and *piggul* 'abomination, stench' (Lev. 7:18) (Sawyer 1967).

The close correspondence between the surviving manuscripts, the earliest of which do not go back before the seventh or eighth century CE, and what ancient evidence we have for the consonantal text, the Dead Sea Scrolls in particular, is striking testimony to the effectiveness of Masoretic methods. Evidence for how it was pronounced in antiquity, before the invention of a vocalization system, is much harder to establish. There are some Greek and Latin transliterations of Hebrew, and some Hebrew inscriptions written in Greek or Latin letters. The cumulative effect of such material, still under investigation by scholars, suggests that the same applies to a large extent to the pointed texts as to the consonantal. There are cases where we can detect the influence of mediaeval conditions on the Masoretic text, the occurrence of a Hebrew word for 'damask' in the pointed text of Amos 3:12, for example. However, as a general rule we can be confident that the Masoretic text preserves with a fair degree of accuracy the sense of the Hebrew text, if not the pronunciation as it was known in the time of Christ.

5

CANONIZATION

We come now to consider the whole question of canonization. This is the complex process which leads to the existence, in many religious communities ancient and modern, as well as in other contexts, of a fixed 'list' or 'canon' of texts believed to be sacred, inspired or in some way special and different from all other texts. In a religious context, decisions are taken by a Church council or a group of leaders like the rabbis at Yavneh, to lay down precisely which books can and cannot be read aloud, and which can and cannot be preached on at public worship. In ancient Rome, the state gave canonical status to certain books or collections of books, such as the poems of Virgil and the Sibylline Oracles, which were officially consulted in times of doubt or crisis, and other texts with a sacred function like the 'Fasti' and the hymns to the gods, which were used on state occasions (Gordon 1990: 184–91). Outside official religion, and over against it, there have been efforts to establish alternative canons. The second-century Gnostic, Marcion, for example, in opposition to orthodoxy fixed a canon containing only the Gospel of Luke and ten Pauline Epistles. In the sixteenth century, Martin Luther decided to remove the apocrypha from the traditional canon of the Western Church, and in the eighteenth century the Swedish scientist and reformer, Emanuel Swedenborg, founder of the New Church, rejected Job, Proverbs, Pauline Epistles and other books as uncanonical.

The official canonization processes of Judaism and Christianity are by far the most familiar, most complex and best-documented examples from our period. We will recognize this by devoting the main part of the chapter to them. We shall be discussing the impact of events, such as the destruction of Jerusalem in 70 CE and the Bar Kokhba revolt in 135 CE. We shall also be discussing the role of Yavneh and the Church Councils, and the efforts of powerful figures like Akiba and Marcion to establish official canons, as well as such matters as the false attribution of texts like the apocryphal gospels and the 'sayings of Rabbi Meir'. But we shall also consider examples from the Greco-Roman world, including attempts to sanction fixed lists of classical works and authors, and the case of the Hippocratic corpus and the Avesta, both for their own sake and for purposes of comparison and contrast. In particular, we shall have to take account of the possible influence on the canonization process of such global events as the literary renaissance under Hadrian and the Antonines in the second century CE and the establishment of Christianity as the state religion of the Roman Empire in the fourth century. Finally, one of the most striking features of this period relevant to our study of canonization is the sheer volume and variety of written works produced. An impressive measure of this is the number of works which Eusebius could draw on for his ten-volume 'History of the Church' (303–23 CE), every page of which refers to the work of some Christian writer of the second to third centuries CE, more often than not lost to us.

The term 'canon' itself is not used in its Christian sense in pagan antiquity. It first meant a 'standard' or 'model': for example, the historian, Dio Cassius (c.164–229 CE), tells us that, for him, Thucydides was 'the canon' (OCD: 286). But the idea of establishing an authoritative 'list' (Latin ordo, numerus) of authors or works is quite common: the 'Three Tragedians', the 'Nine Lyric Poets', the 'Ten Attic Orators' and the like. The 'Five Books of Moses', 'the Pentateuch' as it was known in Hellenistic Greek, is another example. It seems to go back to the great Alexandrian scholars of the third and second centuries BCE whose work of collecting, classifying and interpreting earlier Greek literature we shall have occasion to return to later. The authors in such lists were known as 'the select authors' (hoi enkrithentes) or 'the classics' (Latin classici) and were specially revered. The numbers usually have fairly obvious associations, suggesting, for example, comparison with the 'Three Graces' and the 'Nine Muses', and served a useful mnemonic function in helping students find their way around the classical literature and learn who the great classical writers were. There is some variation both in the numbers and the selection of authors; but, in general, the effect of this kind of numerical classification was to incorporate a degree of uniformity into the educational system by encouraging the imitation of a fixed set of models. It also played an important role in library management by helping to ensure that copies of the great classical works were preserved.

It is important to remember that getting a work copied was relatively expensive and depended on several factors. Someone had to be able and willing to pay a scribe to produce one or more copies of the original. Before the development of the book trade in the first century BCE, and even in conjunction with it, the role of the author's friends and patrons was extremely important. Atticus, Cicero's literary adviser, and Maecenas, the influential ally of the emperor Augustus and patron of Virgil and Horace, are well-known examples from the Roman world.

In the case of religious communities or state institutions, there was official control over the number of copies made and their accuracy. The priests in charge of the Sibylline books, originally housed in the Temple of Jupiter on the Capitol at Rome, had to ensure that legible copies were available to be consulted when required. When the books were destroyed by fire in 83 BCE, they were replaced by oracles collected from the various Sibylline shrines. In 12 CE the emperor, Augustus, himself one of the priests, censored the collection, destroying large parts of it on the grounds that they were politically subversive (Suetonius, *Aug.* 31:1). The copying of the Jewish Torah scroll was, until 70 CE, under the control of the Temple hierarchy who saw to it that all official copies were made exclusively from a master copy held by them in Jerusalem. By contrast, the heretical Jewish monastic community at Qumran had its own scriptorium where the bulk of the Dead Sea Scrolls were copied, conspicuously outside the control of Jerusalem.

Pseudonymity often helped to ensure that a text survived. Some authors blatantly chose to attribute their works to great writers of the past purely in order to get them copied and sold (*OCD*: 1270). But not all pseudonymous works were deliberate forgeries for gain. Most were made innocently and reverently in order to locate the work within a particular literary genre, philosophical school or religious tradition, while at the same time giving it the authority and appeal of an ancient origin. This category would include the 'Epic Cycle', a collection of poems arranged as a narrative running from the beginning of the world to the end of the heroic age, containing poems of differing date and provenance falsely attributed to Homer, and the 'Appendix Vergiliana' referred to in Late Antiquity, which similarly purported to be a collection of poems written by Virgil. Much of the Pythagorean literature and the Sibylline books are also pseudonymous, as are the Wisdom of Solomon, the Book of Enoch and the rest of the Apocrypha and

Pseudepigrapha which survived on the margins of the Christian canon.

The earliest Christian communities must have exercised some control over the copying and circulation of the new literature. But we know nothing for certain of the mechanics of this before the late second century. The handwriting in the earliest Christian manuscripts, including some like the John Rylands 'St John's Gospel' and the Chester Beatty 'Pauline Epistles', which run to over a hundred pages, proves that they were produced by communities whose members included businessmen and minor officials, not by the book trade (*CHB*:1, 62–3). Christian scholarship and education were later influenced by a secular Catechetical School established in Alexandria and libraries at Caesarea, Jerusalem and elsewhere at the beginning of the third century. Eusebius describes the clerical assistance available to Origen's scriptorium at Caesarea where copies of the Bible and biblical commentaries were copied by 'shorthand-writers more than seven in number' (*EH* 6.24.3).

From the fourth century the term 'canon' was applied by Christian writers to the list of books officially recognized as sacred scripture. Its association with the law of the Church, as in 'canon law', indicates the legally binding nature of the official list, but by then it had also acquired theological associations relating to the authority of scripture, its divine nature and origins, its infallibility and the like which we shall consider in a later chapter. There is good evidence that, in both Jewish and Christian tradition, the canon of scripture was a burning issue for the first time in the second century CE. The canon of the Hebrew Bible was discussed and, we are told, finally fixed during the lifetime of Rabbi Akiba (died 135 CE), while the first stage in the process of canonizing in written form the sayings of the rabbis was completed by 200 CE in the Mishnah. The first major dispute about the Christian canon, associated with the name of Marcion, and the oldest official list of New Testament texts known as the 'Muratorian Canon', both date from the second century too.

The second century was, as we have seen, a time when something of a revival of Greek literature and national consciousness took place under the emperor, Hadrian, and the Antonines. In the last decade of the first century and the beginning of the second, important histories and biographies were written, such as Josephus' *Antiquities* and Plutarch's *Lives*, designed to reawaken and record national traditions, Greek, Roman and Jewish. Still more relevant to our present concerns are the efforts made under Hadrian to collect and co-ordinate the mass of ancient knowledge of science and medicine, and incorporate it in encyclopaedic works like those of Ptolemy and Galen. It was under Hadrian's tutelage that the celebrated canon of medical writings known as the Hippocratic corpus was put together by one Artemidorus Capito, and under the Antonines that we first come across a mention of the 'Epic Cycle'. The only surviving Greek hymn-book, a collection of eighty-seven Orphic hymns, was composed in Asia Minor during the second century as well. It is no coincidence that this was also the time when the canons of Jewish and Christian scripture first began to take on their final shape. There is plenty of evidence that Jews studied Greek literature, both in Talmudic references and in the substantial corpus of Jewish Greek literature from the period. In fact, there is even a comparison in the Mishnah between the canon of Hebrew scripture and the canon of Homeric writings (M.Yad. 4:6).

We begin with the Hebrew Bible. As we have seen, the central place of scripture within Judaism can be traced back to ancient Israel. By the time of Ezra (c.400 BCE) at least the first part, the 'Five Books of Moses', known by then as the 'Law' (Hebrew *torah*), must have reached more or less their final form. By the beginning of the second century BCE, the other two parts of the Hebrew Bible, the Prophets and the Writings, were also in existence (Sir. Prologue). However, a considerable degree of fluidity regarding other Jewish texts remained, reflecting the variety of Judaisms that existed at the time. Evidence from Qumran and early Christian sources indicates that other works including Enoch, Jubilees, Tobit and Ecclesiasticus (Wisdom of Jesus ben Sira or Sirach) had some kind of canonical status in at least two contemporary Jewish communities. Quotations from Ecclesiasticus appear quite frequently in the rabbinic literature, sometimes with the formula reserved for biblical texts (BTHag. 12a; Niddah 16b), and fragments of a Hebrew manuscript of Ecclesiasticus have been found in the Jewish synagogue at Massada (c.70 CE) as well as at Qumran and in the Cairo Geniza (c.800). Its popularity is further indicated by the fact that an expanded Aramaic version of it seems to have existed in Talmudic times (BT Sanh. 100b).

The case of Ecclesiasticus, however, does not substantially affect the rabbinic tradition that the Hebrew canon was fixed by the beginning of the second century BCE. In the Mishnah (c.200 CE), as also already in the New Testament, there are references to 'the holy scriptures' (Hebrew *kitve ha-qodesh*) (MMeg. 4:1–2; cf. Rom. 1:2), and its three parts, the Law, the Prophets and the Writings

(MYom. 3:5; cf. Luke 24:44). An early saying in the Talmud lists the twenty-four books of scripture more or less in the order in which they appear in every Hebrew Bible to this day, that is from Genesis to Chronicles (BT BabBat 14b). In view of the earlier comparison with Homer, one is tempted to ask whether the number twenty-four may owe something to the fact that the two epics of Homer, the *Iliad* and the *Odyssey*, were at some time also divided into twenty-four books each, no doubt corresponding to the twenty-four letters of the Greek alphabet. There is another ancient tradition about the number and order of the books, recorded by Josephus (*Against Apion* 1:7f.), Origen (according to Eusebius, *EH* 6:25) and others, who speak of a Hebrew canon of twenty-two books, corresponding to the twenty-two letters of the Hebrew alphabet. This tradition, described by Josephus as hallowed by antiquity and accepted by every Jew from the day of his birth, may also be referred to in the Book of Jubilees, in which case it goes back to the second century BCE (Beckwith 1985: 235ff.).

The number of books in these two canons may vary, but the contents are identical. It was just a matter of the order in which the books were arranged and which books could be taken together as one (e.g. Jeremiah and Lamentations, Ezra and Nehemiah). Josephus' canon had thirteen prophets, probably including Job, Chronicles, Ezra–Nehemiah, Esther and Daniel as well as the traditional eight; and only four books of hymns and precepts in the third part, namely Psalms, Proverbs, Ecclesiastes and Song of Songs. Jesus' saying about 'the righteous blood shed on earth, from the blood of innocent Abel [Gen. 4:8] to the blood of Zechariah son of Berechiah' (2 Chron. 24:21) proves that the Talmudic order also goes back to the first century (Matt. 23:35).

According to Talmudic tradition, the canonicity of five books eventually admitted into the Hebrew Bible was sometimes disputed, even as late as the third century CE. Ezekiel was challenged ostensibly because 'its words contradict the words of the Law' (BT Shab. 13b), but probably the real reason was its dangerous, subversive qualities. There were restrictions on who could read it and under what conditions (M Meg. 4:10; Hag. 2:1) and a cautionary tale was put about to the effect that fire from God's chariot in the opening chapters once burnt a child to death as he was reading it (BT Hag. 13a). Of the other four books, Ecclesiastes caused one of the disputes between the School of Shammai and the School of Hillel (M Eduy. 5:3). Proverbs, Song of Songs, Esther and Ecclesiastes were questioned mainly on the grounds that they are merely human, and not divine (cf. Tos. Yad. 2:14). Esther is unique among biblical books in that the divine name never occurs in it, and the Song of Songs contains erotic language which could be joked about or sung to secular tunes (Tos. Sanh. 12:10). Special problems with Esther, which explain why it was apparently not in the canon of the Qumran community and why, even in the third century CE, prominent authorities rejected its canonicity (BT Sanh. 100a), arise from its connection with the feast of Purim. Not only is the festival not mentioned in the Torah calendars (Lev. 23 and Num. 28–9) and therefore unacceptable as it is considered without scriptural authority, but such a nationalistic feast could make Jews be hated by foreigners (BT Meg. 7a).

All these charges were answered, and Josephus' bullish view of the canon was eventually realized. Rabbi Akiba's defence of the Song of Songs is well known: 'all the Writings are holy, but the Song of Songs is the Holy of Holies' (M Yad. 3:5). There were other arguments too, but probably the main factor in the survival of all these works was the fact that by the time the decisions were being taken, the books in question had long since become so popular, so regularly used and so much part of popular belief and practice in synagogues throughout the world, that it would have been impracticable to reject them. The process of canonization is often an organic one in which books over the years become more and more popular and more and more exclusively associated with particular rituals and beliefs until there can be no thought of separating them.

The Sadducees are sometimes thought to have had a different canon, consisting of the Torah alone. This is an assumption tenuously based on the fact that the Sadducees did not believe in the resurrection of the dead, a doctrine more difficult to find in the Torah than in the Prophets and the Writings. In fact, no mention is ever made of this point of divergence between Pharisees and Sadducees, either by Josephus in his famous discussion of the three Jewish schools, or in the rabbinical literature where there are a great many references to disputes with the Sadducees. It has been suggested that the widespread belief, particularly among Christian writers from the second century, that the Sadducees treated only the Torah as canonical was derived from the fact that in the century or so after the fall of Jerusalem and the destruction of the Temple, the Sadducees joined forces with the Samaritans in the north, who from the beginning rejected the claims of the Jerusalem hierarchy that the Prophets and Writings were canonical (Beckwith 1985: 86–91).

We come now to the so-called apocryphal and pseudepigraphical books, that is to say, books that appear among the Dead Sea Scrolls or are included in some of the Christian canons of the Old Testament, those of the Greek, Russian, Syrian and Ethiopic churches, for example, but never in the canon of the Hebrew Bible. Some of these works, including Ecclesiasticus, Judith, Tobit, and 1 Maccabees, were originally written in Hebrew or Aramaic, but too late to be accepted into the Hebrew canon. Greek versions of such compositions, together with works originally written in Greek, like the Wisdom of Solomon and 2 Maccabees, became popular in many Jewish and Christian communities, and were at some time included alongside versions of the Hebrew Bible in a Greek canon of scripture.

It used to be thought that a Greek canon, called the 'Alexandrian' or 'Hellenistic' canon, existed in Second Temple Period Judaism as an alternative Jewish canon, alongside the Palestinian Hebrew canon we have been considering. This would mean that some of the 'apocryphal' books in the Christian canon were at that time considered canonical in various Jewish contexts. The total absence of any reference to it outside later Christian tradition, however, makes this theory extremely implausible. Philo of Alexandria, for example, knew of no such canon. For him, as for Jesus ben Sira (c.180 BCE) and his grandson, scripture consisted of the Law, the Prophets and the Writings, whether in the Hebrew original or a Greek version. All other books, even those like Ecclesiasticus that were popular in Jewish tradition and occasionally cited as scripture in the rabbinic literature, were excluded as apocryphal or heretical. As Rabbi Akiba put it at the beginning of the second century CE, 'Anyone who reads the heretical books [*sepharim ha-hitzonim* literally 'the outside books'] has no share in the world to come' (M.Sanh. 10:1).

The Essenes seem to have had their own canon for which the Dead Sea Scrolls provide the evidence (*CHB*: 1, 342). Certainly the appearance of 1 Enoch, the Testaments of the Twelve Patriarchs and the Book of Jubilees at Qumran, all of which accord with the Essenes' apocalyptic outlook as well as their distinctive calendar, does not seem to be accidental. Some have suggested that other works, such as the 'Temple Scroll', may also have had canonical status at Qumran. The Apocrypha and Pseudepigrapha, including those discovered at Qumran, also found their way eventually into the Christian canon. The Greek, Latin and Slavonic Bibles contain the Apocrypha with minor variations: the Greek and Slavonic canons include 1 Esdras, the 'Prayer of Manasseh', 3 Maccabees and a 151st psalm not in the Latin canon, and the Slavonic Bible has 2 Esdras, which is not in either of the other two. The Ethiopic canon contains not only the Apocrypha, but also the Book of Jubilees and 1 Enoch from among the Pseudepigrapha. To judge from the first books translated into Ethiopic, the Ascension of Isaiah and 4 Baruch may also have been in the most ancient Ethiopic canon (Beckwith 1985: 478–81).

Before turning to the Christian canon, however, there is another Jewish canon to consider, the canon of oral tradition, the first and most central part of which is known as the 'Mishnah'. The Mishnah is a systematic selection of remembered sayings of the rabbis down to the beginning of the third century, arranged thematically. The date traditionally given for the composition of the Mishnah, under the editorship of Rabbi Judah the Prince, is c.200 CE. The destruction of Jerusalem by the Romans in 70 CE raised the very real possibility that ancient tradition, till now centralized and controlled by the Temple establishment at Jerusalem, would be lost or corrupted. But what happened was that power was transferred from the Temple hierarchy to the rabbis, who took up the task of reconstituting their religion in a form that would survive in Palestine and throughout the world, without the priests and without the Temple rituals. Over the next century, in councils set up first at Yavneh (Greek *Jamnia*) on the coast south of modern Tel Aviv, and later at Usha, Tiberias and Beth Shearim in the north, the rabbis achieved this through the discussions which formed the basis of the Mishnah and all subsequent rabbinic literature (Neusner 1994).

The Mishnah is an entirely original and autonomous composition in structure, form and language, as well as content. It consists of sixty-three tractates of widely differing length, arranged in six thematic divisions or orders, almost as if deliberately to avoid any comparison with the 'Five Books of Moses' and the twenty-four (or twenty-two) books of the Hebrew Bible. Rabbi Akiba, who as we saw took a leading part in fixing the written canon, is credited also with the first systematic arrangement of all this oral material. It was his best student, Rabbi Meir, who is said to have provided Judah the Prince with the basic thematic structure of the Mishnah (BT Sanh. 86a). Rabbi Meir's influence on the whole process is reflected in the tradition that all anonymous sayings in the Mishnah are by him.

The form of the Mishnah is also entirely original and, contrary to a popular misconception among non-Jews, bears no resemblance whatever to a commentary on the Bible. There are relatively few quotations from Hebrew scripture, and where they appear, they are entirely incorporated into the discussion. Paragraphs begin with a question or a statement, usually without any indication as to who the author was. This signals that we are hearing an autonomous and authoritative voice, the voice of tradition, the voice of the Mishnah starting off the discussion, which is then followed by a series of statements mostly attributed to named rabbis. With the exception of Aboth (see below), the form and style are homogeneous throughout the Mishnah – a further means of distancing itself from the enormous stylistic variation within the Law, the Prophets and the Writings. It is not written in 'the sacred language', that is to say, ancient biblical Hebrew, as are, for example, the sectarian documents from Qumran, but in contemporary spoken Hebrew. It is characterized most strikingly by the increasing number of Latin and Greek loanwords, which both gives the impression that these are the actual words of the rabbis quoted, and once again distances itself from the Hebrew Bible.

The Mishnah on any reckoning is a quite extraordinary piece of work. There were of course numerous other rabbinic sayings from that early formative period up to 200 CE that are not included in the Mishnah, and to which the Aramaic term *Baraita* ('extraneous saying') is applied. Some of these can be found in a huge supplement to the Mishnah known as the 'Tosefta', composed about 300 CE, while others appear alongside later material in the talmudic and midrashic literature of the fourth and fifth centuries.

It is also significant that the contents of the Mishnah as well as later the Talmud and Midrash consist of genuinely oral tradition. As we have seen there was a substantial body of Jewish literature written during the last two or three centuries BCE and the first two centuries CE. Many of these works, including the Wisdom of Solomon, Judith, Tobit and Maccabees, found their way into the Christian canon of scripture, but none of it was included in the oral Torah. There are points of similarity and overlap here and there, as well as occasional quotations, but the explicit aim of Rabbi Judah and his successors was to collect and edit only the oral tradition, which by their day had acquired an independent authority quite distinct from any of the written documents, canonical or extra-canonical.

The term 'sacred' (*qadosh*) is never applied to the Mishnah, as it is to the text of the Hebrew Bible, but its editor is sometimes referred to as 'our holy rabbi' *rabbenu ha-qadosh* (BT Pes. 37b; Shab.

156a). Judah was an exceptional person, and some of his editorial skills must be attributed to the Greek education that he had and which he recommended to others (BT Sot. 49b). The last quarter of the second century under the Antonine emperors was a period of peace in which literary activities, especially the collecting and editing of 'classics' as we saw, were encouraged. At this time a significant number of Greek writers lived and worked in Gerasa (modern Jerash), Caesarea, Ashkelon and other cosmopolitan cities in Palestine (Hengel 1989: 20ff.). It was in Caesarea that one of the most famous libraries existed, established by Origen and much used by Eusebius. There are a number of traditions, mostly of an obviously legendary nature, concerning Judah's conversations with the emperor, probably Marcus Aurelius who visited Palestine in 175 CE (BT Sanh. 91a–b). These surely reflect a positive relationship between Jewish and Greco-Roman culture during that short period, which must have affected the motivation, method and character of the Mishnah.

However that may be, within a generation of its completion, the Mishnah claimed the same degree of authority as the Bible. One of the tractates, Aboth or the 'Sayings of the Fathers', is different from the rest and seems to have been added a generation or so later to give the Mishnah a kind of historical context. Aboth begins with the claim that the oral Torah goes back to Sinai just as the written Torah does, and then lists all the 'Fathers' in an unbroken line of oral tradition from Moses, Joshua, the Elders and the Prophets of ancient biblical times down to c.240 CE. From now on Jewish religious literature consisted almost entirely of verse-by-verse commentary on its two canons: the Talmud is a commentary on the Mishnah, the oral canon, and the Midrash is a commentary on the written canon, the Bible. Judaism had now become the religion of the dual Torah; and the oral Torah, now in written form in the Talmud and Midrash, had the same authority as the written Torah.

The fourth century was in many ways almost as traumatic for Jews in the Roman Empire as the first. As Christianity grew more powerful, the body of apologetic literature, both Jewish and pagan, attacking its claims increased in tone and volume. There is very little polemic in the Mishnah and the Tosefta, and it is not till the writings of Celsus towards the end of the second century and Porphyry a century later that pagan writers really start directing their literary efforts against the Christians. Constantine's conversion in 312 CE and the subsequent establishment of Christianity as the state religion of the Roman Empire signalled the triumph of the

Church over its rivals. The reaction of the Jewish sages was to work out again how Judaism could survive and flourish as a powerless minority in such a world. The result was the Palestinian Talmud or 'Yerushalmi' ('Jerusalemite') completed soon after 400 CE. This remarkable work, arranged as a commentary on the Mishnah, combines the teaching of the sages (Hebrew *talmud* MSot. 5:4 or *talmud torah*; cf. Mpeah. 1:1) of the first two centuries with material from rabbinic discussions at Tiberias and elsewhere down to the second half of the fourth century. The older material is in Mishnaic Hebrew, the more recent in Galilean Aramaic.

Over the next two centuries another commentary on the Mishnah, a second Talmud, the Babylonian Talmud or 'Bavli' ('Babylonian') as it is affectionately known, also evolved out of rabbinic discussions, both earlier (in Hebrew) and more recent (in Babylonian Aramaic). Neither Yerushalmi nor Bavli covers the whole of the Mishnah, but of the two, Bavli is much larger and soon became the more popular within Jewish education. It is in effect a vast encyclopaedia of Jewish oral tradition, which from mediaeval times rivalled the Bible as the main sacred text, continually studied and consulted in every Jewish community, and emerging as the main written source of religious authority on which virtually all subsequent Jewish tradition is based.

A type of verse-by-verse commentary on the Bible, known as Midrash, also evolved during this period alongside the huge talmudic commentaries on the Mishnah. Like the Talmud, these contain yet more oral tradition selected from the teaching of the rabbis, especially their synagogue sermons, and are written for the most part in Hebrew. The earliest of these, known as the 'Mekhilta' (on Exodus), 'Sifra' (on Leviticus) and 'Sifre' (on Numbers and Deuteronomy), go back to Mishnaic times and are frequently cited in the Talmud. Together with later commentaries, particularly a group known as Midrash Rabbah 'the great midrash' composed during the fifth and sixth centuries, these texts came to make up a canon of commentaries almost as fundamental to Jewish tradition as the Talmud.

The custom of helping non-Hebrew speakers to understand scripture by giving an oral Aramaic translation of the relevant passage, known as a Targum, probably goes back, as we saw, to the time of Ezra *c.*400 BCE. The question of when such translations were first written down and given some kind of status – canonized – by the rabbis is difficult to answer and will be discussed in the next chapter. The Greek Septuagint was in existence by the first century BCE and certainly acquired some kind of canonical status among the Jews of Egypt, Palestine and elsewhere. Legends about its miraculous origins make this clear. According to the mainly fictitious 'Letter of Aristeas', this otherwise unknown courtier of the Egyptian king had the task of going to Jerusalem to ask the High Priest Eleazar for a team of translators to do the job. Seventy-two translators, six from each tribe, were appointed and on the island of Pharos near Alexandria they each produced identical Greek versions of the Torah in exactly seventy-two days. There is also a reference in the Talmud to 'the beauty of Japheth [interpreted as a reference to Greece; cf. Gen. 10:2] residing in the tents of Shem' (cf. Gen. 10:27; Jastrow 1903:586), a reference to the friendly reception of Greek translations by the Jews. It is constantly quoted and referred to by Greek Jewish authors, including Philo, Josephus and the NT writers. Its adoption by Christians as their scripture soon led to its rejection by Jews. By the time of St Augustine the LXX was believed to be divinely inspired (*City of God*, 18:42–3).

This brings us to the Christian canon. The Greek canon of the Old Testament was the creation of the Church, and probably never existed independently of the Gospels and the other New Testament writings. Apocryphal writings are quoted with increasing frequency by Christian writers from the end of the first century on and by the fourth century the church fathers, in both the Greek and Latin traditions, aware that these writings were never part of the Hebrew canon, labelled them 'apocryphal', but retained them as part of scripture. The Wisdom of Solomon seems to have been a particular favourite. Before the end of the first century it is already cited as scripture by Clement, Bishop of Rome, and a hundred years later it is listed as canonical in the Muratorian Fragment – among the New Testament writings. Wisdom, Ecclesiasticus and Tobit appear already in fragments of the earliest Christian manuscripts of the Greek Bible, such as the Chester Beatty papyri of the second and third centuries; while the great uncial manuscripts of the fourth and fifth centuries all contain the Apocrypha, as well as the New Testament. The conspicuous absence of the Books of Enoch, Jubilees and other Pseudepigrapha from the western and eastern Orthodox canons indicates that by then these works had been finally declared non-canonical. Their survival in Ethiopic, Coptic, Armenian and Syriac translations is a measure of the increasing independence of the eastern churches as, with invasions from Sassanian Persia and later Islam, they broke away from the central authority of Rome and Constantinople. It was only because Greek

Orthodoxy was eventually driven out of Egypt, Ethiopia, Syria, Armenia, Mesopotamia and the East, that Greek had to give way before the Christian vernaculars, Coptic, Ge'ez, Syriac, Armenian and the like, together with their 'heretical' beliefs and the 'pseudepigraphical' scriptures in which they were enshrined.

The addition of the New Testament writings to the Greek Bible and their acceptance as canonical requires some discussion. For the first Christian writers, including Paul and the four evangelists, sacred scripture was of course Jewish scripture. Although as we have seen their canon, like that of the Qumran community, may have been larger than that of rabbinic Judaism and may have included some apocryphal works never accepted as canonical by the Jewish authorities. Clement, Bishop of Rome, Irenaeus, Justin and other writers of the next two or three generations also find their main scriptural authority in the 'Law of Moses and the Prophets and the Psalms' (e.g. Luke 24:44). As scriptural authority for bishops, Clement quotes Isaiah not 1 Timothy 3:1 (1 Clem: 42: 5). But the words of Jesus are quoted already in Paul as in some way authoritative (e.g. 1 Cor. 11:23–6) and soon actually described as sacred in the same terms as written scripture (e.g. 1 Clem. 13:3; 56:3). The words of Jesus are actually bracketed with 'scripture' already in John 2:22: 'When he was raised from the dead, his disciples remembered that he had said this, and they believed the scripture and the word which Jesus had spoken' (cf. Acts 18:28).

The processes by which the words of Jesus were first committed to writing and then subsequently, by the end of the second century, canonized in the forms of the four canonical Gospels, the Gospel of Peter, the Gospel of Thomas and the like are extremely complex and cannot be tackled here (Gerhardsson 1964). There is early manuscript evidence for collections of Jesus' sayings, such as the so-called *logia-papyri* from Egypt, and we know from the Dead Sea Scrolls that collections of messianic proof-texts (*testimonia*) were compiled, which are reminiscent of some passages from the Gospels and Paul. It has also been conjectured that the Latin word for 'parchments' (*membranae*) that Paul uses in his letter to Timothy were notebooks on which words of Jesus had been written down (Roberts 1970: 55f.). There was an early tradition that there once existed a collection of Jesus' sayings in Aramaic, attributed to Matthew, and a widely accepted modern theory of an early 'sayings source' known as 'Q' from its German name *Quelle* 'source', which antedates the three Synoptic Gospels (Matthew, Mark and Luke) and explains the existence of material common to them. But beyond that it is hard to go.

The emergence of the Gospel (Greek *euangelion*) as an entirely new literary form within a society characterized by a strong literary tradition, as well as a very high degree of literacy, is itself a measure of the uniqueness of the new religion. It is possible that behind the production and canonization of each of the gospels there was a particular Greek-speaking Christian community. The earliest mention of Matthew's Gospel, for example, is in the Didache, a kind of Christian manual written in Syria between 70 and 90 CE. It has therefore been suggested that it was produced at Antioch or at any rate first became popular there in some form or another, possibly not yet written down. There is similar evidence to connect Mark with Rome, Luke with Caesarea and John with Ephesus (*CHB*: 1, 269). The popularity of the Gospel of St Thomas within the Coptic Church may suggest that it had its origin in a similar type of situation in Egypt.

However that may be, throughout the first half of the second century CE, there are references to the Gospels and Acts, the Pauline Epistles and Revelation as authoritative for Christians, but they were not yet considered parts of scripture in the way that the Law and the Prophets were. Even Justin Martyr still finds no reason to refer to Paul's Letters, although he does seem to have been aware of the Gospels. It is in the last quarter of the second century that we first come across a reference to one of the Gospels as scripture, and from that time also comes an inscription in which a Phrygian Bishop tells us he never goes anywhere without his 'Paul', that is, Pauline Epistles (*CHB*: 1, 66).

As we have seen, Greek writers under the Antonines were making special efforts to collect and edit their literary and scientific heritage. Perhaps the extraordinary achievement of Judah the Prince owed something to such outside influences too. But a more immediate theological and polemical reason for the Church to tackle the question of their canon of scripture was the challenge of the anti-Jewish Gnostic theologian Marcion. Between 137 and 144 Marcion taught in Rome. He maintained that the true teaching of Jesus had been distorted by the Jews. All the early Christian writings had been tampered with: only Luke's Gospel and ten of Paul's letters, especially Galatians, could be restored. Marcion's radical approach to the question of Christian scripture left him with a strictly defined canon, the first Christian canon of scripture. It consisted of one Gospel and one Apostle whose ten letters, radically edited, made up half of it. It was never accepted by the Church at large, probably, as we suggested above, because the works rejected by Marcion were by then so widely used and popular that it would have been virtually impossible to prohibit their use in churches. Marcion's canon, however, undoubtedly led to the first stage in the Christian canonization process.

By the fifth century both the contents of the Bible and the order of the books were more or less fixed in the Greek and Latin Churches at the great ecumencial councils. One of the earliest complete manuscripts of the Greek Bible, the *Codex Vaticanus*, seems to reflect these decisions in both order and contents, and has been generally adopted as standard in editions of the Greek Bible. Although nowadays normally published in separate volumes as the 'Greek Old Testament' or the 'Septuagint' (LXX) and the 'Greek New Testament', *Codex Vaticanus*, like the other great bible manuscripts of the fourth and fifth centuries, is arranged in a way that highlights the continuity of Christian scripture from Genesis to Revelation as one single sacred text. It is in four sections, which (1) rehearse the ancient history of Israel and the Jews from the creation of heaven and earth in Genesis down to 2 Esdras, (2) sing, study and speculate in the language of Psalms and the other Poetical and Wisdom books, and then (3) look forward in the Prophets from Hosea to Daniel to (4) fulfilment in the Gospels, Acts, Epistles and the final vision of a new heaven and a new earth in Revelation. While Jewish scripture is always published as a single Hebrew text, its traditional structure intact, this aspect of the canon of Christian scripture, especially in its original Greek form, on which most subsequent versions are based, has been largely neglected in the compartmentalized scholarship of the last few centuries. Fortunately with the advent of canonical criticism, and more recently, a new emphasis on intertextuality and reception history, the literary unity of the Christian Bible, from Genesis to Revelation, from Moses to Patmos, is being rediscovered.

We conclude with a few remarks on the situation in Zoroastrianism. A vast canon of Avestan texts, the 'Great Avesta' as it was known, finally attained written form in the fifth or sixth centuries CE in a great scholarly enterprise officially sponsored by the Sassanian kings (224–651 CE). This first written Zoroastrian canon of scripture took the place of the oral canon which had been so zealously preserved down the centuries, although copies of it in its complete form actually only existed for a century or two. Not a single complete copy of the 'Great Avesta' survives, having been

74

destroyed in the Arab, Turkish and Mongol conquests of Iran from the seventh century to the twentieth, and it is known only from fragments and later summaries (Boyce 1984: 11–12).

The canonization process had begun already under the first Sassanian king, Ardashir I (*c.*224–40), when the high priest, Tansar, is said to have fixed the oral canon of Avestan texts, but it was not until the sixth century that the process was complete. A new script was invented for the purpose and the Avestan texts themselves were accompanied by a vast commentary (Zand) in Pahlavi, the official language of the Sassanian empire. The Zand-Avesta, as it is often known, was a vast work made up of twenty-one books (Nasks) containing all kinds of material in prose and verse from the Prophet's own hymns (the Gathas) to legends, law, doctrine, apocalyptic and science. The date of this enterprise, beginning like the Mishnah in the third century CE, and culminating like the Talmud in the fifth or sixth, as well as its sheer scale, strongly suggest that there were common factors operating in that formative period in the history of Zoroastrianism and Judaism. The impact of the fourth- and fifth-century ecumenical councils on Christianity worldwide may also have played a part. With the new-found freedom and the official sponsorship given them by the Sassanian rulers, the Magi must have looked to parallel developments in the West, notably under Constantine, for models on how to establish a state religion, especially one so firmly built on a sacred text.

6

TRANSLATION

Just as in some cases, as we have seen, a sacred text was not committed to writing for many centuries, so there are a number of religious traditions in which a sacred text may be recited only in the original language, even in a congregation where a small minority are familiar with the language or language variety in which it is written. Translation of the Bible into every known language has been such a prominent feature of Christianity since the beginning that it is hard to imagine situations in which this is not the case. Yet in most varieties of contemporary Judaism the weekly reading from the Bible at public worship is still in the original Hebrew. Translation of the Qur'an is actually forbidden by Sunni law, and the Avesta was not even written down, let alone translated into the language of the people, for over 1,000 years. We have noted the role of Old Latin, unintelligible to most, in the ritual of the Arval Brothers in ancient Rome, as well as the custom of consulting the Sibylline books in the original Greek. A Latin translation of the Sibylline books was finally commissioned in the second century CE, but the precise meaning of the Arval hymns was completely lost by the time of Augustus.

There may be various reasons why sacred texts are not translated into other languages. One may be a desire to preserve the original language as meticulously as possible out of a sense of awe and mystery engendered by the belief that the worshippers were listening to the actual words of the original author or founder. That was probably why the Sibylline books and the words of Zoroaster were for so long preserved untranslated. Probably the fundamental rabbinic belief in the unbroken chain of continuity stretching back to Moses at Sinai played a part in establishing Hebrew as the only language in which not only the Bible, but the Mishnah as well, was preserved. Despite modern scholarly preoccupation with the *ipsissima verba* of Jesus and romantic notions of the Syriac Gospels as containing 'the words of our Lord in their original language', Christianity seems in general to be an obvious exception. We will come back later to the question of why there seems to have been so little interest till modern times in preserving the words of Jesus in their original language.

There are also political factors involved in the processes which keep the sacred texts in the obscurity of their original tongue. One of these concerns was the special authority and power of the priests or Magi. In Zoroastrianism, for instance, this was undoubtedly one of the means by which the Magi clung to their unique control in ancient Persia. Only they had the key to understanding the mystery surrounding the true meaning of the words of their Prophet. They decided what to reveal, what to keep hidden. The special powers of the priests in ancient Rome in charge of the Sibylline books was the same, and there has been plenty of political criticism from the time of Martin Luther on about the Roman Church's restrictions on vernacular translations of scripture. Translations can be subversive.

Economic factors are also involved. Like all book production, written translations cost money, and, except in situations where wealth is limitless, decisions have to be taken about priorities. Where translations are for whatever reason considered undesirable, they are not going to be given priority over other publications, notably the extremely expensive process involved in producing Torah scrolls in the original Hebrew. The earliest Aramaic translations of Jewish scripture were almost certainly oral and therefore inexpensive. There is a fourth-century tradition that in synagogues the translator was forbidden to look at the written text of the Torah, while the reader was forbidden to take his eyes off it (*RA*: 161). It was only after the destruction of the Temple at Jerusalem, and with it the Temple hierarchy, that the Aramaic Targums were written down. Greek and Syriac versions of Jewish scripture also date from this period, as does the Zand, the first vernacular translation of the Avesta. The pressures of the outside world, especially under Hadrian and the Antonines, where literary activity and book production reached a new peak, probably influenced both Judaism and Zoroastrianism in this direction.

The role of the hierarchy, however, may not always have been a purely political or economic one. The Temple hierarchy at Jerusalem, and later the rabbinical councils, certainly played an important role in ensuring the survival of Hebrew as the language of scripture. But it must be remembered that the Jewish religious leaders, from Ezra and Nehemiah on, were almost certainly bilingual, using Aramaic or Greek in their contacts with other people, but still speaking Hebrew among themselves, and this removed any need for producing translations for their own use. The study of Hebrew was also a major part of Jewish educational policy with the aim of ensuring that everyone should be able to recite and understand the Torah in its original language. The lack of emphasis on translating Jewish scripture into the vernacular is thus, to some extent, a measure of the success of this policy.

As the centuries passed, the gap between the sacred language of scripture and everyday language widened. Even the scholars had increasing difficulty with the ancient language. By the third century CE, verse-by-verse commentary in Hebrew had evolved in rabbinic Judaism into an important literary genre called 'midrash', together with systems of rules such as the so-called 'Seven Middoth of Hillel' and the 'Thirteen Middoth of Rabbi Ishmael', designed to assist and control interpretation of the sacred text (see pp. 147–9). The tradition was carried on until mediaeval commentaries on the Bible, such as those of Rashi, Avraham Ibn Ezra and David Kimhi, as well as later sixteenth- and seventeenth-century commentaries, came to be printed alongside the original text in all rabbinic Bibles. This whole line of Hebrew exegetical tradition, revived incidentally in the work of modern Israeli biblical scholars writing in Hebrew, always works from a position one stage closer to the original and totally avoids the accidents and constraints of translation. Christian scholars from the third century, writing in Greek, Latin, Syriac and other vernaculars, adopted a similar format in their commentaries on scripture, although the biblical text was given in translation in the same language as the commentary rather than the original Hebrew or Aramaic, and the whole process became that much more remote from it.

Hierarchies are not always seriously concerned to communicate the contents of their sacred texts to outsiders. The missionary zeal of Christianity, which created such a colossal translation industry almost from the very beginning, is exceptional. In rabbinic Judaism converts were, like other Jews, required to learn Hebrew even in situations where translations of Jewish scripture into Greek and Aramaic were available. By the fourth century CE, both the Greek and the Syriac translations of scripture, which originated within Judaism, became the exclusive property of the Church, where they were to replace the Hebrew original as sacred texts.

One final obstacle to the translation of sacred texts is the widespread feeling among the ancients, as well as ourselves, that 'true' translation from one language into another is impossible (Derrida 1991). Something is lost in translation: it is essential to study a text in the original. This view was expressed by the grandson of Jesus ben Sira in his apologetic preface to a Greek version of his grandfather's work: 'Please read carefully and with good will; excuse me where I have got the meaning wrong despite my efforts to translate. When translated into another language, words do not have the same meaning as they have in Hebrew.' According to Augustine some 500 years later, 'there are some words in some languages that cannot be translated into other languages' (*De Doctrina Christiana* 2: 35), and still later Isidore of Seville in his *Etymologiae* (10:123) explains the word *interpres* 'translator' as the one who comes 'between the two parties' (*inter partes*). We shall look in a little more detail at some of the specific problems that arise in translating sacred texts later.

It goes without saying that all translation involves interpretation. In many languages the same word can refer to both. In English, for example, the word 'interpreter' is commonly used for a 'translator' from one language to another, that is to say, for someone engaged in bilingual 'interpreting'; but in some contexts such as the title of the *Interpreter's Dictionary of the Bible*, the same word is clearly not restricted to 'translation'. In ancient Greek, the word *hermeneia* and the verb *hermeneuo*, derived from Hermes the god of communication between heaven and earth, could similarly apply to both translation and interpretation. This reflects the fact that the Greeks did not see the point of translating anything into another language: everyone should speak Greek, and if they did not, they were *barbaroi*. It is revealing that the word *metaphero*, which is occasionally used in classical Greek for 'translate', also means 'change, transfer'. Koine Greek coined the compound *methermeneuo* specifically for bilingual translation (e.g. Matt. 1:23; Mark 5:41).

It was not until the third century CE that Greeks began to appreciate the need to study Latin, and bilingual textbooks known as *hermeneumata* began to appear. From around the same time we can see the influence of the Church on the process of translating Greek texts into Coptic, Syriac, Armenian, Ge'ez and other languages, as well as Latin. The Romans, on the other hand, for the most part gladly acknowledged the influence of Greek literature, and produced many highly proficient translators from Greek, including Virgil and Cicero. It is also significant that Latin, unlike Greek, had a variety of words for bilingual translation available, including *transfero* (cf. translator), *verto* and *exprimo*, in addition to *interpretor*. We will discuss the complex process of reinterpreting Greek myths for use in various Roman religious contexts later.

We begin with the role of Aramaic in international diplomacy and communication from the eighth century BCE, and the situation in Second Temple Period Judaism. It is no coincidence that the words for 'translate' and 'interpreter' in most of the languages of the Middle East, including Hebrew, Arabic, Persian, Turkish and English (if we include the exotic word 'dragoman'), are all derived from Aramaic *targum*. Aramaic was the lingua franca for over five centuries in the ancient Near East, throughout the Assyrian and Persian empires, until it was eventually superseded by Greek after Alexander the Great (323). Its alphabetic script made it infinitely simpler to learn and cheaper to use than any of the alternatives available, until the advent of Greek.

In the Assyrian period scenes depicting the writing down of lists of booty or the like, regularly show two scribes: one writing with a stylus on clay, the other with a brush on papyrus or vellum (*ANEP*: 235–7). The clay tablet, written in Assyrian, was for the imperial authorities, while the other document was an official Aramaic translation for the benefit of the subject peoples, including the people of Israel and Judah, who could not read Assyrian cuneiform. Both scribes were officials acting on orders: one of them was specifically employed to translate from Assyrian to Aramaic, and must have known both languages. Bilingual texts containing an Aramaic version, are extremely common, many of them designed to be used in schools where scribes were trained in the appropriate languages and scripts. International agreements and the like normally had to be bilingual or even trilingual, and if the authorities wished people to be able to read their inscriptions, they had to provide an Aramaic translation. Aramaic appears as one of the official languages on public monuments from Asia Minor to India. Aramaic–Greek inscriptions by the Buddhist king, Ashoka (*c.*268–232 BCE) have already been referred to.

It is in many ways remarkable that, in such a world where so many official texts were either written in Aramaic or accompanied by an Aramaic translation, a complete official Aramaic version of the Hebrew Bible was never produced. The custom of helping non-Hebrew speakers to understand scripture by giving an oral Aramaic translation of the relevant passage probably goes back to the time of Ezra (*c.*400 BCE). The reference in Neh. 8:8 is not in the context of synagogue worship, and there is no explicit reference to translation. But by that time, probably late-fifth century BCE, there is ample evidence that Aramaic was rapidly replacing Hebrew as the main language of large parts of the Jewish community. The need for Palestinian Jews, for example, to communicate with the Persian authorities who used Aramaic as their official language, as well as with their Aramaic-speaking co-religionists in Egypt, Babylon and elsewhere, meant that Aramaic was making ground even in Jerusalem and Judah. Despite Nehemiah's efforts to prevent it, intermarriage between Jews and women whose native language was not Hebrew no doubt also contributed to a situation in which more and more Jews could not understand Hebrew (cf. Neh. 13:23–4). Already parts of Ezra and Daniel were written in Aramaic. In view of all this, there may well be some truth in the ancient Jewish tradition that, in the account of Ezra reading from the Torah to the people, *meporash* 'with an interpretation' (Neh. 8:8) is a reference to the Aramaic targum (BT Meg. 3b; Vermes 1997: 38), although modern scholars mostly take it as meaning nothing more specific than 'clearly, distinctly' (Fishbane 1985: 109; Blenkinsopp 1989: 288).

However that may be, there is little doubt that no written Aramaic translation of Jewish scripture was officially produced until later, despite the fact that the majority of Jews, especially in Babylonia, probably knew little Hebrew. Some of the reasons for this have been discussed earlier. The discovery of two Targums of Job at Qumran proves that by the time of Christ at the latest the use of Aramaic translations of scripture had become part of synagogue ritual (Harrington 1996: 18–22). The Hebrew of Job, incidentally, is notoriously difficult to understand. There were others of which two, known as Targum Onkelos and Targum Jonathan, probably originally from Palestine, are frequently quoted in the Talmud, the former as 'our targum'. These found their way eventually into standard printed editions of the Rabbinic Bible where they remain to this day alongside the Hebrew text of the Bible. There were others, including those known to mediaeval scholars as 'Pseudo-Jonathan' and 'Targum Yerushalmi' (Palestinian Targum), and 'Codex Neofyti I', an important manuscript discovered in 1956 in the Vatican library. All of these certainly contain traditions going back to first-century CE Palestine at least, but the precise date of their composition, the relationship between them and when they were first written down remain problematical. The persistent rabbinic tradition that the Aramaic translation process was primarily oral seems to agree with the extremely scanty evidence for any written Targum before the time of Christ.

The situation farther east, where the large and long-established Jewish communities of Babylonia spoke an eastern dialect of Aramaic, was probably similar. Despite pressure from outside and the no doubt frequent use of oral translation at public gatherings, no official written Aramaic version of scripture was produced before the first or second century CE. But if it is right to assume a Jewish origin for the Peshitta, the Syriac version of the Bible which was eventually monopolized by the Church, then it is possible that a Syriac version existed among the Jews of Mesopotamia just as there were Aramaic and Greek versions circulating in the West. Of the three, only the Aramaic Targumim survived, chiefly because both the Septuagint (LXX) and the Peshitta soon became the exclusive property of the Christian Church. Another factor in this may have been the fact that Aramaic, unlike Greek and Syriac, was written in the same script as the 'sacred language'.

The history of the Greek translation of Jewish scripture is very different. A written Greek version of the Hebrew Bible was in existence by the first century BCE and in regular use among the Jews of Egypt, Palestine and elsewhere. There is no reason to question the tradition that the Septuagint was produced on the orders of Ptolemy VIII Euergetes (c.182–116 BCE) at the suggestion of Demetrius of Phaleron, the president of his great library at Alexandria (*Letter of Aristeas*, 10; OTP:2, 12). He is reported as having said to Ptolemy: 'I am told that the laws of the Jews are worth transcribing and deserve a place in your library…they need to be translated because in the country of the Jews they use a peculiar alphabet and speak a peculiar dialect'. Under the Hellenistic rulers of the last three centuries BCE, there were many officially sanctioned efforts to communicate the sacred traditions of the East to interested Greek-speaking readers. The Egyptian Manetho's *Aiguptiaka* (c.280 BCE) and the roughly contemporary *Babuloniaka* of Berossus, a Babylonian priest, are two well-known examples, which, together with the LXX, indicate that the initiative for translating the Bible into Greek was motivated by intellectual curiosity rather than any religious factor, and came from outside Judaism. Jewish legends about its miraculous origins, however, make it clear that it was soon treated as in some sense a sacred text even within Judaism.

Three Jewish translators, influenced no doubt by the literary and editorial activities encouraged by Hadrian and the Antonines, are known to have produced Greek versions of the Bible in the second century CE. Symmachus and Theodotion, although both described in Christian sources as Jewish proselytes or Christian heretics, are not mentioned in the rabbinic literature at all. The third, Aquila of Pontus, or 'Aquila the proselyte' (*aqilas ha-ger*), is well known in the rabbinic literature, although his Greek translation is seldom referred to (*JE* 2, 36). A scriptural reference to his Greek translation is even found in Psalm 45:3 (Hebr. 45:2) in a wordplay on *yafyafita* 'thou art fairer' and the 'language of Japheth' (Hebrew *yafet*), i.e. Greek (JT Meg. 1.71c; *JE* 2, 36).

This brings us to the vast topic of Christian translations of scripture. We shall look briefly at three aspects of it. First the question of why there seems to have been little interest in preserving the words of Jesus in their original language; second, the impact of Christian missionary zeal upon the language situation in general; and third, the influence of translation on the history of Christianity. In the case of Moses, David, Solomon, Isaiah, the Sibyls, the Arval Brothers, Zarathustra and other religious leaders or founders, as we have seen, efforts were made to preserve their words in the languages in which they were originally uttered or written, Hebrew, Greek, Latin, Persian and the like. The Church historian, Eusebius (*c.*260–339), records a tradition attributed to Papias that Matthew compiled a collection of the sayings of Jesus 'in the Aramaic language and everyone translated them as well as they could' (*EH* 3.39.16). Even if we take this statement at face value, and there is no reason to doubt its historicity, it is significant that Papias assumes that they were never read in the original Aramaic. Why was it that no such effort seems to have been made, either on the part of his early followers or by the Church in later years, to record and preserve the words of Jesus in their original language? There seem to have been a number of factors.

First there is the fact that all the evidence points to Jesus having spoken more than one language. His mother tongue was probably Aramaic, to be precise, a Galilean dialect of Aramaic. Some Aramaic words and phrases used by Jesus have been preserved in the Greek New Testament including *talitha kumi* 'Get up, my child' (Mark 5:41), *mamona* 'money' (Matt. 6:24) and *ephphatha* 'open' (Mark 7:34). His knowledge of Hebrew cannot of course be assessed with any degree of accuracy, but again it is unlikely that somebody with a reputation like that of Jesus as a Jewish religious leader and teacher would not have had a good knowledge of the sacred language. Tradition records that he taught in many synagogues (Luke 4:15), and that in his home town of Nazareth he read aloud from the Hebrew Bible at sabbath worship (Luke 4:16–21). His explanation – 'today this scripture has been fulfilled in your hearing' (v. 21) – was probably given in Aramaic for the benefit of the ordinary people, thereby incidentally distinguishing, for the benefit of those later charged with recording his words for posterity, between his own words and the words of sacred scripture. Finally, even without placing too much emphasis on the stories in the Gospels about his conversations with a Greek woman (hellenis) from Syro-Phoenicia (Mark 7:26), several Roman soldiers and the Roman Governor Pontius Pilate (Hengel 1989: 17), it is safe to assume that, like many Jews in Palestine at the time, he could also speak some colloquial Greek. All his teaching, in other words, may not have been in the same language, and the emphasis was thus inevitably more on what he said than on in what language he said it.

Another possible reason why Jesus' original language was not preserved concerns Aramaic in particular. We have seen that there was in ancient Palestine a prejudice among educated Jews, especially those in Jerusalem and Judaea, against the Galilean dialect of Aramaic, which Jesus spoke (Vermes 1973: 52–3). There is evidence for this in the Gospels where the Jerusalem crowds pour scorn on the idea that the Messiah can come from Galilee (John 7:41, 52). We can imagine the scathing tone of voice in the question addressed to Nicodemus, 'Are you a Galilean too?' (John 7:52). Peter's accent betrays him (Matt. 26:73). They laughed at the way Galileans spoke. There is a well-known story told in the Talmud of a Galilean visitor to Jerusalem. When he asked in the shops for something he called *amar*, everyone laughed at his pronunciation, which could have meant several things: 'you stupid Galilean, do you mean something to ride on [*hamar* 'donkey'], or something to drink [*hamar* 'wine'] or something to wear [*amar* 'wool'] or something to sacrifice [*immar* 'a lamb']?' (BT Erub. 53b).

This was probably one of the reasons why the Galilean Jesus of Nazareth encountered such opposition in Jerusalem and Judaea. There is even a statement in a third-century source that the reason why the teaching of the Galilean rabbis disappeared was the careless way they spoke (BT Erub. 53a), with which may be compared another saying from the same century: 'Galilee, Galilee, you hate the Torah' (Vermes 1973: 57). While no doubt certain elements in the early Church would have welcomed a linguistic break with the Jewish establishment at Jerusalem, there may also have been those who believed Aramaic, especially Galilean Aramaic, was not a suitable vehicle for the words of their divine founder. There was in any case a marked reluctance, as we have seen, to produce written Aramaic translations of scripture or give to Aramaic any kind of sacred status on a par with Hebrew.

Third, Aramaic, like Hebrew, was associated with Judaism in Palestine, and there is plenty of evidence that there were early efforts on the part of Church leaders to remove Jesus from his original Jewish context. 'Judaizers' are already criticized by St Paul (Gal. 2:14). The Ebionites, whose Hebrew name (*ebyonim* 'poor') and recurring association with the apocryphal Gospel to the Hebrews reflect their Jewish character, remained outside mainstream Christianity and were condemned by the early church fathers. The Nazaraeans, another Judaizing variety of Christianity, suffered a similar fate. The almost total absence of any Christian documents written in either Hebrew or Aramaic is adequate proof that from the beginning Christianity sought to define itself as something different and separate from Judaism. Origen and Jerome consulted rabbis about the meaning of scripture, and there have been some notable Christian hebraists (McKane 1989). But it is not until modern times that Christian missionaries, directing their efforts towards the Jews, have started publishing Hebrew translations of the New Testament.

Finally, there were positive factors in the Church's apparent lack of interest in preserving their founder's words in the original language, and their preference for Greek. In the first place, there was among the earliest Christian leaders and writers a passionate desire to communicate with as many people as possible, especially the gentiles. This clearly outweighed any feelings that there was something special about the *ipsissima verba* of Jesus. The beginning of Acts makes this clear, where the first thing that happens when the Holy Spirit comes into the world at Pentecost is the reversal of the Tower of Babel story and miraculous communication occurs between crowds of people who speak different languages. Language and communication are recurring themes throughout the Book of Acts, especially in the account of the missionary journeys of Paul through Syria, Asia Minor and the West. Greek had pride of place as the chief language of international communication throughout the world.

Greek was also the language of new religious movements, and a language ideally suited to expressing the niceties of philosophical discourse. Its use in that capacity has a long history. Libraries were predominantly stocked with Greek works. Virtually every educated person studied Greek more than anything else. Jewish scripture, which was taken over in its entirety by Christians, as well as what was later known as the apocryphal Jewish literature, was already available in Greek. It was not only natural, but unavoidable, that Greek would take pride of place in early Christianity, and the words of Jesus were translated into Greek almost as far back as we can trace them. Some of our earliest versions of Jesus' words are to be found in papyrus documents in Coptic from Egypt, and within two or three centuries Christian writers were citing Jesus' words in Latin, Syriac, Armenian and other languages. The enterprise of translating scripture into all the languages of the world was well under way. But even then most of these translations were translations from the Greek, and the influence of Greek on them was profound.

The impact of the spread of Christianity on language is a huge subject in its own right. There is space here only for a few examples from the first centuries CE, with a brief discussion of two linguistic developments for which Christianity in several cases can claim much of the credit, namely the raising of a vernacular to the status of sacred language and the invention of a script in which it could be written. While Greek was the language of social and intellectual communication between most educated people, even in Rome, until the end of the second century, it was not most people's first language or mother tongue. The first Christian efforts at communication, illustrated by the journeys of St Paul for example, and the letters of St Clement, Bishop of Rome, were in Greek. A few conspicuous exceptions are carefully recorded (Acts 22:2; 26:14), but we know that for the first century at least, Christians, including in particular the many Jewish converts in their number, mostly spoke Greek. Latin began to be used regularly by the theologians only in the second century: Tertullian wrote in Greek and Latin, Justin Martyr only in Latin. Even Syriac-speaking Tatian from northern Mesopotamia, who studied under Justin Martyr in Rome, probably wrote his famous Diatessaron version of the four Gospels in Greek at first. But while from the fourth century on, the Church authorities in Rome and Constantinople continued to promote Latin and Greek, one of the most striking features of early Christian expansion was the production of Bible translations in the vernacular. We shall look briefly at four examples, Syriac, Coptic, Armenian and Gothic.

Syriac was originally the local Aramaic dialect of Edessa (modern Urfa in south-east Turkey) and the earliest evidence for it antedates

Christianity. As we have seen, it is possible that Syriac-speaking Jewish communities in the area produced an early translation of the Hebrew Bible, the influence of which can be detected in the Peshitta. But it was without question the influence of Christianity that made Syriac into the language in which the largest surviving body of Aramaic literature is written. Perhaps the greatest of all Syriac writers was Ephraem the Syrian (*c*.306–73), who lived in Edessa throughout most of the fourth century and wrote voluminous works on theology and ecclesiastical matters of all kinds, as well as hymns and poems of the highest quality. His works were soon translated into Greek, Armenian and Latin, and the very large number of surviving manuscripts of these versions is a measure of his popularity throughout the world (Brock 1994).

By the end of the fourth century there were in existence several Old Syriac translations of the New Testament. In the early fifth century all previous versions were superseded by an official Syriac version of the whole Bible, known as the 'Peshitta', which is still in use today in Syriac-speaking Christian communities. The tradition recorded in Eusebius (*EH* 3.1.1) and elsewhere that St Thomas evangelized Persia and India may not be historical, but there is good evidence for the fact that by then, or soon after, Syriac-speaking Christianity had spread into Persia, Central and South Asia, as well as Arabia and West Africa. It was undoubtedly due to Christian expansion in those early centuries that the Syriac script became one of the most successful and widely used in the Middle East. As well as Greek and Latin, texts in Armenian, Sogdian (Afghanistan) and even Malayalam (South India) were written in the Syriac script. There was even a special term for Arabic written in the Syriac script, 'Garshuni', which gives some indication of how widespread the influence of Christian Syriac had become.

In Egypt, as we have seen, Greek was the language of a large majority of the Jews. The earliest translation of Hebrew scripture was into Greek, and a significant proportion of apocryphal scripture, like the Wisdom of Solomon, was originally written in Greek in Egypt. Philo of Alexandria, a towering example of Egyptian Jewish literary achievement, wrote in Greek. It is likely that other religious groups in Egypt, such as the cults of Isis and Serapis, were already using Greek too. But by the end of the second century CE, Christians were using documents written in Coptic, the language of the ordinary peasant folk. Christian writers had produced Coptic versions of most of the Bible, as well as other writings. As a result of this Christian literary initiative, the Coptic language ceased to be the vernacular of the uneducated masses, and became instead the sacred language of the Coptic Church, where it has remained in use to this day in Egypt and elsewhere. The Coptic script, which consists of Greek letters supplemented by seven derived from the Egyptian writing system, may not have actually been invented by a Christian. However, as in the case of Syriac, if it had not been for the fact that Christians adopted it, it would not have survived the advent of Islam.

Christian influence in Ethiopia came not only from Alexandria and the Greek Church in the north, but also from Syrian missionaries to Arabia in the east. There are stories, no doubt at least based on fact, about a Syrian Christian from Tyre called Frumentius (c. 300–80) who accidentally found himself in Ethiopia and carried out missionary work there on behalf of Athanasius, Bishop of Alexandria. Christianity became the state religion soon after and, although no ancient manuscripts have survived, the first efforts to translate the Christian liturgy and scripture into the vernacular, known as Ge'ez, probably began then too. The resulting language was strongly influenced by Christian Greek and Syriac, and required the adaptation of an earlier writing system, originally derived from south-west Arabia, to cope with Greek and Latin loanwords (Ullendorff 1968: 172–8). It was thus once again due to the linguistic skill and energy of Christian missionaries that Ge'ez became the official language of Ethiopia for 1,000 years until it was superseded by Amharic. It remains the sacred language of the Ethiopian Church to this day.

A similar story can be told of the impact of Christianity in the same century on Armenian, Georgian, Gothic and other languages, with, in most cases, rather more historical details than have survived from Ethiopia. In Armenia, which adopted Christianity as its state religion at the beginning of the fourth century, Bishop Mesrop (c. 345–440), a fervent nationalist committed to eradicating Syrian influence from his church and an enthusiastic scholar, invented the Armenian alphabet so that he could provide his compatriots with a vernacular translation of scripture. He also adapted it to cope with Georgian. In southern Germany, with the same goal, Bishop Ulfilas (c. 311–83) devised the Gothic script which found its way, thanks to the wandering westward of the Goths during the next three centuries, to Spain, North Africa, Italy and Gaul. The invention of the Glagolitic and Cyrillic scripts by St Cyril (826–69) and his associates falls outside the scope of this volume, as do countless other examples down the ages of Christian contributions to the history of writing systems. In some of these cases, the writing down of vernacular literature may at first have had self-indulgent or narrowly political motives and may have been aimed at a relatively circumscribed section of the population, but there can be no doubt that in every case the provision of a means of writing literature in the vernacular marked a turning point in the social and cultural history of the nation.

Two features common to most of these translation initiatives need to be noted. First, they took place in the fourth century, that is to say, in the immediate aftermath of the Christianization of the Roman Empire, and were undertaken under the direct authority of the Church. Frumentius was made a Bishop by Athanasius at Alexandria, and Ulfilas by Eusebius in Constantinople. Mesrop ended his days as Patriarch of Armenia. Without state support they would probably not have been so successful. This was also the time when the Christian Church began to take final decisions on matters of doctrine and ecclesiastical structure, and when Judaism was defined as a religion now fully and finally separated from Christianity. It was also, as we have seen, the time when the sacred texts of Zoroastrianism, now the state religion of the Sassanian dynasty in Iran, were canonized and for the first time translated into Pahlavi with a commentary in the same language. There was a period of a century or two just before the spread of Islam when state religions were established in many countries, for example Iran, Armenia, Ethiopia and Egypt, as well as the Roman Empire itself. It was in this context that history produced one of the most fruitful partnerships between language, literature and religion there has ever been.

Another point to be emphasized in our discussion of this explosion of translation activity is that, as we have already mentioned, in almost every case the new translations were based on Greek. This leads us into our next topic, namely the influence of translation on the development of Christianity. As we saw, Greek was by far the most widespread medium in which Christianity first spread throughout the world. Hebrew scripture had already been translated into Greek before the time of Christ, and apart from a few relatively small groups of Judaizers, such as the Ebionites and the Nazaraeans, Greek was the language in which the texts of Judaism and Christianity were first circulated. The Syriac, Armenian, Coptic, Gothic and Latin versions of Christian scripture were thus heavily influenced by Greek. This can be seen in the numerous loanwords, such as *pistis* 'faith', *nomos* 'law' and *episkupa* 'bishop' in Syriac, or *evangelium* and *baptisma* in Latin. Ge'ez is an interesting exception where the presence of Hebrew and Aramaic loanwords like *mitzva* 'good deed', *targum* 'translate' and *mal'ak* 'angel' suggests that significant Jewish influence in south-west Arabia and West Africa preceded Frumentius and the other Christian initiatives in the fourth century and later (Ullendorff 1968: 120–5).

This is not the case in the other Christian languages where the direct influence of Greek far exceeds that of Hebrew and Aramaic. That being the case, I propose to limit our discussion of the influence of translation on the history of Christianity to a brief consideration of the specific question of what happens when Hebrew words are translated into Greek, and whether the fact that one is a Semitic language and the other Indo-European is significant. This transfer had already happened before most of the Christian versions of scripture were produced. Even where there is evidence that translators consulted rabbis on the meaning of the Hebrew, as there is for Jerome whose concern for *hebraica veritas* is well known, heavy dependence on the Septuagint is never in doubt.

Two general points before we look at some detailed examples. A fundamental concern of the translators and their employers was the achievement of literal accuracy in the Greek version of Hebrew scripture, in striking contrast to the Aramaic Targums, which are notoriously free and often in effect paraphrases rather than translations. This is expressed in different ways by many ancient scholars and commentators. There was the traditional Jewish reverence for the sacred language, backed up by neo-platonic views on the true meaning of language. This is clearly reflected in the legend referred to earlier of the seventy-two translators, who all miraculously produced the same version of the Septuagint. The three Jewish versions produced in the second century CE by Aquila, Theodotion and Symmachus illustrate in different ways the same concern for literal equivalence. Aquila, the most respected of the three in rabbinic tradition, even thought it necessary or desirable to represent Hebrew particles like the object marker *et* in Greek, despite the fact that in Greek it is represented by the accusative case.

Even more significant in this context is Origen's *Hexapla* (completed *c.*245) – an enormous work of scholarship consisting of a synoptic text in six parallel columns showing the Hebrew text beside a transliteration of the Hebrew into Greek, the versions of Aquila, Symmachus and Theodotion, and, in the famous fifth column, the Septuagint itself. We can assume that the Septuagint translators made every effort to achieve the closest possible equivalence between their source language (Hebrew) and their target language, and also that they were well versed in both. Where there are serious discrepancies, and there are a good many, in some books more than in others, this may in some cases be because our manuscripts of the Hebrew text are not identical to the manuscripts in the hands of the ancient translators.

The other general matter concerns the question of whether there is a greater problem involved in translating from a Semitic language to an Indo-European one, than from one Indo-European to another or one Semitic language to another. There used to be a widely held view that the Hebrew mind, as reflected in the Hebrew language, was different from the Greek mind (Boman 1960). The Hebrew tense system, it used to be said, which is different from the Greek system in many respects, indicated a different view of time so that, for example, Hebrew speakers did not distinguish so clearly between past, present and future as the Greeks did. There are fewer abstract nouns in biblical Hebrew than in Greek, and this meant that Hebrew speakers could not formulate abstract philosophical ideas as effectively as the Greeks. Such improbable generalizations, equivalent to suggesting that the absence of a word for 'dirty' in biblical Hebrew proves that the ancient Hebrews were unusually clean, have now for the most part been discredited (Barr 1961).

The language of the Hebrew Bible does have some interesting characteristics, but these inform us, for the most part, about the nature of the corpus rather than the structure of the Hebrew mind. It is only a relatively small sample of the language people actually spoke. That is why many everyday items of vocabulary are missing or very rare, such as words for 'dirty' (0x), 'ladder' (1x) and 'sneeze' (1x). On the other hand, the absence of abstract philosophical terms, like substance, quality and reality, is clearly due to the fact that the Bible does not contain philosophical discourse for which such terms are required. It does not necessarily imply that there was anything about the Hebrew mind or the Hebrew language that made it impossible to express such concepts. Illustrations of this are provided by the Hebrew words for 'soul', 'paradise' and 'resurrection', which for good historical reasons were not needed by the biblical writers. However, under the influence of Greek and Persian forces they became normal items of vocabulary in the Hellenistic and Roman periods: *neshamah* 'soul' (in biblical Hebrew it means 'breath' – there is no word for 'soul'); *pardes* 'paradise' (a

Persian loanword) and *tehiyyat he-metim* 'resurrection of the dead' (a Hebrew phrase not recorded before then but quite possibly ancient) (Sawyer 1973).

There certainly were problems for the Greek translator of biblical Hebrew, but these had little to do with any in-built structural differences between Hebrew and Greek or between a Semitic and an Indo-European language, and were probably no greater than for any other translation task. But our concern here is to assess the effect of translating biblical Hebrew into Hellenistic Greek (Hill 1967). As we saw, unlike those responsible for the ancient Aramaic translations, which were originally oral and often more paraphrase or commentary than translation, the Greek translators aimed at an accurate and literal translation. The problem is that no two words in the same language, let alone in different languages, ever have exactly the same semantic range, and translation thus inevitably alters the meaning of the source language. Let us look at a few crucial examples. First, the word for 'blood': biblical Hebrew *dam* always suggests something closely associated with death and revulsion, and thus the Hebrew equivalent of an expression like 'to be of the same blood' would be something like 'to be of the same flesh' or 'of the same bone' (Gen. 2:23). The Hebrew expression translated 'blood of the covenant' cannot refer to 'blood-brotherhood' or a similar bond, but to the frightening ritual by which it was initiated (Exod. 24). In Christian Greek and English this does not apply and a whole new way of interpreting the Sinai covenant ritual and the words of Jesus at the Last Supper (Luke 22:20) became possible (Christ 1977).

Another example is the important biblical Hebrew word *tzedaqah*, the semantic range of which is reflected in English 'righteousness' (e.g. Amos 5:24), 'deliverance' (e.g. Isa. 51:6, 8) and 'triumph' (Judges 5:11). The Greek translators represented it almost everywhere by the abstract word *dikaiosune* 'righteousness'. The question is: how much of the original Hebrew meaning is carried over into the target language, and how much is lost? Is it possible, for example, for a Greek writer to introduce into his or her language a new item of vocabulary consisting of a Greek word with a Hebrew meaning derived from an equivalent word in Hebrew. This is known as semantic borrowing or calque. The Greek phrase *ho huios tou anthropou* 'the son of man' is an uncontroversial example in which the common Hebrew idiom *ben adam* (or the Aramaic equivalent *bar nasha*) 'a human being, one, someone' has been literally translated into Greek where the phrase has no meaning apart from the Hebrew from which it is derived. *Dikaoisune* is much more problematical and raises a number of questions: how far did the Greek translators want readers to understand it in a new borrowed Hebrew sense? What did first-century Jewish writers like Paul mean when they wrote the word *dikaoisune*? Whatever they intended, what was to prevent Greek-speaking Christian readers from taking it in its normal Greek sense and distancing themselves, consciously or unconsciously, from the original Hebrew scriptures?

The translators were Jews, devoted as much to the Hebrew original as to their task of representing it in Greek (p. 116). They were often brilliantly successful, as their choice of *doxa* for *kabod* 'glory', *ktizo* for *qanah* 'create' and *skene* for *mishkan* 'tabernacle' illustrates. But the choice of Greek equivalents like *nomos* 'law' for Hebrew *torah* 'teaching', *prophetes* for *nabi* 'prophet' and 'Hades' for 'Sheol' (e.g. Isa. 14:15; 38:18), to which we might add occasional historic innovations like *parthenos* in Isaiah 7:14 and *episkopos* in Isa. 60:17, inevitably introduced radical new lines of thought. Overall, the effect of translating Hebrew scripture into Greek was to construct a radically different text, one which, in the history of Christianity, virtually took the place of the Hebrew original as the Church's sacred text, and which the Jewish authorities soon rejected as alien.

It is arguable that that first written translation of the Hebrew Bible was the single most radical shift in the history of its interpretation. As we have seen, in the hands of readers ignorant of the original Hebrew, the Greek of the Septuagint may often have meant something different from what the Greek translators had intended, and certainly different from the original Hebrew. The process of translating from the sacred language of a relatively small minority group, many of whom no longer spoke it as their first language, into an international language spoken by most educated people – the lingua franca of philosophers and scientists all over the world – made it inevitable that the Greek version of Jewish scripture would soon have a life of its own, in most contexts independent of the Hebrew original and deprived of many of the subtleties of semantic borrowing known only to a minority of Jewish scholars.

That first shift, from Hebrew to Greek, a century or more before the time of Christ, was never repeated in subsequent translations. The influence of the LXX on all subsequent versions, from the Latin, Syriac, Coptic and other ancient versions down to Martin Luther's German Bible and *King James' Authorized Version*, was far more direct and unambiguous than that of the Hebrew original on the LXX. In the Latin of the Vulgate, for example, there is far more direct borrowing of key terminology from Greek than there is from Hebrew in the LXX. Important and influential Greek loanwords in Christian Latin include *Genesis*, *Exodus*, *Deuteronomium*, *Psalmi*, *propheta*, *Christus*, *angelus*, *holocaustum*, *lepra* 'leprosy', *evangelium*, *baptisma*, *synagoga* and *zelotes* (e.g. Exod. 20:5). The Vulgate derived *virgo* in Isaiah 7:14 from the LXX, and *caper emissarius* 'scapegoat' in Leviticus 16 is a calque of the Greek *apopompaios* 'sent away'. These and countless other LXX loanwords, many of them via Latin, Syriac and other early Christian translations of the Bible, found their way into almost every language in the world. Despite the efforts of a few Hebrew scholars down the ages and their claims to be concerned, like St Jerome, with the original Hebrew, it was the Greek Bible that has been most influential in the history of Christianity and indirectly in the history of western culture.

This was the case in Palestine where there is virtually no evidence of Hebrew-speaking Christians. Greek and Aramaic were the first languages of Christianity, because they were the everyday languages of most people, and the Jewish scriptures were at first read and studied almost exclusively in Greek translation. In Rome, Christians used first Greek then Latin. In Egypt, most of the earliest Christian documents are in Coptic. The use of Armenian, Syriac and Mandaean among eastern Christians, Ge'ez in Ethiopia and Gothic in parts of Europe makes it abundantly clear that the local churches maintained a degree of independence from the world powers and fostered close relations with the ordinary people in every country in which they established themselves. Vernacular translations of scripture in all these languages were produced in the first few centuries CE.

There is another interesting contrast here, between official and unofficial religion, or between orthodoxy and heresy. Rome from 325 CE sought to impose its authority on the religious beliefs and practices of its subjects, as well as its language. The Goths maintained their independence, both linguistically and doctrinally, for several centuries – hence the need for Ulfilas' famous translation of the Bible. Similarly, as parts of eastern Christianity threw off Greek influence and produced their own vernacular translations of scripture, they developed their own distinctive beliefs and practices. This explains why, for example, certain books of the Bible, like Enoch and Jubilees, which were rejected as non-canonical by Greek Orthodoxy and by Rome, have survived in Ethiopic or Armenian versions. There is also a close correlation between those who use the vernacular in Jewish worship and their relations with the orthodox hierarchy.

7

BELIEFS AND CONTROLS

In this chapter we will consider various types of religious belief, from official doctrine to popular tradition, concerning the nature and origin of sacred texts. On the one hand, priests and scholars representing the religious establishment promulgated a system of doctrines, such as the verbal inerrancy of scripture and divine inspiration, and special procedures, including official lectionaries for public worship and rules governing the pronunciation, writing down and protection of sacred texts. On the other hand, the people responded by surrounding such sacred texts with an aura of sanctity and reverence, which gave rise to all kinds of colourful legends and superstitions. These then had the effect of reinforcing the official doctrines and guaranteeing the unique authority of scripture.

This situation existed in many communities in the Greco-Roman world. The Sibylline Oracles had such a role in ancient Rome, for example, and the Avesta in parts of Persia. But once again the role of the Torah in ancient Judaism is unique in many respects, as well as exceptionally well documented, and it is with ancient Jewish beliefs and practices that we begin our discussion. The Jewish case will then provide us with a paradigm for our discussion of beliefs about date and authorship, inspiration, rules and regulations in general. Most of the Jewish sources referred to, in particular the Talmud and Midrash, were not written down until the fifth century or later. However, all of them clearly contain material from several centuries earlier and can, with caution, be used as evidence for some general conclusions on beliefs and practices at the beginning of the common era.

The simplest and most widespread explanation of the origin of scripture is that it was composed by one or more inspired individuals. Thus the first part of the Jewish Bible has been known from ancient times as the 'Five Books of Moses', and the Mosaic authorship of the Torah or Pentateuch has been one of the central themes of Jewish and Christian thinking about the Bible ever since. The belief goes back to the Bible itself, to the story of Israel at Sinai, where Moses' unique role is repeatedly stressed, for example: 'Moses went up to God...' (Exod. 19:3)...the Lord said to Moses, 'Write these words...' (Exod. 34:27). There is a reference to Moses' successor, Joshua, copying from 'the book of the law [torah] of Moses' (Josh. 8:31–2), and the 'law of Moses' is frequently mentioned elsewhere (e.g. 2 Kings 14:6; 23:25; Mal. 4:4; Neh. 8:1). By the first century CE, the terms 'Moses' and the 'Torah' are virtually interchangeable. Christian writers cited the Torah as follows: 'What did Moses command you...?' (Mark 10:3); 'Moses wrote...' (Mark 12:19); 'whenever Moses is read...' (2 Cor. 3:15). The Qumran sectarians did the same (e.g. CD 5:8–9; 8:14 DSST 36, 38), and in rabbinic usage 'Moses our teacher' *moshe rabbenu* appears regularly in similar contexts.

How Moses thus came to be accepted as author of the Torah and thus the unquestioned ultimate source of religious authority for Jews, is a historical question to which we shall return later. The claims to this unique role are actually made explicit in the Torah itself, which ends with the words 'Never since has there arisen a prophet like Moses whom the Lord knew face to face. He was unequalled for all the signs and wonders which the Lord sent him to perform...' (Deut. 34:10–11). He was the yardstick against which other authorities were measured: David, Isaiah (BT Makkot 24a) and, in the unfavourable comparison of Christian Judaism, Christ (2 Cor. 3). Tradition turned a blind eye to anachronisms that worry modern commentators (e.g. Gen. 12:6), and accepted that Moses was the author of the Torah. By the same token he was also the author of other manifestly later works such as Psalm 90, the apocryphal Testament of Moses and the Qumran document known as the 'Words of Moses' (*DSST*: 276–81). There is even a Talmudic tradition that he wrote the Book of Job (BT BabBat 14b), and another that he was the original author of the Mishnah. It is recounted that Moses actually wanted the Oral Law (the Mishnah) to be written down at Sinai as well, and that God did not permit this because he wanted to keep the true meaning of the Hebrew Bible out of the hands of the gentiles: only those who have the key (that is, the oral tradition) are in a position to understand it (RA: 159–60).

Belief in the direct continuity from Sinai to the chief sources of contemporary authority was embodied in the Mishnaic tradition referred to earlier (M.Aboth 1:1) that there was an unbroken chain of people, most of them identifiable, stretching back to Moses at Sinai. The chain ran from Moses to Joshua to the Elders (Josh. 24:31) to the Prophets to the 'Great Assembly' (in Ezra's time) to Simeon the Just to Antigonus of Soko, and from him through a series of 'pairs' (*zugot*) of leaders such as Hillel and Shammai, down to the present, that is, the third century CE. The ancient Mosaic authority of contemporary institutions was given additional substance by highlighting the numerical association between the seventy-two elders who received a share in 'the spirit that was upon Moses' (Num. 11:24–30), the seventy-two translators responsible for the Septuagint translation in the third century BCE and the seventy-two elder statesmen, most of them priests, who constituted the Sanhedrin, the Jewish court at Jerusalem until the end of the Second Temple Period in 70 CE. With the destruction of Jerusalem in 70 CE, and with it the temple hierarchy and the Sanhedrin, that substance evaporated and was replaced by the mishnaic chain of tradition discussed earlier. According to the Christian doctrine of the apostolic succession, the authority of contemporary Christian institutions at Rome was traced back in a similar way through named individuals to St Peter, the first Bishop of Rome, who in turn had been given the 'keys of the kingdom' by Jesus himself (Matt. 16:13–20). The 'keys' were required, incidentally, to unlock the true meaning of scripture, which therefore remained in the safe keeping of the Church and under its control.

Most of the other books of the Hebrew Bible are also attributed to divinely inspired individuals, though there is some disagreement among the authorities over who wrote what. One tradition divides up the books among eight 'authors': Moses, Joshua, Samuel, David, Jeremiah, 'Hezekiah and his company' (cf. Prov. 25:1), the 'men of the Great Synagogue' (cf. M.Aboth 1:1) and Ezra (BT BabBat 14b–15c; cited in *CHB*: 1,116). According to this list, Isaiah, Ezekiel and others did not actually write anything themselves, but this does not affect the authenticity of what they say. It is simply taking account of the fact that the books attributed to these authors contain biographical material clearly written by someone else. In the Hebrew text of the Bible, Solomon is given as author of Proverbs, Ecclesiastes and the Song of Songs, to which can be added the apocryphal Wisdom of Solomon, the Psalms of Solomon and the Odes of Solomon. Writers in this list are not the same as authors, which may help to explain the anomalous attribution of some of the 'Psalms of David' to other people, including Moses (Ps. 90), and

Solomon (Pss. 72; 127). It has been well said that all the Psalms are by David, but some more than others.

The Gospels attributed to Matthew, Mark, Luke, John, Thomas, Peter, Philip and other apostles of Christ provide interesting parallels to this process. It is highly likely that none of these works was written entirely by the author to whom it was attributed. The 'sacred words of Jesus' (1 Clement 13.3; 56.3) raise a similar problem, which is made more acute both by the firmly held belief in his divine nature, and by the short time-scale from his life in Palestine to the circulation of his sayings throughout the Roman Empire less than one hundred years later. To modern critics many of the sayings attributed to Jesus in our sources are at best approximations of what he actually said, at worst creations of the early church. Attempts have been made to separate what he actually said from what early Christian writers tell us he said, and to recover or reconstruct his *ipsissima verba*. The same processes were involved in the case of the sayings of the rabbis, recorded in some cases within less than a century of their death and many of which, like those of Jesus, are almost certainly apocryphal. Another example is the attribution of the whole Avesta to Zoroaster, despite the fact that, like the Pentateuch, it contains clear evidence of multiple authorship.

This type of attribution of literature to famous individuals, known as pseudonymity, was extremely common throughout our period both within the Jewish tradition and in the Greco-Roman world. Indeed, from ancient times Christian authorities identified numerous works of this type as pseudepigrapha, that is, 'with a false superscription'. A second-century writer rejects the Gospel of Peter and other NT 'pseudepigrapha' as heretical (Eusebius, *EH* 3.25.6) and there is an interesting list of OT pseudepigrapha given in a sixth-century work, itself falsely attributed to Athanasius of Alexandria (*c.*296–73) (*OTP* 1: xxi–xxvii). Modern scholars since the eighteenth century have published collections of these fascinating and important works, notably R.H. Charles' *Apocrypha and Pseudepigrapha of the Old Testament* (1913), James Charlesworth's more recent two-volume *Old Testament Pseudepigrapha* (1985), which contains the edited texts of more than fifty works, M.R. James' *The Apocryphal New Testament* and Hennecke *et al*'s *New Testament Apocrypha* (1963–5).

Modern historical critical interest in questions of date and authorship has enlarged these lists of pseudepigrapha to include most of the Bible as well, for example: the 'Five Books of Moses', the biblical books attributed to Isaiah, Jeremiah and Daniel, the Psalms of David, the Proverbs of Solomon, the Four Gospels, some of the Letters of Paul and Peter, and the Revelation of St John are all now considered to be pseudepigrapha in the sense that they bear a false (i.e. historically inaccurate) superscription, although the term is hardly ever applied. The distinction between the Bible and the Pseudepigrapha, in other words, has less to do with date and authorship than with decisions taken by religious authorities centuries ago, for theological or ecclesiastical reasons, on which texts are canonical and which are not. Scholars interested in the history of ancient Judaism and Christianity nowadays ignore the ecclesiastical division of the relevant literature into Old Testament, New Testament, Intertestamental, Apocryphal, Pseudepigraphical or the like, and handle all the relevant texts from c.200 BCE to c.600 CE in the same way. The importance of the Book of Enoch, for example, in reconstructing Christian origins, as well as some of the shorter texts among the NT apocrypha, is increasingly being recognized (Barker 1988).

We are concerned here, however, with ancient attitudes to pseudonymity, not modern. What did the authors, or at any rate those responsible for adding such false superscriptions, hope to achieve? In seeking an answer to this question we must take account of the wider context of the Greco-Roman world. In the first place, a distinction was made between good and bad motives. Eusebius devotes a lengthy section of his *Preparation for the Gospel* to the subject. Literary property was an important issue among the Greeks and deliberate fraud or plagiarism was condemned. The medical writer Galen in the second century CE was worried by a forgery of his work (*OCD*: 605). Another factor in some cases was the attitude of the state to certain publications. An oppressive regime led to authors sometimes being forced to hide behind a pseudonym. It has been suggested that those who wrote the Book of Daniel and some of the other politically sensitive apocalyptic works of the period, which contain coded references to contemporary political figures and events, chose to conceal their identity for this reason. Certainly there is evidence that some of the Neo-Pythagorean philosophers from the beginning of the second century BCE hid behind names like Orpheus to escape repression by the state, and there are important pseudonymous texts ascribed to Pythagoras and other Pythagoreans dating from the third century BCE to Byzantine times (*OCD*: 1284)

One thing that is clear is that the custom by which authors attributed their writings to the one whom they considered to be their model or the founder of their school, was widely practised and, other things being equal, seems to have been a convention accepted by everyone. It was a way of acknowledging one's intellectual or religious origins and claiming continuity with them, just as we saw in relation to rabbinic claims that the oral Torah goes back to Moses at Sinai. *Mimesis* or *imitatio* was a fundamental feature of Greek and Roman educational technique, and writers were trained from the earliest stages to imitate models from among the great literary figures of the past (Quintilian, *Institutio Oratorica* 10:2). *Imitatio* was not plagiarism, nor should it be slavish or uncritical. Emulation was encouraged as well as comparison between various models. But the basic assumption that it was right to base one's creative activity on a profound reverence for the great literary or other figures of the past was common to all.

The situation in the ancient Near East was not dissimilar. The scribal tradition common to Egypt and Babylonia put great emphasis on copying the same texts, generation after generation. There were forms and techniques associated with particular literary genres, covering everything from lists and legal documents to fables, funeral laments and educational treatises, which survived unchanged for many centuries. The influence of this universal phenomenon on the Bible can be seen in the so-called 'Wisdom books' of Proverbs, Ecclesiastes and Sirach (Ecclesiasticus), in which, for example, the ancient literary fiction that an elder ruler or king is addressing his son is studiously kept up: 'Hear, my son, your father's instructions...' (Prov. 1:8; 2:1; 3:1, etc.; Ecclesiastes 12:12; Sir. 2:1; 3:1; 4:1, etc.). Even the number of sayings seems to have been conventional, Solomon's 'thirty sayings' of biblical tradition (Prov. 22:20) apparently being modelled on the 'Thirty Sayings of the Egyptian sage Amenemope' (McKane 1970: 369–74). The fundamental principle that education is first and foremost a matter of learning to respect one's distinguished literary ancestors is a recurring theme throughout the exhortatory prologue to the Book of Proverbs (chapters 1–9) and nicely summarized in ben Sira's eulogy of the scribe as one who 'will seek out the wisdom of the ancients...and preserve the discourse of distinguished men' (Sir. 39:1–2).

If it was no crime to imitate ancient writers, where the aim was not to steal or plagiarize, but to emulate, then it was not necessarily considered unacceptable to take the process one step further and write under the pseudonym of one of the chosen models. This immediately suggests that the rejection of pseudonymous writings as forgeries must therefore have often been due to factors other than a concern for historical truth. When, for instance, the Emperor Augustus ordered 2,000 volumes of the Sibylline Oracles to be destroyed as forgeries in 12 CE, this was certainly more because he disapproved of their content than out of a concern for historical truth. Three oracles written by Hellenistic Jews (Sib. 3–5), with no connection whatever to any of the Sibyls, were not questioned. Similarly, the Church's decision to reject the Book of Enoch, the Gospel of Thomas, the Acts of Paul and the rest of what they described as pseudepigrapha, was due to their content, their provenance and perhaps their date rather than the fiction of their title.

An illuminating example is provided by the first-century BCE Greek work known as the 'Wisdom of Solomon', accepted as canonical by most of the Christian Church but excluded from the Jewish canon of scripture. There is ample evidence from as early as the second century CE that its Solomonic authorship was not taken literally by everyone. The 'Muratorian Fragment' describes it as 'written by the friends of Solomon in his honour' (Beckwith 1985: 247). If that is what 'authorship' means in this case, one wonders whether our modern historical critical attitude towards this ancient convention is not misplaced. There are to be sure plenty of examples of ancient writers, Christian and Jewish, apparently taking what to our eyes are manifestly false claims at face value. Tertullian, for example, devotes a whole chapter to discussing how the Book of Enoch, Noah's great grandfather (Gen. 5:21), could have survived the flood, and there is plenty of rabbinic speculation, as we shall see, about Moses' actual role in the origin of the Torah. But to ancient eyes surely the tradition that Enoch wrote the book that bears his name and Moses wrote the Pentateuch are stories like all the other stories about divinely inspired characters in the Bible, stories to be read and studied in their own right, stories about divine revelation and the nature of sacred texts rather than accounts of what actually happened. Even today it can be argued that the tradition that Moses wrote the Pentateuch is more important, from a religious, theological and literary point of view, than the fact that he did not.

This brings us to a second widespread aspect of traditional views about the nature and origin of sacred texts. The author is normally believed to have been divinely inspired, and the role of the deity in the process in relation to that of the author is of the greatest

significance. In most cases the author is a prophet or one who shares many of the characteristics of a prophet. This applies, for example, to Moses, Samuel, Isaiah, Daniel, Ezra (2 Esdras 1:1), Jesus, Zoroaster, Orpheus, the Sibyls and many others. Many such as Enoch, Ezra and John of Patmos give an account of miraculous journeys to heaven or Horeb or Jerusalem where they meet the deity face to face, and receive instruction on what to write, so the divine authority of their words cannot be questioned. This is the point of Jeremiah's challenge to the 'false prophets': 'For who has stood in the council of the Lord so as to hear and to see his word?' (Jer. 23:18). Even where such details are not given, divine authorship is never in doubt.

The priority of divine authority over that of the prophet is expressed in various ways. It goes back to the claim constantly made by the biblical prophets that they are speaking the 'word of the Lord', not their own words. The role of the 'inspired prophet' may then in effect be reduced to that of a dumb instrument in the hand of the deity. It is from this view that such traditions as those about Amos' lack of professional training (Amos 7:14) and the illiteracy of Muhammad arose: the less human participation in the process, the greater the emphasis on its divine authorship. According to Muslim tradition, the Holy Qur'an is actually the word of God, written in Arabic before creation and transmitted through the mouth of Muhammad, but absolutely untouched by him or any other human agency.

By contrast, in both Jewish and Christian tradition, itself rooted in the Bible, the human authors are usually highly respected figures and given credit for their role. The stories about how Moses, Jeremiah and others at first raised objections to the divine imperative, and then only reluctantly agreed to act as prophets, highlight the importance of the human element in the process. A rabbinic variation on this theme depicts Moses objecting to the content of what he is being asked to write, implying that he is critically aware, at least, of what he is writing: 'When he came to the verse, "And God said, Let us make man", Moses said, "Sovereign of the Universe, why dost thou furnish me with such evidence for heretics?" "Write, said He, Whoever wishes to err, may err" ' (Gen. R. 8:18). Incidentally this reference to Moses' writing, which is by no means the only one, reminds us that the illiteracy theme which was an important part of Muslim teaching about the divine authorship of their scripture, has no place in Jewish tradition. Moses wrote the Torah with his own hand, and that

means a human element is involved right from the beginning. In his commentary on Psalm 45:1 ('My tongue is like the pen of a ready scribe'), Theodore of Mopsuestia (392–428) says that a writer of scripture is 'like a pen in the hand of the Holy Spirit, the real author. The Spirit fills his mind with divine thoughts as the scribe fills his pen with ink' (*CHB*: 1, 492). But there are indications elsewhere that, like most of his contemporaries, he left room for the human writer's free-will.

Another theme which has a similar function in developing this teaching about the role of the prophets, is that of their faith and courage to continue with their work of communicating God's word in the teeth of social or political opposition. The tradition that the prophets were persecuted and killed by the authorities is a common one. The martyrdom of Isaiah under Manasseh, recounted both in the Talmud and in a second-century Christian work known as the 'Ascension of Isaiah' (OTP: 2, 143–176), is the most elaborate example of this, but there are other references in the Bible (Jer. 20:2; Matt. 23:37). There is also a rabbinic tradition that Moses told his people of the suffering he had endured when he received the Torah:

> Moses said to Israel, Know you not with what travail I gained the Torah! What toil, what labour I endured for its sake! Forty days and forty nights I was with God. I entered among the angels, the Living Creatures, the Seraphim, of whom any one could blast the whole universe in flame. My soul, my blood I gave for the Torah. And I learnt it in travail, so do you learn it in travail, and as you learn it in travail, so do you teach it in travail.
>
> (*RA*: 135)

No doubt such teaching about the divinely inspired authors of scripture was influenced by contemporary martyrs like Akiba, Hananiah ben Teradion, Polycarp, Perpetua and others. The continuity going back to Sinai which we have seen to be so crucial in the case of the authors of the oral Torah is reinforced by recognizing in contemporary leaders, as does the passage from the Midrash just quoted, the same qualities of faith, courage and devoted scholarship which characterized Moses, Isaiah and the other authors of scripture. The relevance of such comparisons between heroes of the past and contemporary aspirations for modern

thinking about the function of pseudonymity in the ancient world needs no further comment.

The role of the prophet was sometimes downgraded in order to stress the divine authorship of the original. There is a legend in the Talmud, for example, that Moses, traditionally praised for his humility (Num. 12:3), refused to accept any credit for the Torah:

> Satan went to Moses and said to him, 'Where is the law which God gave to you?' Moses replied, 'What am I that God should have given the Torah to me?' Then God said, 'Moses are you a liar?' Then Moses said, 'This lovely and hidden thing in which day by day you took your pleasure, should I take credit for it?' Then God said, 'Because you have made yourself small, therefore it shall be called by your name, as it says, Remember the Law of Moses.' (Mal.3:2).
>
> (BT Shab. 89a; *RA*: 168–9)

It will be noticed that here, as in some of the examples mentioned earlier, Moses is not actually the author of the Torah, although it is called the 'Law of Moses'. There is in fact a whole series of traditions to the effect that the Torah was written in heaven by God before creation. According to one, when Moses went up to heaven to receive the Torah, he found God sitting weaving crowns for the letters (BT Men. 29b; *RA*: 168). The pre-existent Torah was written with black fire on white fire (Midrash Psalm 90, para. 12). What happened at Sinai, in other words, was that it was delivered ready-made to Moses and the human role in its composition is reduced to a minimum.

The term 'Torah' traditionally often includes not only the 'Five Books of Moses', but also the Prophets and the Writings that make up the whole of Hebrew scripture. It also refers to the oral Torah as much as to the written Torah as we have seen. Thus the following charming traditions which appear in many parts of the rabbinic literature were intended to stress the divine pre-existence of the whole 'Dual Totah'. When God was about to give the Torah to Moses, the angels at first complained: 'The beautiful Torah which you have hidden away since creation...do you now propose to give it to a mere mortal?' (BT Shab. 88b). When God gave the Torah to Israel, the earth rejoiced and the heavens wept (Pes.R. 95a).

The pre-existence of the Torah was supremely expressed in the Jewish belief that it was to be identified with the biblical concept of wisdom (*hokmah*), 'created at the beginning of his way, the first of his acts of old' (Prov. 8:22). The common word 'Torah' itself is

not normally translated 'Law', but rather 'teaching, instruction' as in Proverbs 1:8, 3:1, 4:1, 8:33 and regularly throughout the Hebrew Bible. This brings 'Torah' into close association with 'wisdom'. An elaborate example from the second century BCE is to be found in the Wisdom of Jesus ben Sira (Ecclesiasticus) where Torah describes how she first 'dwelt in high places…and walked in the depths of the abyss' and then 'made her dwelling' in Israel (Sir. 24).

A Christian variation on this theme occurs in the prologue to St John's Gospel, which describes how the Word existed before creation and then 'became flesh and dwelt among us'. Here the Greek philosophers' term *logos* 'word, reason, natural order' takes the place of Hebrew Wisdom/Torah, but the allusion to the cosmology of Proverbs 8:22 and Sirach 24 is unmistakable. Possibly the masculine term *logos* was thought more appropriate in its application to Christ than the feminine word *sophia* which would have been a more literal rendering of the Hebrew word for wisdom used in Proverbs and Ben Sira. In Greek translations of Jewish scripture *logos* occurs in such familiar phrases as 'hear the word of the Lord' and 'the word of the Lord came to me', where it refers to prophetic utterances. The parallel between the two beliefs is very close: just as in rabbinic tradition, the divine and pre-existent wisdom of God came into the world in book form at Sinai, so, in the Christian doctrine of the incarnation, it came into the world in the form of a human being. The Christian parallel nicely illustrates the crucial role of the Torah in Judaism, exactly corresponding as it to the role of Christ in Christianity. While Christians hear the voice of Christ in the words of Proverbs 8 – 'I love those who love me…whoever finds me finds life' – Jews hear the voice of Torah.

One final example of the Jewish expression of their belief in the independent existence and immortality of the divine words of the Torah appears in a legend concerning the martyrdom of Hanina ben Teradion, a contemporary of Akiba. It is said that he held a Torah scroll in his arms when he went to the stake and, as the flames started to burn the leather sheets of the scroll, he told his disciples he could see the letters flying off, presumably back to heaven (BT Ab. Zar. 18a). The scroll was made of perishable stuff, but its words were divine.

Between belief in the role of great human personalities, prophets, sages and others, and belief in the divine origin of sacred texts, there is the doctrine of divine inspiration. It takes various forms according to the status of the inspired person, the degree of

institutionalization of the phenomenon and the nature of the written sources available. In ancient Greece and Rome a distinction was drawn between the term *prophetes*, which normally refers to inspired cultic functionaries at an institution like the oracular shrine at Delphi, and *mantis* used of ecstatic or charismatic individuals not necessarily formally attached to any institution. In biblical narrative a similar distinction can be drawn between the 'inspiration' of groups or guilds of people whose experience is described in dramatic language (Num. 11; 1 Sam. 10), but who are not named and whose words are not preserved, and individual cases of the 'spirit of the Lord' influencing famous individuals, like Isaiah, Ezekiel and Jesus, whose words are at least as important as their experience. Paul's distinction between prophecy and speaking in tongues, both described as 'gifts of the spirit', is similarly motivated by his concern for order in the young churches he was concerned with. Belief in the notion of divine inspiration is the same in all these cases and affects our discussion only insofar as the words of the inspired individuals have been preserved and become sacred scripture.

In rabbinic traditions about the relationship between the divine and human in the process of divine revelation there are two related phenomena, both appearing in the well-known legend of Rabbi Eliezer to be considered now (BT BabMetz. 59a–b). The first is the notion of a *bat qol* 'a heavenly voice', which can intervene in human debate with a contribution that claims divine authority, and may or may not be accepted by all the participants. The story goes that a *bat qol* intervened on the side of Rabbi Eliezer in a heated debate about the ritual status of a certain type of oven. What is very interesting is that Eliezer was rejected by the majority on the grounds that God's contribution to debates of this kind is restricted to what happened at Sinai. The Torah is no longer in heaven: at Sinai it was delivered once and for all into the hands of a human community who must work out their own problems without further divine intervention. Rabbi Eliezer, on the other hand, made the same kind of claim to divine authority for his own views, as all the other inspired individuals in the tradition, from Moses and Isaiah on. Although the legend makes it clear that he did have divine approval, he was rejected just like many other inspired individuals including Isaiah, Jesus and Haninah ben Dosa.

The other phenomenon to be considered in this context is the figure of Elijah. He too intervenes from time to time in human situations, often to settle some kind of hitherto insoluble dispute.

There are many references to him 'meeting' rabbis who are rescued or advised or helped in some way by him. He was believed to have a particular role in cases where no solution to a problem could be found and the technical term *teyqu* 'let it stand (the question is undecided)' is used. The four letters of the talmudic term were ingeniously taken as an acronym of the following sentence: 'the Tishbite [Elijah: 1 Kings 17:1] will solve difficulties and problems'.

The concept of divine inspiration was perhaps first worked out in detail among the leaders and writers of the early Christian Church. The first attested occurrence of the term *theopneustos* 'inspired (or breathed) by God', as applied directly to the sacred writing, is in 2 Tim. 3:15–17. Elsewhere it is rare, applied to a person, a river or the like (Sib. Or. 5:308), but here it applies to Jewish scripture. Later, in the patristic literature it covers the Gospels, Letters of Paul and all the other Christian additions to scripture as well. The notion that the writings of scripture are 'inspired' is frequently expressed by reference to the activity of the Holy Spirit. Thus, for example, the Psalms are attributed to David and the Holy Spirit almost in equal proportions: 'Sovereign Lord…who by the mouth of David, your servant, said by the Holy Spirit' (Acts 4:25). Elsewhere the process is described in the formula 'the Holy Spirit spoke through the mouth of David' (Acts 1:16), or 'God spoke through the mouth of his prophets' (Acts 3:21). After three centuries or so of theological debate, the Church encapsulated its doctrine of inspiration in the briefest of formulas in the Nicene Creed: 'And I believe in the Holy Spirit…who spake by the Prophets'.

In some contexts, the writings of Philo, for example, and the montanists, including Tertullian, the role of the prophet was compared to that of a musical instrument in the hands of a divine musician. Following biblical examples, this view of the process of divine inspiration envisages a moment of divine possession in which prophets completely lose consciousness and the words uttered are not theirs, but those of God speaking through their lips. In other words, as in examples cited earlier, the degree of human participation in the process is virtually zero. The church fathers, however, wished to dissociate the inspired writers of scripture from the ecstatic prophets of paganism and insisted that what happened in the case of the inspired Christian scriptures was that the Holy Spirit acted on human faculties, on the evangelists' memories, for example, in such a way as to transform their human words into the

Word of God. The process thus varied from one individual to another and from one period or locality to another.

Verbal inspiration is a specific type of inspiration according to which every word, every letter of the sacred text, is divinely inspired and therefore inerrant. The distinction which defines some extreme forms of modern fundamentalism is hardly found in antiquity, although there is plenty of good evidence from both Jewish and Christian sources that every letter did have significance. For example, in cases where there were alternative ways of spelling the same word, the choice of one or the other in a particular context was believed by Jewish commentators to have been deliberate and required explanation. The Hebrew word translated 'formed', for example, in Genesis 2:7 and 19 is spelled in two ways, one with one Yodh, the other with two Yodhs. The rabbis noticed that when it refers to the creation of a human being it is spelled with two Yodhs (v. 7), while when it refers to the creation of animals it has only one, and concluded that this is because human beings have two inclinations in their nature, an evil inclination and a good inclination, while animals have only one. Incidentally, the letter in question, Yodh, is the smallest letter in the Hebrew alphabet, paired with the 'tittle', a tiny stroke used in the formation of some letters, in Jesus' saying on the everlasting significance and authority of every tiniest detail of the Torah: 'For truly I say to you till heaven and earth will pass away, not a jot or tittle [RSV 'not an iota, not a dot'] will pass from the law until all is accomplished' (Matt. 5:17–18). Like the rabbis, the church fathers believed that scripture, including the more recent books of the New Testament, contained nothing superfluous. Origen argued that 'there is not one jot or tittle written in the Bible which does not accomplish its special work for those capable of using it' (Wiles 1970), and Jerome maintained that 'every word, syllable, accent and point is packed with meaning' (Kelly 1975: 62).

It is against this background that we must understand the rules that governed the manufacture, copying, handling and reading of sacred texts. Torah scrolls had to be written on leather in ink and in a particular form of the Hebrew script (MYad. 4:5). Detailed rules were laid down governing the materials used in the manufacture of the scrolls, and the craftsmen required special training under religious supervision. Copying of the Torah from dictation was prohibited, and every scroll had to be copied from another scroll. Before 70 CE, the whole industry was controlled by the Temple hierarchy where a kind of master copy was held, known as the

'Scroll of the Temple Court' and believed by some to have been actually written by Ezra (MMoed Katan 3:4). The disposal of damaged scrolls was also controlled. Synagogues had a special storeroom, later called a *geniza*, in which both the coverings and the scrolls themselves had to be hidden away (*ganaz*) when they were worn out or in a state of decay (cf. MShab 9:6). The best-known *geniza* is the Cairo Geniza, accidentally discovered by Solomon Schechter in 1899, which contained centuries of manuscripts of inestimable value to modern scholars, and still yielding their secrets under the aegis of the Cambridge Geniza Project.

Central to this whole question was the belief that sacred writings (Hebrew *kitve qodesh*) 'make the hands unclean', a phrase that is roughly equivalent to the term 'are canonical'. Whatever the precise meaning of the Hebrew term *tame*, as applied to animals, birds, fish and insects in the food laws of Leviticus and Deuteronomy and normally translated as unclean or impure, it is clear that it does not always carry the strong negative overtones of 'polluted' or the like which unclean suggests to English ears (Douglas 1999). Its use in connection with sacred books in rabbinic Hebrew suggests that the emphasis is more on not touching or damaging them in any way, in other words, treating with respect rather than abhorrence. There is a curious comment on this attributed to the great Rabban Yochanan ben Zakkai (first century CE), in which he seems to imply that the uncleanness transmitted by the Holy Scriptures is somehow connected to the special love with which they have to be treated: he says 'as is our love for them [the Holy Scriptures] so is their uncleanness' (MYad. 4:6). Incidentally, in the Mishnaic period the commercial value of a Torah scroll was considered greater than that of a whole synagogue (MMeg. 3:1). Conversely, the Hebrew term for 'to suppress, declare non-canonical' was *ganaz* 'to hide away' (cf. Geniza earlier): there were efforts to 'hide away' the books of Ezekiel and Qohelet (Ecclesiastes) (BT Hag. 13a; BT Shab 30b). The Greek term 'Apocrypha' has the same etymology. Hebrew authorities also applied the term *hitzoni* 'external, i.e. heretical' to extra-canonical works (e.g. MSanh. 10:1).

Study of the Torah was constantly recommended. When two or three discuss the Torah together, the divine presence (*Shekinah*) rests between them (MAb. 3:2). It is the best of all the crafts in the world 'for it guards you from evil while you are young, and in old age it grants you a future and a hope' (MQidd. 4:14). Proverbs 6:22 summed it up for the rabbis: 'When you walk [that is, in this life], it leads you; when you lie down [that is, die], it will watch over you; and when you awake [that is, rise from the dead], it will talk with you'. Another tradition derived from Deuteronomy. 4:11 envisages the rabbis encircled by fire when they are studying Torah (BT Sot. 21a; cf. Rashi).

There were also rules controlling the unrestricted reading or exposition of certain parts of scripture. These were authorized by reference to such texts as Deuteronomy 29:29 ('The secret things belong to the Lord...') and a passage from the apocryphal Book of Ecclesiasticus or the Wisdom of Jesus ben Sira, cited more than once in the rabbinic literature: 'Seek not what is too difficult for you nor investigate what is beyond your power. Reflect on what has been assigned to you; for you do not need what is hidden' (Sir. 3:21–2; cf. BT Hag. 13a; Gen. R. 8:2). Genesis 1:1–3 and Ezekiel 1:4ff. were considered too dangerous for individuals to read on their own or without supervision by a qualified rabbinic scholar. The first few verses of Genesis were the scriptural source of early esoteric speculation on the origin of the universe, and the Ezekiel vision was the starting point of Merkavah ('Chariot') mysticism (MMeg. 4:10; MHag. 2:1). The dangerous or subversive effect of these texts upon individuals is further emphasized in the Talmud by several cautionary tales. The story of the child who was said to have been consumed by fire while reading the Book of Ezekiel has been mentioned already (Chapter 4). Rabbi Elisha ben Abuya (also known as Rabbi Aher 'the apostate') is said to have concluded from his mystical experience of heaven that there were two Gods (BT Hag. 14b), and in the most famous of all these stories, the great Rabbi Akiba was the only one of 'the four who entered paradise' to come back unhurt (BT Hag. 15b; Scholem 1965:14f.). According to Mishnaic law the expounding of the laws of incest (Hebrew 'nakedness') in Leviticus 18 was also restricted (Mhag. 2:1), no doubt for fear of embarrassing or over-exciting adolescents, while Origen tells us that the same applied to the Song of Songs (de Lange 1976: 34f.).

8

NAMES AND NUMBERS

The 'correctness of names' is the subject of one of the later dialogues of Plato (c.429–347 BCE). In the first part of the *Cratylus*, Socrates argues with Hermogenes, a friend of Cratylus, that the meaning of names in general is not arbitrary or due to irrational convention as Hermogenes maintains, but so 'correct' in their meaning and application to individuals that they must have been deliberately and logically given by lawgivers at some time in the past. He points out that already in Homer a distinction is drawn, more than once, between the names by which gods and men call the same things (e.g. *Iliad* 2:813f.; 14:291; 20:74). He argues that the gods must have had a reason for using particular names and moreover that the gods' names for things must be the correct ones.

Socrates first illustrates this by proposing, probably with tongue in cheek, etymologies for all the names he can think of, sometimes two or more different ones for the same name, and some of them considerably more convincing than others. Apollo is not the 'destroyer' many people imagine him to be (cf. *apollumi* 'to destroy'), but 'the god who both purifies (*apolouo*) and delivers (*apoluo*)'. Dionysus is the giver (*didous*) of wine (*oinos*). Aphrodite was named after her birth from the foam (*aphros*). Athena is 'the mind of God' (*he theou noesis*) or 'she who knows divine things' (*ta theia noousa*). Hermogenes' own name, which means 'son of Hermes', causes some amusement since neither of its two meanings, 'successful money-lender' (Hermes was patron of bankers and merchants) or 'skilled speaker' (*hermeneuo* 'to interpret'), is at all appropriate. Other problems with a rational theory of the correctness of names arise in the discussion, and Socrates concludes that, while originally or in an ideal world every name has an appropriate and rational meaning, the situation is more complex and more fluid (citing the philosopher Heracleitus), so that we can no longer know in every case what it is.

Speculation on the meaning of names was widespread in the ancient literatures. Homer relates the name of Odysseus to a word for 'pain' (*Od.*: 1.62). Aeschylus derives Zeus from *zen* 'to live' (*Suppl.*: 584), and, in a better-known example, Helen from Greek words for 'destroy' and 'ship' (*Agam.* 681–90). Plautus begins his *Amphitryo* with puns on the names of Mercury as god of mercantile enterprises (*mercator*), and his Greek counterpart Hermes as the interpreter, messenger (*nuntius* from Greek *hermeneus*). Elsewhere he plays on the fact that the names of many Roman deities are actually abstract Latin nouns, like Pax, Fortuna, Amor, Felicitas, Virtus, Salus and the like, the meanings of which are self-explanatory. In practice, almost any such noun can be personified, the only exceptions are neuter nouns like *auxilium* 'help' and *gaudium* 'joy' which grammatically are inanimate.

In some contexts it may not be entirely clear whether one is dealing with an abstract noun or the name of a deity, *pax* or Pax, *fortuna* or Fortuna, *amor* or Amor. The distinction is clear enough in English, but in a script which does not have upper case and lower case forms, it is not always so easy to determine whether *PAX* is an abstract noun for 'peace' or the goddess who was honoured in Rome by Augustus' famous *Ara Pacis* 'altar of Peace' (9 BCE) and the Flavian Temple of Peace (75 CE). The ambiguity is nicely exploited by two characters in Plautus' *Bacchides* discussing the following guest list for a party: Amor, Voluptas, Venus, Venustas, Gaudium, Iocus, Ludus, Sermo, Suavisaviatio. Venus certainly is a deity, Amor may be, but Gaudium certainly is not; Venustas is a word-play on the name of Venus, and Suavisaviatio ('Sexy kissing') looks like a deliberate attempt to ridicule the whole system: *an deus est ullus Suavisaviatio?* 'Is there any god with the name Suavisaviatio?' (*Bacch.* 120; Feeney 1998: 88).

There is an interesting correspondence here between biblical language about God and Greek and Roman usage, despite obvious theological and linguistic differences. In Semitic languages, including Hebrew and Syriac, where there are only two genders, masculine and feminine, and the deity is normally represented grammatically by masculine forms, there are nonetheless a number of feminine words for aspects of the divine, which, like the few female images just discussed, have been given prominence in modern feminist usage. The conspicuous mention right at the beginning of the Bible of 'the spirit (feminine) of God moving over the surface of the waters' (Gen. 1:2) is one of these, and in both Jewish (Hebrew) and Christian (Syriac) tradition the Spirit has been interpreted as a female aspect of the godhead. Another example is *shekinah* 'presence' which is used already in the rabbinic literature almost as a synonym for God (p. 138).

'Torah' is another feminine term frequently personified as in a rabbinic interpretation of Proverbs 6:22 mentioned earlier (p. 110), and this brings us to one final example. In Proverbs 1–9 and elsewhere wisdom (Hebrew *hokmah*, like Torah, feminine) is depicted almost as a goddess, with 'long life in her right hand and in her left hand riches and honour' (3:16), playing at the feet of Yahweh as he creates the world (8:30) and inviting people into her house of seven pillars to eat her bread and drink her wine (9:1, 5). Her origins go back to traditions about the Egyptian goddess of truth and justice, Ma'at, who is represented in similar imagery, or perhaps to a Greek cult of Aphrodite, the goddess of love: 'I love those who love me' (Prov. 8:17; McKane 1970: 362f.). Theologically impossible for Jewish orthodoxy, the identification of wisdom with Christ, the son of God, made it possible for Christians to conceive of an independent divine being known as Wisdom.

After this brief digression on personifications, we return to the subject of popular etymologies. The origin and meaning of names has an important role to play in Hebrew tradition as well. The Book of Genesis, which is very much concerned with origins, naturally contains numerous examples. In many cases the author makes the connection between the name and its proposed etymology explicit, as in his explanation of Eve's name as 'mother of all living' (3:20), Abraham's as 'father of a multitude' (17:5) and Jacob's as the 'one who took hold of Esau's heel' (25:26). Place-names are explained in the same way, for example: 'Isaac called it Rehoboth, for the Lord has made room [from *rahab* 'to be spacious'] for us' (26:22) and Jacob 'called the place Mahanaim because that was where he had met an army (*mahaneh*) of angels' (32:1–2). Elsewhere the association between a name and its meaning is transparent enough, as the example from Homer's *Odyssey* given earlier, not to need any special highlighting: 'the Lord God formed the human creature (*adam*) out of dust from the "ground" ' (*adamah* 2:7). Isaac's name (Hebrew *yitzhaq*), revealed in an oracle (Gen. 17:19), obviously alludes to the fact that Abraham 'fell on his face and laughed' (*yitzhaq*) with disbelief at the news that his aged wife was going to have a baby (v. 17). There are examples in biblical Greek too where Jesus' words to Peter need no explanation: 'You are Peter and on this rock (*petra*)

I will build my church' (Matt. 16:18). A less obvious example of this, requiring a knowledge of Hebrew as well as Greek, occurs in Acts 28:1: 'After we had escaped, we heard that the island was called Malta, (Greek *Melita*: cf. Hebrew *melitah* 'escape').

Modern etymological studies, based on the vastly increased resources and improved techniques of comparative linguistics, have established the etymology of most words in Greek, as well as Latin and Hebrew, beyond all reasonable doubt. In the last two centuries or so there has been a quantum leap in our knowledge of the early history of these languages, their relationship to other languages both within the Indo-European and Semitic language families and outside them, and the rules governing sound changes and correspondences between them. The abbreviation 'etym.dub.' appears only in a minority of entries in the standard dictionaries. But it is only quite recently, in the world of biblical scholarship at any rate, that the relationship between a word's etymology and its meaning has been clarified. Socrates' conclusion that the situation is more complicated than it looked at first sight has been proved to be absolutely correct. In more modern parlance, a word's (diachronic) semantic prehistory or etymology may or may not be relevant to its (synchronic) meaning in a given context. The only way to establish whether it is, is to analyse its meaning synchronically as it is used by a particular author or in a particular literary context or at a particular time. The historical fact that the Hebrew word for toothpaste, for example, is etymologically related to the word for Messiah (from Hebrew *mashah* 'to anoint') will in almost every context be totally irrelevant (the present discussion of 'etymologizing' being a rare exception).

For two centuries the study of biblical Hebrew suffered greatly from the misuse of comparative linguistic data. Eighteenth-century scholars claimed to have discovered the true and original meanings of words, long since lost or forgotten, by identifying etymological relationships with other Semitic languages, particularly Arabic. One of the pioneers of this method, the Dutch scholar, Albert Schultens, entitled his book *Hebrew Origins or the most ancient nature and character of the Hebrew Language recovered from the interior of Arabia (Arabiae penetralibus revocata)* (1761). This soon became the recognized method used by biblical scholars to identify and describe the meaning of Hebrew vocabulary, and was incorporated into virtually every grammar book, dictionary and commentary from then until quite recently. It found its way into some of the new translations of the Bible, most notably the *New English Bible* (1970) which, under the influence of the late Sir Godfrey Rolles Driver, included philological errors like *tzanah* 'to break wind' (Judges 1:14), and had to be drastically revised and corrected almost as soon as it was published. The *Jerusalem Bible* (1966) was also much affected by the Ugaritomania of such scholars as Mitchell Dahood who, in his translation of the Psalms, introduced numerous new meanings for Hebrew words on the basis of newly discovered Ugaritic (a dialect of Canaanite) vocabulary.

Since the publication of James Barr's *Semantics of Biblical Language* (1961) and *Comparative Philology and the Text of the Old Testament* (1968), in which he exposed what he called the 'root fallacy' in many influential biblical and theological writings, such 'etymologizing', although still apparent in some quarters, has yielded to more sophisticated semantic analysis and lexicography. Statements like the root meaning or the literal meaning of *hoshia* ('to save') is 'spaciousness' (cf. Arabic *wasi'a* 'to be spacious') have become less common in recent scholarly discourse (Sawyer 1990b: 441–63). The editors of the successful new Sheffield *Dictionary of Classical Hebrew* (1993) decided that etymological data could be dispensed with entirely.

The meaning of a word can usually be defined without reference to its root or its etymology by establishing its semantic relation to other words in the same language. *Bara* (create) can be defined, for example, as different from *yatzar* (form), *'asah* (make), *banah* (build), etc., in some respects, and closer to *sim* (put) and *qanah* (buy, possess) in others. The ancient versions of the Bible often provide us with early evidence of how some items of vocabulary were understood. The rendering of *bara* by ancient Greek translators as *ktizo* (found, colonize) in many passages (Deut. 4:32; Psalm 51:10; Isa. 45:7, 8) confirms the abstract and legal associations of *bara* in contrast to most of its synonyms. The importance of the ancient and mediaeval Jewish sources, which are of course historically closer to biblical Hebrew than Arabic or Ugaritic, has also been increasingly recognized by recent commentators. This is especially true when we consider that the most commonly used text of the Hebrew Bible is based on a mediaeval manuscript (Sawyer 1986).

On the other hand, as we have seen, folk-etymologies are common in many literatures. Monolingual etymological or pseudo-etymological explanations of the meaning of words can be and have been used by a great many authors, ancient and modern. This can be done with good effect, making excellent sense and adding an interesting dimension to the story-telling technique. The question in such cases is not whether the proposed etymology is correct or not, but how and for what purpose the author uses it. The structure of Hebrew in some respects lends itself to such etymologizing, in the relative transparency of its morphological structure, for example, and in the nature of its consonantal script (Sawyer 1967). In other words, despite recent, and entirely justified, scholarly cautions about the misuse of etymological data, root-meanings frequently do have an important part to play in the history of religious language and literature. We shall look at two aspects of this phenomenon as it relates to our main subject: religious factors in naming and religious beliefs about the power of names.

Much anthropological research has been done on the practice of giving names to individuals. There is a great deal of variety. In some societies, for example, the meaning of a name and its appropriateness to the individual are less important than its association with an ancestor or other member of the group. By contrast, research on biblical names revealed that in ancient Israel, that is before the Babylonian Exile in the sixth century BCE, the names of forebears were strictly avoided to emphasize the uniqueness and 'absolute identity of the person with the name' (Lauterbach 1970: 30). There was only one Abraham, one David, one Isaiah, etc. During the Second Temple Period this changed. The names of respected ancestors were frequently reused, and by the beginning of our period we come across a fair number of Joshuas (Aramaic *Jeshua*, Greek *Jesus*), Simeons (Greek *Simon*), Miriams (Greek *Maria*), etc. In Hellenistic times individuals deliberately chose to break their links with ancestral tradition by adopting Greek names. The corrupt high priest, Jeshua (174–171 BCE), changed his name to Jason, hero of Greek legend (Josephus, *Ant.* 12.5.1).

In the Bible there are many traditions about significant name changes. Jacob is given the name Israel, after struggling with the angel at Penuel, to mark his new status in God's plans for his people (Gen. 32), although this is more a literary device than evidence for ancient naming practices. The same applies to biblical explanations of names like Moses (Exod. 2:10), Naomi (Ruth 1:20) and the other examples given earlier. Isaiah's well-known naming of his two sons, Shear Jashub and Mahershalalhashbaz, no doubt belongs to the same category, where the emphasis is on the meaning of the names rather than the individuals bearing them (Isa. 7:3; 8:1–4; cf. 10:20–2). The naming of Immanuel by his mother in the same context (Isa. 7:14; cf. 8:8, 10; Matt. 1:23) is another example of the same literary technique. On the other hand, the renaming of Saul as Paul on his conversion to Christianity (cf. Acts 13:9) foreshadows the widespread practice according to which individuals are given a special Christian name on conversion, at baptism or on entering a monastic order to mark a change of spiritual status.

An especially significant element in many societies is the use of theophoric names, that is, compound names containing a reference to the group's deity. The practice is very widespread and at first sight would appear to be a fairly reliable indication of the religion of the group, since it is unlikely that parents would choose to give a child a name associated with a rival or alien religion. Familiar examples are Babylonian Nebuchadrezzar (*Nebo* 'protect the boundary') and Egyptian Rameses ('son of Ra'). Several of the Zoroastrian kings of Pontus were called Mithridates 'gift of Mithras', the Carthaginians named their children Hannibal 'Baal is gracious' and the like. A very large proportion of Hebrew names are composed of short sentences with the element *El* 'God' or some kind of abbreviated allusion to the name Yahweh/Jehovah. Thus Ezekiel means 'El is strong (*hazaq*)', Eliezer 'God helps (*'azar*)' and Michael 'who is like *El?*'. Jonathan means 'Yahweh gives (*nathan*)', Elijah 'Yahweh is my God (*el*)' and Isaiah 'Yahweh saves (*yasha*)'. In some cases, known as hypocoristic names, the name of the deity is dropped to make the name simpler and easier to use, for example: Nathan, Dan and Joseph. Moses is probably an Egyptian example in which the original Egyptian deity, Ra as in Ra-moses (child of Ra), or Thuth as in Thut-moses (child of Thut) has been dropped. Theophoric names were not common in ancient Roman society, but in ancient Greece some of the commonest Greek personal names are theophoric, like Apollonius, Dionysius, Demetrius, and compounds containing the element Dio- (Zeus), such as Diogenes (son of Zeus) and Diodorus (gift of Zeus).

Actually there is plenty of evidence that theophoric names do not always correspond to the religion of those who use them. Even in these cases the 'correctness of names' can be questioned. Biblical heroes, such as Samson, Esther and Mordecai, and all those named after them in later times, derive their names respectively from the Canaanite sun god, Shamash, and the Babylonian deities, Ishtar and Marduk. The evidence of early Christian names also confirms this. The Greek names Isidore (gift of Isis) and Heliodorus (gift of the sun-god) obviously had their origin in pre-Christian religions, but continued to be popular among Christians. Perhaps such names represent an attempt on behalf of new converts to find common ground between their new religion and the old. Christians continued to name their children Apollonius, Dionysius, Aphrodite, Hermes and the like for several centuries. In the same way the Christians of Carthage used popular Punic names such as Muttumbaal (gift of Baal) translated into Latin (Warmington 1964: 257). It took a long time for Christians to adopt biblical names, probably because of their Jewish associations, but also because of the widespread and deep-seated desire already mentioned to maintain continuity with their ancestors. It was not until the time of Constantine that names like John and Peter became popular in their Greek and Latin forms, as well as such names as Theodotus (given by God), Theodora (gift of God) and Donatus (given) which are Greek and Latin versions of Hebrew theophoric names. It is clear from all this that the relationship between the etymological meaning of a name and its application to a particular individual is far from straightforward. Other factors, such as family connections, religious affiliations and other types of association, often have a more significant role to play in naming customs than meaning.

We come now to belief in the power of names and naming. Biblical tradition regularly makes a connection between knowing somone's name and having power over that person. The first human being is instructed to assert his authority over all the beasts of the field and the birds of the air by giving them names (Gen. 2:19–20), and in fulfilment of the curse of Eve (3:16), over her too (3:20). This is parallel to the act of creation, described in the previous chapter, by which primeval chaos is brought under control by the divine creator's word or command (e.g. 'let there be light'), and the ordered elements of the cosmos are given names: day, night, sky, earth, sea. In the language of the Babylonian creation epic, *Enuma Elish*, which has much in common with the cosmological imagery of the Bible, naming actually takes precedence over any other word for creating, forming or controlling: 'When on high the heavens had not been named/Firm ground below had not been called by name…'. The story of Jacob's struggle all night with the angel illustrates the same connection between naming and controlling. Jacob innocently reveals his name to the angel, but when Jacob asks the angel what his name is the angel retains his psychological advantage over Jacob by refusing to tell him (Gen. 32:29).

In such a context, the revelation of the divine name to Moses in the burning bush story (Exod. 3) is all the more significant. The story tells how the Lord has 'come down' to rescue his suffering people in Egypt, and to appoint Moses as their leader. When Moses asks what his name is, the Lord replies: 'EHYEH ASHER EHYEH', which could be interpreted along the lines of the answer given by the angel at Jabbok: 'I am who I am', implying that he has no intention of telling Moses his name. The context, however, certainly suggests that this is a defining moment in the history of the saving actions of Yahweh, expressed in terms of the deity telling Moses what his name is, and thereby, so to speak, putting himself at his people's disposal in a new way. The full name 'EHYEH ASHER EHYEH' does not appear elsewhere in the Bible, although it is referred to in the rabbinic and mediaeval literature. A shortened form of it 'Ehyeh' occurs in verse 14 where Moses is instructed to tell his people that Ehyeh has sent him to them. But then in the next verse it is made clear that Ehyeh is intended to be an alternative form of the name Yahweh: 'God also said to Moses, "Tell the people of Israel that Yahweh...has sent me to you. This is my name for ever." ' As in some of the examples noted earlier, the author, without explicitly pointing it out, clearly wants us to associate the two names, Ehyeh and Yahweh. Not only does Yahweh reveal his name to Moses; he also gives him a clue as to what it means.

The name 'Ehyeh asher ehyeh' is thus usually understood to be a sentence in which Yahweh introduces himself 'I am the one who is' in such a way as to highlight the connection between his name Yahweh and the verb 'to be'. Ehyeh means 'I am' and Yahweh 'he is'. Both Ehyeh and Yahweh are considered here to be forms of the verb *hayah* in Hebrew, the meaning of which requires a comment. The nearest translation equivalent of *hayah* in English is the verb 'to be', but *hayah* regularly occurs in more dynamic, less abstract contexts: it is the verb used in such expressions as 'it came to pass' or 'happened' and 'the word of the Lord came to the prophet'. Its meaning in Hebrew here thus comes closer to 'I am the one who acts or intervenes' than 'I am the one who is'. It must also be pointed out that the Hebrew verb system makes less of a distinction between present and future than English grammar does and this gives Yahweh's name a forward-looking dimension, perhaps reflected in the words 'for ever' in verse 15: 'this is my name for ever: the one who acts – and will act'. There are other interpretations of Exodus 3:14. The first Greek translators, for example, found a more philosophical, monotheistic meaning in the words: 'I am the one who exists' (*eimi ho on*), that is, in opposition to all other deities whose existence is thus by implication denied, but this is less appropriate in the Exodus context where action is more important than abstract philosophy.

It is the power and function of the name that is our chief interest here, however, not its meaning. Jewish beliefs and practices concerning the personal name of their God provide us with an excellent example of a very widespread phenomenon. In the rabbinic literature, it is known as 'the Name' (*ha-shem*) or 'the Special Name' (*shem ha-meyuhad*) or 'the Four-letter (consonant) Name' (*shem ben-arba otiyyot*) (BT Qidd. 71a). The tetragrammaton, as it is known in English, from early times was surrounded by taboos. According to a second-century CE tradition, anyone who pronounces the Name will receive divine retribution after death in the same way as those who deny the resurrection of the dead or the divine origin of the Torah (MSanh. 10:1). Blasphemy is not as serious a crime as pronouncing the Name (MSanh. 7:5). There are even restrictions on angels' pronouncing the name (Sifre Deut. Ha'azinu 306, 132b; RA: 97). Scribes were advised to take special care when writing the tetragrammaton, and in some of the Dead Sea Scrolls a special archaic script different from the rest of the manuscript was used to write the sacred name. In some manuscripts of Aquila's Greek translation of the Bible, the tetragrammaton is written *Π Ι Π Ι* (*pipi*) which is a bizarre hybrid attempt to portray the Hebrew letters of the tetragrammaton in Greek capitals. It is not uncommon for modern writers to represent the name in English as YHWH, without the vowels, or, as in the RSV, by capitalizing the four letters of the substitute word LORD.

Only priests were permitted to pronounce the tetragrammaton. On Yom Kippur (the Day of Atonement) when the High Priest came out of the holy of holies and recited the ancient threefold blessing which begins 'The Lord bless you and keep you...' (Num. 6:24–6), he pronounced it, and all the people and priests in the temple court knelt down, bowed and prostrated themselves, saying 'Blessed is the name of the glory of the kingdom for ever and ever' (MYoma 6:2). There is an extended and even more graphic account of this most sacred moment in the apocryphal Book of Ecclesiasticus (50:1–21).

The tradition was originally probably no more than a mark of respect, just as first names are normally avoided by children addressing their parents, or courtiers addressing their monarch. Anthropologists cite societies in which it is simply unacceptable to address people by their given names. Special greeting names are sometimes used, or, more often, kinship terms. In Jewish religious tradition, the divine name was most commonly avoided by substituting Adonai 'the Lord' or simply 'the Name'. It is still the custom in both Jewish and Christian tradition, in most texts of the Bible for example, to avoid the name Yahweh or Jehovah. Some Christians treat the name Jesus with the same respect, substituting 'Our Lord' for his name, and bowing their heads when the name 'Jesus' is used, for example in the reading of scripture (Philipp. 2:10).

In early christological discourse the divinity of Jesus and his complex relationship with the God of scripture were implied by the use of terms for 'Lord'. Both Greek *kurios* and Latin *dominus* were used in this way. In Aramaic, too, the word *mar* 'Lord' acquired special religious overtones when applied to a deity and even on occasion to human persons. It is said, for example, that Rabbi Abba Hilkiah, grandson of the miracle-working Honi the Circle drawer, attracted the Aramaic title *mar* 'Lord' apparently because he too had supernatural powers (Vermes 1973: 118f.). In New Testament usage, Jesus is also addressed as 'Lord', partly no doubt, like Abba Hilkiah, in his capacity as miracle worker, and the significance of the Aramaic formula *maranatha* 'our Lord, come!', cited by Paul at the end of his first letter to the Corinthians (1 Cor. 16:22), has to be seen in this light. The name of Mary, the mother of Jesus, also acquired similar awesome religious overtones, and is also avoided by many Christians who refer to her instead as 'Our Lady'.

The use of sacred names for magical or thaumaturgical purposes is also well documented. There is an amusing reference in Apuleius' novel *The Golden Ass* (second century CE) to the belief that the invocation of the awful name of the Emperor could deliver a man from his miseries. Unfortunately, the ass could not enunciate the word Caesar correctly and had to remain in his misery (*Metamorphoses* 3.29). In a Jewish version of the apocryphal legend of the martyrdom of Isaiah, the prophet pronounced the tetragrammaton in a desperate attempt to escape from his persecutors (BT Yeb. 49b). According to another Jewish legend, Adam's first wife, Lilith, used the Name to escape from the garden of Eden where she felt threatened and repressed by Adam (Ginzberg 1975: 34–5). Moses killed the Egyptian by pronouncing the Name over him (Exod. R. 1:29). Despite the official prohibition on using the Name for magical purposes, which can be traced back to the Fourth Commandment (Exod. 20:7; Deut. 5:11), there is evidence that the Name was used in healing formulas. Rabbi Akiba (c.120 CE) condemns those who utter charms over a wound, in particular the formula 'I am YHWH, your healer' from Exodus 15:26. There are references in the Talmud to the use of the name Jesus in healing incantations (e.g. BT Ab. Zar. 27b). In the Gospels, Jesus himself is depicted as using the Hebrew term *Ephpheatha* 'be opened' when he healed a deaf person (Mark 7:34; Vermes 1973: 238).

Particular taboos surrounded the written form of the Name as we have seen, and its magical powers are frequently referred to in Jewish literature from ancient times. In Talmudic tradition, it was inscribed on a chain and a ring mentioned in the legend of Solomon and Asmodeus (BT Gitt. 68b). According to a later Midrash on Psalm 114:3 (Hebr. 114:2), the Red Sea fled because it saw the tetragrammaton engraved on Aaron's staff. Amulets are already referred to in the Hebrew Bible among the ornaments and jewellery both of Israelites (Isa. 3:18) and non-Israelites (Judges 8:26; Nah. 3:4). They are also regularly mentioned in passages where the protection or life-giving power of the Torah is compared to that of precious jewels (e.g. Prov. 1:9; 3:22; 6:21): her words can be 'life to those who find them and healing to all their flesh' (Prov. 4:22). By contrast, the dangerous powers of such things are said to have been the cause of the death of Jewish warriors in the Maccabean campaigns (2 Macc. 2:13).

There is much discussion of amulets (Hebrew *qemi'ot*) in the Talmud. Distinctions were drawn between amulets that had successfully cured someone or more than one person and those that had not, between those that had the name of God inscribed on them and those that did not, and between some amulet-makers and others. Tefillin and mezuzahs were considered legitimate amulets (e.g. Targum Song of Songs 8:6), while other amulets, such as those made from splinters from wooden idols and the use of them for magical purposes, were forbidden. Men, women, children and animals all wore amulets. Furniture could be protected by having the tetragrammaton inscribed on it. All manner of diseases could be cured by the use of amulets. There is an interesting Talmudic ruling concerning the preservation of amulets on the sabbath: 'even if they contain in their letters the name of God or passages from the Torah, they should not be saved from a fire: let them burn where they are' (BT Shab. 115b). This indicates that in the rabbis' estimation such things were entirely normal, but not precious enough to override the sabbath (*JE* 1: 546–50; Trachtenberg 1939: 132–52).

A very large proportion of amulets that have survived from the Talmudic period have the tetragrammaton written on them. The text of one cited in the Talmud is supposed to be a potent cure for rabies: *yah yah YHWH tzvao'ot* 'Yah Yah the LORD of hosts' (BT Yoma 84a). Others bear the name of the demon creature associated with a particular disease in the superstitious belief that wearing such an amulet would protect the wearer from that disease. Sometimes the letters of the name were written in intricate patterns: this is what the Talmudic reference to the tetragrammaton being contained 'within the letters' of an amulet inscription means. In an interesting glimpse into the world of ancient superstition, the Talmud records a method of combating *shabriri* 'blindness' by reciting the name of the disease repeatedly, omitting the first letter each time in the belief that the strength of the spirit would diminish until it lost its power over the victim (BT Pes. 12a; BT Ab. Zar. 12b). This form of incantation is better known in relation to the magical formula ABRACADABRA, first mentioned in a treatise by Serenus Sammonicus, a physician and prolific writer under the Antonines. Its origin is unknown: some suggest a connection with Hebrew *ha-berakha* 'blessing' and *dabar* 'word'. Written in the form of an inverted cone, it became one of the commonest amulet inscriptions in the Middle Ages (Trachtenberg 1939: 80–2). Another magical formula of unknown origin is *abraxas*, first mentioned by Irenaeus (*c.*130–202) as a name given by Gnostics to the highest being, and frequently occurring with other divine names, including the tetragrammaton, on amulets.

The much discussed ROTAS-SATOR square discovered at Pompeii in 1936 is another example.

S A T O R
A R E P O
T E N E T
O P E R A
R O T A S

This remarkable cryptogram incorporates the divine names PATERNOSTER 'Our Father' and 'A(lpha) and O(mega)' (cf. Rev. 21:6; cf. Isa. 41:4; 44:6), as well as containing a conspicuous cross formed by the word TENET. The twenty-five letters contain the eleven letters of Paternoster, each repeated twice except for the N at the centre, plus the letters 'A' and 'O' also repeated twice. The pattern of letters then makes up a five-word Latin sentence meaning something like 'The sower Arepo holds the wheels with care', but it is the twice-repeated religious message apparently hidden in the letters that really counts: 'Our Father (is) Alpha and Omega'. Composing word-squares of this kind seems to have been a favourite pastime at Pompeii as others have been found there, and the respected fifth-century CE Roman writer, Sidonius Apollinaris, mentions in passing that palindromes and such like provided endless amusement for the Roman landed gentry.

Despite the appropriateness of this for Christian use, and its subsequent appearance in a Christian context in Syria, Hungary, Italy, England and elsewhere, its origin is almost certainly pre-Christian. There is no evidence for a Christian presence at Pompeii and highly unlikely that even if there were Christians there at such an early date, they could by then have invented a cryptic rebus of this kind. Furthermore the cross was not adopted as a Christian symbol till the time of Constantine. There is a Mithraic explanation of the origin of the square, largely dependent on some ingenious gematria (Moeller 1973). The numerical value of the letters TENET (in Greek $T+H+N+H+T=666$) corresponds to that of the name Aurelion which means 'solar' (Rev. 13:18). The TENET cross in the cryptogram is then a symbol of the sun-god, and identical with the sign of the cross which was marked on the foreheads of Mithraic initiates.

The simplest and probably the most attractive solution is that it had a Jewish origin. There is good evidence that Jews had settled in Pompeii in considerable numbers before its destruction in 79 CE. There are other Jewish inscriptions in Latin, and their fondness for alphabetic acrostics, word-games and magical formulae, in Hebrew, Aramaic and Greek, has already been mentioned. The invocation 'Our Father' (Hebrew *abinu*) is of course Jewish as well as Christian, occurring already in the Hebrew Bible (Isa. 63:16; 64:8), and associated in the Talmud with two first-century CE rabbis, R. Eliezer and R. Akiba (Taan. 25b; cf. also Matt. 6:9). The Alpha-Omega (Hebrew *Aleph-Tau*) symbol is Jewish too (cf. Isa. 41:4; 44:6), and even the cross, represented by the archaic form of the letter Tau, or X, had magical significance in Jewish tradition as well (cf. Ezek. 9: 4–6) (Fishwick 1964: 46–50).

This brings us back to Jewish beliefs about the power of names, and, in particular, to the belief that even individual letters of the alphabet can have power as instruments of creation. The great first-century CE sage Rabban Yohanan ben Zakkai is the earliest of many authorities for the belief that God created the world with the letter He (Gen. R. 12:10; cf. MHag. 2:1 (77c); BTMen. 29b) (Sawyer 1993: 97). Scriptural authority for this belief is to be found in Genesis 2:4 where the consonants of the Hebrew word *behib-bar'am* 'in their being created (when they were created)' may be read as *be-He bera'am* 'with (the letter) He, he created them'. A century or so later, Rabbi Jonah, speaking in the name of Rabbi Levi, claimed that it was with the letter Beth that the world was created: 'as Beth is enclosed on all sides except one, so you are forbidden to investigate what is above, what is below, what was before, and what will happen after...'. We saw earlier how speculating about the creation and the secrets of the universe was severely restricted by the rabbis.

Later still in *Sepher Yetzirah* (the Book of Creation), there is a much more elaborate account of how God used all twenty-two letters of the Hebrew alphabet to create the world, arranging them in groups of three, seven and twelve corresponding to the three elements (wind, water, fire), the seven planets and the twelve signs of the zodiac. It is significant that both in Hebrew and Greek the word for 'letter' has a much wider range of meaning than in English. Hebrew *'ot* can also mean 'sign, miracle', and *stoicheion* in Greek is the regular philosophical term for the basic element of matter. Without entering into the question of the extent of Pythagorean influence on rabbinic cosmology, suffice it to say that in both traditions the alphabet had a role to play in expounding the integrating principle of the universe.

This brings us to the numerical values of the letters of the alphabet, and how they too are used in religious texts. From the Hellenistic period the letters of the Greek and Hebrew alphabets served as numerals as well as letters, the first nine functioning as single digits, the rest as tens and hundreds. The one-to-one relationship between letters and numerals thus made possible a peculiar type of exegesis in which the numerical value of words could be exploited, often for polemical purposes. It was known in the Talmud as gematria, a Greek loanword derived somehow from *geometria* 'geometry' or perhaps from *grammateia* 'learning' (cf. Sir. 44:4), and listed among the thirty-two principles of hermeneutics attributed to Rabbi Eliezer ben Jose the Galilean who lived in the second half of the second century CE. Thus, for example, the seven letters of *nrwn qsr* 'the emperor Nero', written in the Hebrew script, add up to 666 (50+200+6+50+100+60+200=666), the number of the beast in Revelation, and the three letters of *yeshu* 'Jesus' (10+300+6=316) come to the same total as *elohe nekhar* 'the alien god' in Deut. 31:16 (1+30+5+10+50+20+200=316). In the Sibylline Oracles, the names of emperors are often given as numbers, and there is an enigmatic riddle on the Name of God, still unsolved: 'I have nine letters, I have four syllables...the first three have two letters each, the last has the rest. Five are consonants. The entire number is $2 \times 8 + 300$, $3 \times 10 + 7$ (Sib. 1:141–5; *OTP* 1, 338).

The number of fishes hauled ashore by Simon Peter in the last of Jesus' resurrection appearances is given explicitly as 153 (John 21:11), and may be an early Christian example of gematria, although, if it was, its meaning has been lost. Another early Christian example appears in the Greek Epistle of Barnabas written towards the end of the first century CE: 'Learn therefore, children of love, that Abraham...looked forward to Jesus...for scripture says, "Abraham circumcised of his household 318 males..." ' (Gen. 14:14; cf. 17:27). Eighteen is IH, the first two letters of the name IHSOUS 'Jesus' (and also, incidentally, of the tetragrammaton), and 300 is Tau which stands for the cross (Barnabas 9:7–8). This gematria was then accepted and quoted with approval by Clement of Alexandria, Tertullian, Augustine and many others. Jewish interpreters noted instead that the number 318 is the equivalent of the name Eliezer $(1+30+10+70+7+200)$, the only one of Abraham's servants to be named (Gen. 15:2; BT Ned. 32a). We referred earlier to a possible example from Mithraism.

It has a particularly prominent role to play in the history of Jewish interpretation. There are many examples of gematria in the Talmud and Midrash. The numerical value of Satan (Hebrew *hasatan*) is 364 and this teaches us that Satan has dominion over Israel every day of the year, except the Day of Atonement (BT Yoma 20a). The somewhat unusual word *totza'ot* 'means of escape (when death threatens)' in Ps. 68:21 (English versions 20) is explained in the Talmud by gematria as a reference to the 903 causes of death (BT Ber. 8a). Another example from the Midrash highlights the dangers of drinking too much wine by noting the numerical equivalence (seventy) between *yayin* 'wine' $(10+10+50=70)$ and *sod* 'secret' $(60+6+4=70)$: 'When wine comes in, a secret goes out' (Numbers R. 10, 4:8). Gematria became a very much more widespread and influential method of Jewish interpretation in the mediaeval period and later, in particular in the mystical literature.

The same applies to other linguistic devices, first encountered in the biblical or rabbinic literature, but far more commonly used in mediaeval times. One of these, a bizarre type of code called *atbash*, in which the first letter of the Hebrew alphabet is substituted for the last ('a' for 't'), the second for the second last ('b' for 'sh'), etc., actually occurs in the Bible. In Jeremiah 25:26 the name *Babel*, Hebrew for 'Babylon', is written Sheshak where 'B', the second letter of the alphabet from the beginning, has become 'sh', the second from the end, and 'L', eleventh from the beginning, has become 'K', eleventh from the end. Another example appears in Jeremiah 51:1 where the Hebrew *leb-qamai* 'the heart of those who rise up against me' is an atbash for *kasdim* 'Chaldeans', another name for the Babylonians. It may be that originally this device was used to conceal subversive language from an oppressive regime for fear of reprisals. Certainly the two Jeremiah contexts are violent rhetorical attacks on hostile regimes with the king of Babylon in a very prominent position. Later uses of atbash, however, are more concerned with discovering hidden, mystical meanings and designed for fellow Jews, not outsiders.

Another method of extracting hidden meanings from the sacred text involves treating the letters of a word as an acronym. This method, known in the Talmud as *notarikon*, from Latin *notarius* 'stenographer', is also listed as one of the thirty-two Middot referred to earlier. A good example concerns the biblical explanation of Abraham's new name in which the six letters of the Hebrew phrase translated 'father of a multitude' (Gen. 17:5) are said to be the initials of the following impressive description of the first patriarch: 'father, young man, beloved, king, distinguished and faithful' (BT Shab. 105a). Another makes sense of the puzzling word *nimretzet* used to describe a curse in 1 Kings 2:8. By means of *notarikon*, it is understood to refer to five aspects of King David's sin: 'adulterer, Moabite, murderer, oppressor, abomination' (BT Shab. 105a). The list has marvellous relevance when one realizes it was addressed to David in an incident recalled by him on his death-bed.

9

STYLES AND STRATEGIES

In addition to using special languages and language varieties, a sacred text, like any other piece of literature, is normally written in a style considered appropriate for its purpose. In this chapter we shall consider some examples, mostly biblical, of how language and religion interact in this respect. Suspicion of honeyed words, clever arguments and verbal pyrotechnics is common. Cato the Censor (234–49 BCE) summed it up in a memorable dictum: *rem tene, verba sequentur* 'hold on to the content, and the words will follow' (*OCD*: 1314). In religious texts, concern for truth might take precedence over literary form. But skill in the subtle handling of language is praised in every culture whether in love poetry, story-telling, religious instruction or public speaking. In the language of Proverbs, 'A word fitly spoken is like apples of gold in a setting of silver' (25:11). Psalm 45, described in its title as a 'love song', begins with a claim by the author to have a tongue 'like the pen of a skilful scribe'. The Roman poet, Horace (65–8 BCE), rather more eloquently, singles out speech style, along with laughter, as one of his lover's particular attractions: *dulce loquentem Lalagen amabo, dulce ridentem* 'I love the sweetly talking, sweetly laughing Lalage' (Horace, *Odes* 1, 22:23). Proverbs has many references to the words of the wise and to the need to listen to them and imitate them: 'incline your ear and hear my words...for it will be pleasant if you keep them within you and if all of them are ready on your lips' (22:17–18; cf. 7:1).

A characteristic of the preaching of Jesus, Paul and others, much commented on in early Christian sources, was *parrhesia*, a term notoriously difficult to translate. In ancient Athens it referred to the democratic right of every free citizen to speak in public. In biblical and Jewish usage it came to be almost synonymous at times with general terms for 'freedom' (e.g. Lev. 26:13 LXX) and in particular with the confident style adopted by the first Christian preachers (Acts 4:13; 28:31). In some contexts, however, it must mean something like 'in plain language' as opposed to cryptic or allusive language (Mark 8:32; cf. 4:33; John 16:25) (Brown 1970: 734f.). Either way it provides an interesting example of how a variety of people from different backgrounds, either consciously or unconsciously, come to speak in a clearly identifiable style as a result of their being passionately committed to the same cause.

A frequent theme in the traditions about great prophets and orators of antiquity is their initial lack of skill with words and their need for treatment, divine or human, before their work could begin. There is a tradition, for example, that Moses had some kind of speech impediment when God's call first came to him. Exactly what is meant by the biblical phrase 'uncircumcised lips' (Exod. 6:12) is uncertain: 'ears' and 'hearts' are elsewhere described as 'uncircumcised' (e.g. Jer. 6:10; 9:25; Ezek. 44:7, 9), but the implication is that Moses did not believe he had the skill required by someone commissioned to speak in public. The call of Jeremiah gives us a more detailed example: initially he, too, claims to be unable to speak in public ('I am only a boy'), but in his own words, 'the Lord put out his hand and touched my lips, and said, "Now I have put my words in your mouth" ' (Jer. 1:6–9). Isaiah is another equally well-known and very similar example in which the prophet's lips are touched by a coal from the altar (Isa. 6). Later in the book, this type of divine intervention in relation to linguistic ability is described as being given *leshon limudim*, a much-discussed phrase probably meaning simply 'a skilled tongue' (50:4). No such supernatural assistance was available to Demosthenes, one of Greece's greatest orators (384–322 BCE), who is said to have had a stammer, and to have had to practise speaking on the sea-shore with pebbles in his mouth and the roar of the sea to contend with (cf. Cicero, *De Oratore* 1.61).

The power of language, to work both good and evil, not by magic as in the examples we were considering in a previous chapter, but by language skill, is also often referred to in the literature. It is a recurring theme in the Book of Proverbs and the Wisdom of Jesus ben Sira (Ecclesiasticus): 'death and life are in the power of the tongue, and those who love it will eat its fruit' (Prov. 18:21; cf. 10:20; 12:18–20; 15:4; Sir. 5:13; 28:17). The words for 'tongue', 'lips', 'mouth' and 'speaking' are among the most frequent in these texts. The same applies to the traditional teaching of ancient Egypt and Mesopotamia

(McKane 1970: 51–208). A particular feature of ancient Mesopotamian teaching on this topic was its elevation of silence to the status of a much-praised virtue (Whybray 1965: 59–61).

In Greek literary tradition, it was Theophrastus (*c.*372–286 BCE), a pupil of Aristotle, who first analysed rhetoric in terms of its effect on the audience: creating both pleasure (*hedone*) and shock (*ekplexis*) in one's audience was in his view an effective strategy for persuading them of the truth of what was being said. The little Book of Ecclesiastes, which brings the Hebrew Bible almost as close to the Hellenistic world as it gets, ends with a description of the sayings of the wise as 'goads' and 'nails firmly fixed' – striking images of effective persuasion and utter reliability probably drawn from contemporary rhetoric. The success of public speakers was often noted. Rabbi Meir (second century CE) was remembered as one who captivated his audiences with his learning, wit and originality. The tradition that there were no *darshanim* after the death of his gifted contemporary ben Zoma probably refers to his brilliance as a preacher as much as to technical exegetical skill (BT Sota 49a). Cicero reluctantly acknowledges Julius Caesar's gifts as a speaker (Cicero, *In Brutum*: 262), while he and Demosthenes were for their contemporaries and later writers, notably Quintilian, without equal.

The key to such success is to be found in the speaker's choice and handling of what linguists call register. A register is the variety of language proper to particular situations. People naturally switch from one register to another, from the language they use, for example, when addressing their children to the language they need for negotiations with colleagues in business or international politics. Children frequently speak in one register at school and another at home. In bilingual contexts, such registers are often in two different languages, a phenomenon known as 'diglossia' where children speak one language with their parents at home and another at school. Other registers, more deliberate or contrived, would include the deferential language used when addressing a superior. In a common biblical example of this, the first and second person pronouns are avoided – presumably as implying too intimate a relationship – and 'my lord', 'your servant', etc., are substituted throughout, for example: 'Speak, Lord, for thy servant is listening' (1 Sam. 3:10; cf. Gen. 44:7–9). Studies of the register used among friends in secular Greco-Roman societies reveal certain stylistic features found in Paul's Letters, especially his Letter to the Philippians (Mitchell 1997: 225–62), and tell us something of the writer's linguistic or literary strategy. Another recent study of the language of Paul's Letters has shown how the notion of mimesis (e.g. 1 Cor. 4:16; 11:1; 1 Thess. 1:6; 2:14) can function as a strategy of power (Castelli 1991).

Our first example of the deliberate use of particular styles in religious literature concerns the register of language addressed directly to a deity (Sawyer 1972: 18–27). In most cases, including biblical language, this is a register particularly easy to identify. Until comparatively recently, it was the custom throughout English-speaking Christendom to address God as 'thou' in such a way as to make a clear distinction between language addressed to God and language addressed to anyone else. Some English versions of the Bible like the *Revised Standard Version* (1952) actually made the same stylistic distinction between this register and the rest of the Bible, using 'thou-forms' consistently whenever language was addressed to God. Often it is clearly distinguished from what precedes it and what follows it by a conspicuous change of style from prose narrative to verse form, for example (1 Sam. 2:1f., Jon. 2:2f.). Sometimes it is introduced by indications that a special effort is being made by the speaker aware that he is in the presence of his God: 'he stood before the altar in the presence of all the assembly of Israel and spread forth his hands towards heaven and said...' (1 Kings 8:22).

A wide variety of styles is used in this register from querulous colloquialisms (Gen. 18:15; Exod. 4:13) to highly formalized hymns or prayers (e.g. 2 Sam. 22:2–51). The speaker may be anyone from the cultic leader of Israel (Exod. 32:11–14) to a servant girl (Gen. 16:13), from a lion (Isa. 21:8) to a crew of Phoenician sailors (Jon. 1:14), and the location anywhere from the Temple in Jerusalem (Ezra. 9:6–15; cf. 10:1) to the belly of a fish (Jon. 2:2). The language of Greek and Roman prayer can also range from formal utterances like that of the priest Chryses to Apollo in Homer's *Iliad* (1:37–9) to the briefest of cries like *Mars vigila!* 'Mars wake up!' (*OCD*: 1243). Unconventional and irreverent content dressed in formal style appears in Jeremiah's so-called 'Confessions': 'You have deceived me, O Lord' (Jer. 20:7; cf. Psalm 22:1).

Two biblical examples of prayer-style are particularly illuminating: those introduced by the verbs *hitpallel* 'to pray' (or the noun *tepillah*) and *qara* 'to call, invoke'. Prayers of the first type are normally quite long and elaborate, and characterized by a concentration of formulaic expressions, confessions of sin, declarations of faith, intercessions, etc. Most are poetic compositions similar to the Psalms (1 Sam. 2; Jon. 2; Hab. 3) or prose prayers written in the very distinctive Deuteronomic style to be discussed later (2 Sam. 7; 1 Kings 8; 2 Kings 19; Jer. 32; Dan. 9; Ezra 9; Neh. 9). With very few exceptions prayers of this type are spoken by kings, prophets or other leaders of Israel, and contextualized at cultic locations. Prayers introduced by *qara*, on the other hand, are short, unconnected with any cultic location or official, and normally begin with the name of the deity addressed. While the first, described as formal prayer (*tepillah*), introduces into the narrative many of the traditional trappings of the liturgy, however inappropriate to the context, the second can hardly be called prayer in the liturgical sense at all, but is instead more of a call for help, invoking the name of the deity. It is perhaps significant that the second, less formal style of addressing God is nonetheless given the special status of having its own aetiology: 'at that time [that is, after the Cain and Abel story] people began to call (*qara*) on the name of the Lord' (Gen. 4:26). Both styles, although totally different, are clearly considered appropriate and effective strategies for communicating with the deity.

Our second example concerns the style of Leviticus and raises questions about the nature and purpose of this part of the Pentateuch (Sawyer 1997). Style can be described at the level of grammar and syntax, as well as vocabulary, and with the advent of the computer it is much easier to investigate minute grammatical data than it used to be (Andersen and Forbes 1992). Of course statistical data can be misleading, especially in the case of a text like the Hebrew Bible in which complex, arbitrary and frequently unknown factors have operated, from the speaker's and author's original choices in ancient Israel to the fixing of the canon and all manner of scribal activity right down to the mediaeval period. In most respects – frequency of verbs, nouns, the definite article, passive forms, pronouns, prepositions, numerals – Leviticus is normal in comparison with the rest of biblical Hebrew. But there is one remarkable feature of the language of Leviticus which stands out and seems to be significant. It is the extreme infrequency of imperatives: thirty-five per thousand words compared with three or four times that number in the rest of the books of the Bible. Imperatives are ten times more frequent in the Psalms for example. When we remember that a large proportion of the imperatives that do occur in Leviticus are those addressed by God to Moses (e.g. 'speak to the people…'; 'take Aaron and his sons…'), then the lack of direct commands addressed to the people is very remarkable indeed and requires some explanation.

The book is described at the end as a collection of 'commandments which the Lord gave to Moses for the people of Israel on Mount Sinai' (27:34), and there are throughout the book a good many other similar descriptions (14:1; 16:29; 18:4). But the language in which God addresses the people through his prophetic spokesman seems to be almost devoid of the normal direct means of phrasing obligations. The author seems instead to want us to imagine a society or a state in which certain procedures will be carefully carried out. Sanctions are there, including the death penalty. But the emphasis is on how things will be rather than on obligations. Direct commands in chapters 18 and 19 seem to be exceptions rather than the norm. At the end of chapter 26, the sanctions are mitigated, as they are at the end of Deuteronomy: the unique and memorable 'yet in spite of everything' (26:44) makes this clear. One of the problems with the niceties of Hebrew style is that they are impossible to translate: should it be 'he shall bring...' or 'he will bring...' or 'let him bring...' (Lev.4:4)? The word *torah* is another problem for translators, not unrelated to the present discussion: should it be 'this is the law of the leper...' (AV) or 'this shall be the ritual for the leprous person' (NRSV) or 'this is (Moses') teaching about people suffering from leprosy' (Lev. 14:2)? Is Leviticus a lawbook as is usually thought, or, remembering the tradition that Moses is first and foremost a prophet, could it be seen rather as a vision of a future age? (cf. Douglas 1999).

Let us move on to the Book of Deuteronomy, which is an excellent example of the matching of style to function. Deuteronomic style is relatively easy to define and can be recognized both in the Book of Deuteronomy itself and in other books, including Samuel, Kings and Jeremiah (Driver 1913: 98–103). It is characterized by a set of striking phrases and images such as 'the iron furnace of affliction' and 'with a strong hand and an outstretched arm'. But the author's skill is evident also in his use of other literary techniques (Polzin 1980). By setting the scene of the last book of the Torah in the hills overlooking the promised land, he is able to relate the situation of his readers directly to that of Moses' followers. For both, the challenges and opportunities of life as the people of God are still in the future; both are equipped with a constitution and a hope. The geographical setting is stressed at the beginning and the end of the book, but there are constant references to it elsewhere as well (3:27; 4:44–9; 9:1; 11:31; 29:1; 31:1–8;

32:48–52). This effect is further enhanced by the repetition of words and phrases like 'today', 'all of you here, alive, today' and many others which address the readers and listeners directly in the second person.

The personal appeal is also strengthened by the consistent choice of the terms 'my God' and 'our God' (which in Hebrew are single words) in preference to 'the Lord' or 'the God of Israel', etc. The use of the covenant metaphor is also extensive and distinctive in Deuteronomy, and may be a brilliant literary invention by the author, designed to highlight the special relationship between God and his people Israel. Many have argued that this thoroughly biblical image is more ancient than Deuteronomy, but it does not appear as prominently in the utterances attributed to the eighth-century prophets as one might have expected, and no other work makes so much use of the image as Deuteronomy. However, the passionate emphasis on a personal relationship between the people and their deity actually goes beyond the strict demands of the legal metaphor of a covenant relationship (30:6), and is further expressed in repeated references to the uniqueness of God (e.g. 4:35, 39; 6:4; 32:39), and the parent–child analogy (1:31; 8:5; 32:18).

It is in this context that we must look at another and much-discussed stylistic peculiarity of Deuteronomy, namely the frequent vacillation between singular and plural forms of the second person. The words of Moses are addressed, sometimes in the same verse, to both a single individual and to a plural group. Scholars have resorted to source criticism to explain this: one source was addressed to an individual, others to a group, and then combined into a single text preserving the differences despite obvious inconsistency. So conspicuous is this feature of Deuteronomic style, however, preserved in ancient Greek and Latin translations, though undetectable in most English versions, that it can hardly be explained as due to clumsy editing or scribal error. More likely this is a deliberate stylistic device, like the repetition of 'today', 'all of you' and the other features mentioned earlier, designed to ensure that everyone feels personally addressed both as an individual and as a couple or a family or a community. The same change of person occurs in Exodus 22:21–3 and other ancient Near Eastern literature (Weinfeld, 1992:173–4).

In this connection we may consider briefly an important stylistic feature of one of the best-known religious texts, the Ten Commandments. One version of it appears in Exodus 20:2–17, but in this context we are concerned exclusively with the one that appears in Deuteronomy 5:6–21. Unlike much of the rest of the book, where, as we have seen, the author vacillates between singulars and plurals, the Ten Commandments are phrased exclusively in the singular, represented in the *King James' Authorized Version* by the familiar forms beginning 'thou shalt not...'. The effect of this is to heighten the sense of awe surrounding these ten obligations by presenting them as addressed directly by the deity to the individual. From the first words ('I am the Lord your God who brought you up from the land of Egypt...') to the last, each individual hears the words as though no-one else is involved: they are exclusive, direct and personal in a way that other commandments and instructions are not. What is the effect of this stylistic feature on the universal application of the Decalogue? In the first place, second person masculine singular forms are sometimes used, though not very often, in biblical Hebrew, as in English, for impersonal constructions (e.g. Gen. 13:10; Prov. 19:25; 30:28; Isa. 7:25. Gesenius–Kautzsch para.144h). The nearest English equivalent would then be 'one must not kill...one must not commit adultery...', and what has just been said about the 'exclusive, direct and personal' nature of the Ten Commandments would not necessarily follow. Second, the context makes it clear that some of the Ten Commandments at any rate are addressed only to city dwellers (5:14), property-owners (5:14) and adult males (5:21). It is therefore possible that, in some contexts, only these groups were intended, and the relevance of these and other biblical texts to peasants, the poor and to women in general would be less obvious. This brings us to the question of gender-specific language and its role in religious language.

Priests, religious leaders and writers, the rabbis, the church fathers, the Magi, etc., are exclusively male. The same applies to the *Quindecimviri* in charge of managing the Sibylline Oracles in ancient Rome, books purporting to have been written by women prophets, and the 'exegetes' attached to the oracles at Delphi and elsewhere who interpreted the cryptic sayings uttered by the woman prophet at the centre of the institution. Modern interest in the roles of Miriam (6:4), Deborah (Judg. 4–5), Hannah (1 Sam. 2), Judith, Mary, Beruriah and other women in political leadership, worship, scholarship and elsewhere according to ancient biblical and rabbinic legend is hardly reflected in Jewish or Christian tradition. The same applies to the ample evidence from Paul's Letters (e.g. Rom. 16), ancient Jewish inscriptions and alternative forms of Christianity like Montanism, for women leaders in the early church and ancient Judaism.

The language and imagery of the texts we have been considering is predominantly patriarchal. It is only in the last decades of the twentieth century that this has been seriously observed and analysed. A striking example of male intervention in the handing down of biblical tradition appears in the story of Deborah, who is said to have ruled Israel in precisely the same manner as Gideon, Jephthah, Samson and the other legendary judges. At the beginning of the story, she is described as 'a woman prophet' and an *eshet lappidot* 'a woman of fire (lit. flames)' (Judg. 4:4), in other words, a strong, independent woman in her own right, just like the character depicted in the rest of the narrative. Later tradition, however, in order to fit her into its own patriarchal categories, interpreted *lappidot* as the name of a man so that a husband is invented for Deborah. She is no longer an independent woman: she is 'the wife of Lappidoth', totally unknown elsewhere but rather disingenuously identified by the rabbis with Barak (v. 6). Similar readings of the biblical stories of Eve, Sarah, Miriam, Ruth, Naomi, Hannah, Judith, Mary and other women come to the same conclusion: convincing alternative interpretations more sympathetic to the women's role in the narrative are possible, but have had little or no effect on Jewish and Christian tradition till now.

The power of language to control and abuse has now been the subject of much writing, often from the point of view of the victims down the centuries: women, Jews, blacks, gays and lesbians. A recent study of *Excitable Speech* analyses 'linguistic vulnerability', 'sovereign performatives', 'implicit censorship' and other aspects of this crucial question with fresh brilliance (Butler 1997). Nowhere has the power of language to dominate and control been more effective down the centuries than in the male hierarchies in control of most of the world's religions. A conspicuous example of this in some of the sacred languages we have been discussing is the frequent abuse of women and their bodies in biblical literature (Bal 1989; Exum 1993). Phyllis Trible's classic *Texts of Terror* challenges the reader to think seriously about what is going on in four biblical stories of rejection, rape and murder. What is being done to the women in these stories, and what does that tell us about the concerns and attitudes of the authors of such stories and their pious interpreters down the ages? Other recent writers have examined the effect on readers and interpreters of the constant and often pornographic use of women as literary images, such as prostitutes to symbolize Israel's lust for paganism (Hosea) or pathetic victims of male violence to symbolize the defeat and destruction of a city (Isa. 47; Rev. 18) (Sherwood 1996; Camp and Fontaine 1993).

There are a few exceptions like the touching story of the 'daughter of Zion' in Isaiah 40–66 (Sawyer 1989). But in general female images mirror male prejudice fairly closely. This aspect of the language of scripture, together with texts blaming women for the existence of sin and evil in the world (Sir. 25:24), and marginalizing or silencing them (1 Tim. 2:8–15) cannot easily be explained away or reinterpreted. Furthermore, because the Church is still to a large extent bound by decisions taken in the first Christian centuries by a predominantly male hierarchy, they cannot be removed from the canon, as perhaps they would have been if the Montanists or some other variety of Christianity with a less negative attitude towards women had had a part to play alongside Tertullian and Augustine in the decision-making process (Trevett 1996).

Images of God in Jewish and Christian tradition are also almost entirely male. The few exceptions do not amount to very much, but have been the subject of recent interest both among literary scholars and among Jewish and Christian women seeking scriptural authority for a less patriarchal God. The reference in Genesis to the belief that both men and women are created 'in the image of God', for example, has been used to authorize a more transcendent concept of the biblical god as one who is beyond all human comparison (cf. Exod. 20:4; Isa. 40:18; 44:7), and therefore as one of whom no image, not even that of father or king or lord, can claim to be exclusively valid or appropriate. Those rare passages in which the deity is compared to a mother comforting her children (Isa. 66:13; Ps. 131:2; cf. Luke 13:34) or suffering the pains of childbirth (Isa. 42:14; Deut. 32:18) then assume greater signifi-cance in contemporary contexts as scriptural authority for rewording or revising the language of prayer. The following prayer derives almost all of its imagery from Isaiah: 'God our mother,/you hold our life within you,/nourish us at your breast,/and teach us to walk alone' (cf. Isa. 46:3–4; 49:14–16; 66:7–13) (Morley 1988: 25). An example from Reform Judaism is the liturgical use of the feminine term *shekinah* 'presence', an ancient synonym for God: 'Blessed are you (feminine), O Shekinah, who made me a woman'.

The last style to be discussed here is the polemical style used in denunciations. It is a style frequently adopted by religious writers passionately committed to their own tradition or point of view, but it has a long history in secular literature as well. *Vituperatio* 'denunciation' (Greek *loidoria*, *psogos*, *kakegoria*) was a recognized element in a public orator's training. Quintilian, in his hugely influential treatise on rhetoric entitled *Institutio Oratoria* (*c*.95 CE), discusses praise and blame (*vituperatio*) at some length, rejecting the view of Aristotle and others that such speeches never had a practical function other than to delight and entertain their audiences. He acknowledges the fact that some speeches, such as eulogies in praise of the gods, were primarily for entertainment, but he also cites the examples of funeral orations which clearly have a social or political function, and the speeches made by witnesses in law courts, praising or denouncing the character of the accused to prove that such techniques are by no means employed only to entertain (Quintilian, *Inst.* 8.6.45).

Abusive compositions written primarily for entertainment did exist in ancient Rome. The function of iambic verse was originally abusive: Horace understands iambi as *criminosi* (*Odes* 1:16.2) and the product of rage (*Ars Poetica* 79), while other Roman writers explain them as pugnacious (Ovid, *Ars Amatoria* 521) and vengeful (Statius, *Silv.* 2.2.115). The *fescennini*, ribald songs of Etruscan origin traditionally sung at weddings, may at one time have been recited to ward off evil spirits, but came to be pure entertainment (e.g. Catullus 61:119–80) (*OCD*: 593). There was legislation against defamation of character and slander in both Greece and Rome, but it did not prevent prominent orators, like Demosthenes and Cicero, from using *vituperatio* in language at times extremely tasteless to our modern ears to achieve their ends in court or senate.

Quintilian recommends attacking a man's origins and parentage, just as in a funeral oration one might begin by tracing the noble ancestry of the deceased. There are biblical examples of this: 'your father was an Amorite, your mother a Hittite' (Ezek.16:3; cf. 23). The Galilean origins of Jesus and some of his followers were ridiculed as we saw (p. 84). Children are blamed for the crimes of their parents: the words 'his blood be upon us and on our children' put into the mouths of Jews present at the trial of Jesus (Matt. 27:25) is a terrible example of this. Conversely, founders are blamed for the crimes of their descendants: one might argue, for example, says Quintilian in an unexpected aside, that Moses is hated because the people who profess the religion he founded, the *superstitio Judaica*, are so unpopular (*Inst.* 3.7.21). Demosthenes' speech against the man who challenged his claim to the gold crown (awarded for an outstanding contribution to the state) is a case in point. As well as heaping abuse on his adversary's moral failings and professional

incompetence – 'evil monster... sycophant...ape...honey orator...'
– he refers to his humble origins in such epithets as 'country
bumpkin' (Demosthenes, *De Corona*).

Cicero provides an even more explicit example in his speech,
delivered to the Roman senate in 55 BCE against Lucius Calpurnius
Piso, father of Julius Caesar's wife Calpurnia. He begins with
references to his mother and his native town. He goes on to list his
crimes and failings, addressing him as monster: 'at first we knew
nothing of your filthy vices, the crassness of your intelligence and
the sluggish impotence of your tongue'. In the peroration he
envisages what will happen to the accused when he is found guilty.
He does not want the death penalty: death would be too good for
him.

> But to see you abject, despised, scorned by your fellows, a
> thing that despairs of itself and lives abandoned by itself,
> that peers into every corner and quakes at every whisper...a
> shivering, trembling, fawning wretch – this I have desired
> to see.
>
> (Cicero, *In Pisonem*: 99)

A biblical example which is interesting not only as an insight
into internal politics in ancient Judah, but also in the way it has
been used by Christian writers and preachers, is to be found in the
Book of Isaiah. In Isaiah, as in the other prophets, there is plenty of
vituperatio directed at foreign nations, Babylon (13–14), Moab
(15–16), Syria (17), Ethiopia (18), Egypt (19) (cf. Jer. 46–51;
Ezek. 25–32; Amos 1–2). Some of the invective directed at Zion's
enemies in Isaiah is exceptionally ferocious: 'With their faces to the
ground they shall bow down to you and lick the dust of your feet...
I will make your oppressors eat their own flesh and they shall be
drunk with their own blood like wine' (Isa. 49:23, 26; cf. 47). This
is a style with an ancient pedigree going back to the so-called
'Execration Texts' of ancient Egypt and elsewhere. But much more
significant are the ferocious insults and abuse directed at Judah,
both by the eighth-century prophet in chapter 1 ('sinful nation...rulers of Sodom...people of Gomorrah...') and, more subtly,
in chapters 56–66 where internal disputes in Judah seem to have
given rise to unusually bitter feelings (65:13–15; 66:1–5). There is
a rabbinic tradition that Isaiah, though much loved as the 'prophet
of the consolation', went too far in criticizing and maligning his
own people. What really happened in the Temple, according to a

well-known Midrash, was that Isaiah had his lips burnt as a punishment for presuming to call his people 'a people of unclean lips' (6:5) (Ginzberg 1954, 4:263).

Isaiah thus gave the Church scriptural authority to direct all manner of abusive language at the Jews. If their own prophet criticized them for their blindness (Isa. 6:9–10), their disbelief (65:2) and even the crime of deicide ('your hands are full of blood' 1:15; cf. Matt. 27:25), how much more is the Church justified? When Justin Martyr (c.100–65 CE), John Chrysostom (c.347–407), Augustine (354–430) and many others called the Jews 'rulers of Sodom' (1:9), 'dogs' (56:10) and 'drunkards' (29:9), accusing them of stubbornness (65:2) and treachery (3:9–11), they cite Isaiah. When they want to tell the Jews it is their own fault that they were rejected (29:13–4), their city destroyed (3:1) and their lives ruined (57:1–4) they can cite Isaiah as scriptural authority. When they want to warn the Jews of the terrible fate that awaits them if they persist in their foolish and stubborn ways, they quote some of the appallingly bitter invective with which the Book of Isaiah, like Cicero's speech against Lucius Calpurnius Piso, concludes:

> Thus says the Lord God, 'My servants shall eat, but you shall be hungry, my servants shall drink but you shall be thirsty…my servants shall sing for joy but you shall cry out in pain… (65:13–14)…and they shall go out and look at the corpses of the people who have rebelled against me; for their worm shall not die, their fire shall not be extinguished and they shall be an abhorrence to the whole human race' (66:24).
>
> (Sawyer 1996: 108–13)

The Book of Isaiah as a sacred text has played an enormously influential role in the history of both Judaism and Christianity from the earliest times. It is known to Christians since Jerome as more evangelist than prophet because 'he describes all the mysteries of Christ and the Church so clearly that you would think he is composing a history of what has already happened rather than prophesying about what is to come' (Sawyer 1996: 1); and to Jews as the prophet of consolation, author of the beautiful readings (taken from chapters 40–61) prescribed to be read in the synagogue on the seven sabbaths following the fast on the ninth of Ab; and the three sentences used to conclude the prayers said in the house of the bereaved (66:13; 60:19; 25:8). Its use in the polemical context we have been considering illustrates how such a sacred text can also be used mercilessly to hurt and repress a vulnerable minority.

10

INTERPRETATION

Our final topic concerns the history of how the sacred languages and sacred texts we have been considering were received, interpreted and transmitted. The process of interpreting and explaining the meaning of a text begins as soon as it exists. Indeed, in the case of an oral utterance by a prophet or a teacher, the process begins even before then when it is first heard and remembered, and only later, sometimes, as in the case of the words of Zoroaster, many centuries later, written down. Very little is known of those early preliterary stages in the process, mainly because we are almost entirely dependent on written records, mostly of uncertain date. The scientific quest for the original words of Jesus or Isaiah or Zoroaster has given way in recent years to a renewed critical study of the texts as we have them, and as they have been used and interpreted by the communities who believe them to be sacred. The reception, interpretation and transmission of written texts in their final sacred or canonical form will be the main subject of this chapter, but first we shall look at some preliterary stages in the process.

The writing down of the oral Torah, that is, the sayings and discussions of the rabbis, began in the second century CE, probably partly as a response to the destruction of Jerusalem in 70, and partly under the influence of literary developments elsewhere in the Roman Empire. Two factors helped to ensure that 'what they had actually said' was recorded as accurately as possible. In the first place, the attribution of a saying to a particular person, who says he heard it from another person or who claims to be speaking in the name of someone else, has the effect of constructing a chain of tradition back in history to a point progressively nearer to what actually happened. Furthermore, many of the characters mentioned by name in the Talmudic literature have personal traits and attributes which can give the sayings attributed to them an added degree of authenticity. Of course there is no way of proving beyond doubt that any of them actually said what the Talmud attributes to them. But the constant emphasis on this aspect of the oral tradition is proof, if proof is needed, that one of the concerns of the author was to record what was actually said and by whom. How successful he was, we will never know. We do know that he had other concerns as well in his selection and editing of material, which would often conflict with concern for historical accuracy.

The second factor in this process of oral transmission is the evolution of a variety of conventional literary forms and devices, which facilitate accurate memorizing. Without going into great detail here, this has always been an essential aspect of the transmission process, both in its oral and its written stages. Prophets, poets, preachers, teachers and others chose to speak or write in an appropriate conventional literary form (*Gattung*) with the idea that this makes it easier for the audience to relate to and remember. Thus, for example, a teacher of ethical wisdom, like the legendary Aesop, might choose the literary type known as the fable to communicate his teachings, while others like Jesus preferred the parable, a short story designed to illustrate some ethical or theological truth, and others like Solomon used the royal instruction fiction in which an old king passes on the fruits of his experience to his son. Prophets, poets and psalmists had many poetical forms available from short laments and dynastic oracles to elaborate hymns and love poems. Conventional forms could be used with heavy irony as in Isaiah's famous lament for the king of Babylon (14). Alphabetical acrostics were also used like the poem 'In praise of the virtuous woman' at the end of Proverbs, in which the twenty-two verses begin with the twenty-two letters of the Hebrew alphabet (Prov. 31:10–31), or Psalm 119 in which the twenty-two stanzas each contain eight verses all beginning with the same letter: Aleph, Beth, Gimel, etc., through the alphabet. These and other conventions, which greatly facilitate memorizing on the part of the hearers, may have played an important role in ensuring that some of the *ipsissima verba* of the original speaker survived, despite later ill-informed or tendentious editing.

The third question concerns the role of disciples or scribes in the process of remembering and recording spoken utterances. Ancient Greece was predominantly an oral society until the fifth century BCE. The evidence for popular literacy before then, in the form of graffiti for example, is very scanty. Even such things as legal contracts were dependent on the oral testimony of witnesses, while the Homeric epics and the lyric poetry of Sappho and her contemporaries were handed down orally for centuries. One of the earliest references to a book appears in the tradition that *c.*500 BCE the philosopher Heraclitus placed a book he had written in the Temple of Artemis at Ephesus. Thereafter, the works of Herodotus, Aeschylus, Sophocles, Aristophanes, Thucydides, Plato, Aristotle and all the classical writers were in written form from the beginning and the issue of who recorded it does not arise.

As we saw in a previous chapter, writing was widespread throughout the ancient Near East much earlier, and there is good evidence of writing in ancient Israel from the eighth century BCE at the latest. There is no reason, for example, to question the passing references in the Book of Proverbs to the writing of 'thirty sayings of admonition and knowledge' (22:20) and the copying of the proverbs of Solomon by 'the men of Hezekiah' (25:1). The important conclusion to draw from this reference to the transmission of a text concerns the locus of the process: the writings of King Solomon were preserved for 200 years in the palace at Jerusalem, presumably in some kind of royal library under the supervision of trained scribes or copyists. It is probable that ancient liturgical compositions, like some of the Psalms, were similarly transmitted from generation to generation in the Temple, in written or oral form, under the supervision of the priestly hierarchy, and the same may have been true of parts of the 'Five Books of Moses'.

The process whereby the spoken words of the prophets were collected and recorded is much more difficult to reconstruct. There are very few explicit references to disciples or scribes in relation to the prophets. The Hebrew of Isaiah 8:16 is problematical, and the divine imperatives addressed to Habakkuk ('write the vision...' 2:2), Jeremiah ('take a scroll and write on it...' 36:2) and Ezekiel ('eat this scroll...' 3:1) do not prove that these three prophets wrote down their own prophecies. The reference to Baruch, Jeremiah's amanuensis (36:4), is also exceptional. The most these few references to writing in the Prophets can do is to confirm what we already know: that from the time of Habakkuk, that is, the end of the seventh century, writing became more widespread, and that by the end of the sixth century or the beginning of the fifth, roughly contemporary with a parallel situation in ancient Greece, a predominantly oral society was becoming predominantly literate. They tell us nothing about the situation in the eighth century BCE, the golden age of biblical prophecy, and who it was that remembered and recorded the words of Hosea, Amos, Micah and Isaiah.

It is likely that one important factor in the situation was the detailed and devastating way in which much of what they had foretold actually came true. In the year *c.*740 BCE Amos said, 'As a shepherd rescues from the mouth of the lion two legs or a piece of an ear, so shall the people of Israel who dwell in Samaria be rescued' (Amos 3:12). In the year 722 that was exactly what happened as a result of large-scale Assyrian military campaigns in the region. This must have heightened the awe with which people regarded the prophets, and increased the credibility of the rest of their words. It was no doubt in Jerusalem and Judah that the prophets' attacks on their Samaritan neighbours to the north were most appreciated, and gloating over the fall of Samaria was most exuberant. At least three of the four eighth-century prophets, Amos, Micah and Isaiah, are said to have been Judaeans. But we know nothing at all about exactly who recorded their words, how and where.

All the books attributed to them are clearly literary compositions from a later age. They are the result of a cumulative process involving adding material which reflects, for example, the nationalism of Josiah's reign (Clements 1980), the destruction of the Temple in 586 and the period of rebuilding and restoration after the fall of Babylon in 538 (Ackroyd 1968). Common themes run through each book suggesting that those responsible for this long and often complex editorial process claimed some kind of special relationship with the original prophet, but to what extent we can speak of a 'Hosea tradition' or an 'Amos legacy' or an 'Isaiah school' in a concrete sense implying some kind of dedicated society or association within the general context of Judaean literary tradition, it is impossible to say. All we can say with reasonable confidence is that most of the books which make up the Hebrew Bible were in existence in more or less their final form by the end of the third century BCE.

The case of the 'original words of Jesus' has been partly discussed already (see pp. 83–5). In the present context it will suffice to make one observation. In contrast to the situation of the Hebrew prophets, there is constant reference throughout all our earliest sources to the existence of disciples. Like the schools or groups of disciples surrounding the great rabbis, these were men close enough to Jesus to be familiar with what he said and what he meant, and were explicitly commissioned to communicate it orally to others. The obvious danger that the disciples might forget exactly what he had said or get it wrong was solved, not by encouraging anyone to keep a written record, but by reference to divine intervention: 'do not be anxious how you are to speak or what you are to say: for what you are to say will be given to you at that time; for it is not you who speak but the Spirit of your Father speaking through you' (Matt. 10:19–20).

On a more practical level, the oral memorizing of what Jesus actually said was no doubt assisted, as it was in the case of the prophets of ancient Israel and the rabbis in his own day, by his use of conventional literary forms like parables, woe sayings and the like. There is evidence that it was also actively encouraged by the first leaders of the Church, including Peter (Acts 11:16), Paul (Acts 20:35) and Clement, Bishop of Rome: 'Most of all remember the words of the Lord Jesus...that we may walk in obedience to his sacred words (*hagia logia*)' (1 Clem. 13:3). None of the words attributed to Jesus in these passages from Acts and 1 Clement appear verbatim in any of the extant gospels, and the words of Jesus may well have been transmitted orally in Rome and elsewhere till the end of the first century or later (Kelber 1997). Written records of the life and teachings of Jesus, attributed pseudonymously to the original disciples Matthew, John, Peter and Thomas, or their contemporaries Nicodemus, Mark, James and Mary, probably did not replace oral tradition till well into the second century CE. Decisions on which of these texts were to be treated as authoritative or canonical, and also, to return to the subject of this chapter, on how they were to be interpreted, were not taken until still later.

We can distinguish two clear factors in the origins and early background of what was to become so crucial an issue in both Judaism and Christianity, the interpretation of scripture: one broadly secular, the other religious. First, there was the enormous influence of Hellenistic literary and linguistic scholarship. The presence in Alexandria during the third century BCE, as well as Pergamum in Asia Minor, and later in Athens, Caesarea, Rome and elsewhere, of huge libraries, some of which were under the enthusiastic tutelage of the Ptolemies, containing virtually every book written in Greek, gave new impetus to the study of ancient literature. One of the chief interests of the Alexandrian scholars was to establish what the original text was, and it was they who first compared all the available manuscripts of a work and devised a system of notation for marking scribal errors, from which Origen derived the system he uses in his *Hexapla*. They also introduced the *apparatus criticus*, that is, marginal notes written around or below the main text indicating variant readings, scribal errors or the like. The system was adopted in many of the surviving Greek, Hebrew and Syriac manuscripts of the Bible.

But their scholarship went beyond textual criticism. The almost legendary Aristarchus of Samothrace (*c.*216–144 BCE), known as *ho grammatikotatos* 'the most scholarly scholar' and even *ho mantis* 'the prophet' on account of the special skills and judgement he displayed in his writings, was tutor to one of the Ptolemies and head of the library at Alexandria, as well as prolific writer, and his influence on subsequent developments at Alexandria was very great. He is said to have been the first to write 'Commentaries' (*hupomnemata*) on Homer, Hesiod, Aeschylus, Euripides and many other classical texts. In these he discussed, among other things, the meaning of rare words, literary comparisons, and matters of style, form and metre. He is also traditionally credited with inventing one of the main principles of exegesis adopted by the rabbis and others a few centuries later: *Homeron ex Homerou saphenizein* 'explain Homer from Homer', that is, use one passage from the same author to clarify another. The rabbinic equivalent, included among seven hermeneutical rules attributed to Hillel, is *ke-yotze bo be-maqom aher* 'like something similar in another passage'.

Another strand within Hellenistic approaches to the study of ancient texts, which was to be equally influential later, was allegorical interpretation – the search for a meaning different from the obvious or literal meaning of a text. Allegory as a literary device is common enough in the ancient literature: there are examples in Homer and Plato, as well as in the Hebrew Bible. Such hidden or underlying meanings were referred to as *ainigmata* 'riddles' by the Greek and Latin literary critics. The Hebrew equivalent is *mashal* 'proverb, parable', sometimes in conjunction with *hidah* 'riddle' (Ezek. 17:2; Prov. 1:6). The Greek terms *allegoria* and *allegoreo* (Latin *allegorizo*) are not attested much before Philo, Josephus and Paul (Gal. 4:24).

The allegorical interpretation of texts which were not originally intended as allegories, however, is something different. Two distinct factors seem to have operated in this development, both due to the very high regard in which an author was held. Homer, for example, could be described as 'the divine Homer' and Moses as 'in all respects the greatest and most perfect of men' (Philo, *Vit. Mos.* 1.1). So, on the one hand, there was the desire to protect him or her from the charge of being banal or naive or immoral by maintaining that, as we would say, his or her words are not to be taken too literally. Thus, references to the 'hand of God' or the creation of a woman out of the side of a man (Gen. 2) taken literally are just silly, and have to be interpreted allegorically. On the other hand, the same reverence for the author prompted scholars to seek authority for their own views in his or her writings, to bridge the gap, so to speak, between an ancient text and contemporary ethics and philosophy. This gave them licence to employ all manner of exegetical tools, including allegory, to do so. Philo in his *Legum Allegoriae* argues that, whatever the original meaning and purpose of the prohibition on eating birds of prey (Lev. 11:13ff.), for him and his contemporaries it was to teach people not to be rapacious. This approach implies that texts have more than one meaning, a view given much emphasis incidentally in recent literary theory, and in effect opened up an endless series of hermeneutical paths for the reader or interpreter to explore.

The approach was not uncontroversial. Plato, and later Aristarchus, the founding father of Hellenistic scholarship, rejected it – as do modern historical critical interpreters of the Bible who regard it as trivial or misguided. Within the rabbinic tradition, Rabbi Ishmael (died *c.*140 CE), to whom, like Hillel, a famous set of 'Hermeneutical Rules' is attributed, also sounded a note of caution against contrived or far-fetched interpretations: *dibberah torah kileshon bene adam* 'the Torah speaks the language of ordinary people'. There were voices raised in the early Christian tradition against extravagant allegorization of scripture. In the East, the School of Antioch, under the leadership of John Chrysostom, Theodore of Mopsuestia and others in opposition to the Alexandrians, placed much emphasis on the literal meaning of the text. In the West, both Irenaeus (died *c.*200) and Tertullian (died *c.*225) expressed doubts about allegorization, which they associated with Gnostics and other heretical groups. Another Latin writer, Arnobius (died *c.*330 CE), sums up Christian suspicion of allegorical interpretation as follows: 'How are we to know that these passages are to be allegorized? Do you know the intention of the authors of these stories better than they knew it themselves?' (*CHB*: 1, 429). Despite doubts about such methods of interpretation, the search for other meanings beyond the plain meaning of the text became the norm in both rabbinic and patristic exegesis.

The influence of the Alexandrians, and in particular Philo, was decisive, particularly, as one would expect, on the Greek Fathers, but through them on every part of Christianity, East and West.

Already in the New Testament there are examples of allegorical interpretation, one of them actually described as such:

> Now this [the story of Hagar and Sarah] is an allegory: these two women are two covenants. One is from Mount Sinai, bearing children for slavery; she is Hagar...she corresponds to the present Jerusalem for she is in slavery with her children. But the Jerusalem above is free, and she is our mother....
>
> (Gal. 4:24–6)

Clement of Alexandria (*Stromata* 5:4) frequently uses allegorical method and, citing Paul, argued that the 'primary sense is only for babes in religion' (*RA*: 620). The first great Christian biblical scholar, Origen, was steeped in the traditions of Alexandrian scholarship, particularly Philo, and sought to apply their methods systematically to Greek scripture. He found three meanings in scripture, literal, moral and spiritual, corresponding to the threefold make-up of human psychology as body, soul and spirit, and this provided the underlying theoretical basis for his approach. Not every text yields all three meanings; sometimes the literal meaning is important and sometimes the distinction between moral and spiritual is not always clear. But the insight that texts should normally be approached as having more than one meaning, and that even the bare facts of a simple historical narrative, like parts of the Gospels, have symbolic meaning as soon as they are read or interpreted or applied, set the course for Christian exegesis down to modern times.

By the fourth century, many such interpretations of scripture had became fixed parts of official Christian tradition, and powerful tools for the Church to use in their efforts to define their identity and reject alternatives. A similar process can be seen in the history of rabbinic exegesis, running very much in parallel with patristic developments, and in the establishment of Talmudic and Midrashic texts by the sixth century, which were to define Judaism in ways that still operate to this day. The Greek allegorizing tradition of the Alexandrians, in particular Philo, did not have so much influence on Jewish exegetical tradition as it did on Christian tradition. There are some examples, including allegorical interpretations of the High Priest's breastplate (Wis. of Sol. 18:24), the tabernacle (Josephus, *Ant*. 3.7.4) and Rabbi Akiba's famous defence of the Song of Songs on the grounds that it is an allegory of the love between God and

Israel. The introduction to the Midrash Rabbah on Song of Songs stresses the importance of allegory: 'Do not underestimate the value of allegory (*mashal*), because through it one gets to the basic truth'.

But it is said that after the death of Rabbi Meir (second century CE) there were no more *moshle meshalim* 'allegorizers' (MSot. 9:15), and after the death of ben Zoma there were no more *darshanim* 'expounders of the text'. It is probably true to say that, after the second century, extravagant allegorizations and creative exegeses came to be associated, like the LXX and Peshitta, with the Christians and were increasingly avoided by the rabbis. During those three or four formative centuries, there was the feeling that their case could often be better served by adhering as much as possible to the plain meaning of the original Hebrew. The most elaborate types of exegeses did not flourish until the Middle Ages.

But the insight that texts have more than one meaning was as fundamental to rabbinic exegesis as to patristic. One of the most striking features of the rabbinic literature is that it records many differing views even when all but one are rejected. There is the famous story, referred to earlier, about Rabbi Eliezer ben Hyrcanus, whose opinion received divine approval in the form of a *bat qol* and a personal appearance of Elijah the prophet, but was rejected by the majority (see p. 107). The result is that the study of texts was always carried out in an atmosphere in which the discussion of varying interpretations was encouraged. Every word has forty-nine aspects (Num.R. 2:3). Reading a text is like striking sparks from a rock (BTSanh. 4a–4b).

This brings us to the second aspect of this earliest stage in the history of interpretation that we must consider. We are concerned with the special case of sacred texts. As we have seen, religious and ethical issues arose within the context of Hellenistic approaches to Homer and other literature, but the interpretation of a sacred text within an explicitly religious context, for predominantly religious purposes, required special controls. The implications of such exegetical activities often went far beyond the ivory towers of the library or museum to affect the lives of people and institutions throughout the world. The reason why Bishop Irenaeus opposed the extravagant allegorization of scripture was not a purely academic one: he was concerned that his opponents, especially the Gnostics, were using it to give their own views on scriptural authority. The same applies to Tertullian, Jerome, John Chrysostom and many others whose critique of allegorization was prompted by fears that it posed a serious challenge to their authority. Origen's own highly developed but open-ended methods of interpretation, motivated more by intellectual curiosity than concern for theological or ecclesiastical correctness, came in for much criticism for the same reason, especially after his death.

In the case of religious texts, the decision on which was the 'correct' interpretation, that is to say, the one to be espoused by official teachers, preachers, law-makers, those who formulated creeds and the like, clearly had particular importance. It was not a purely academic issue to be debated endlessly and inconclusively by the chattering classes. The task of interpreting was in the hands of specially trained cultic officials, working under authority and using approved methods of exegesis. We shall look first at the role of such official exegetes in this process, and then at some of the attempts by religious authorities to define and control exegetical method.

We begin with some examples from ancient Greece and Rome. In Athens and other Greek cities in antiquity, officials known as *exegetai* were appointed to expound various sacred texts including ancestral laws and the Eleusinian mysteries. There were also professional interpreters called *prophetai* attached to oracles like the one at Delphi, whose function was to act as mediators between the divinely inspired Pythia (or Sibyl) herself and the inquirer. These *prophetai* shaped the words of the original oracular pronouncement, and clearly were in a position to adapt or expand it. Only they heard the original utterances and there will always be controversy about their precise role in the transmission process, but we can be sure that the ancient and powerful international organization known as the 'Delphic Amphictyony', which had political control over the Oracle, ensured that their interpretations were politically favourable to themselves or their allies.

The Emperor Hadrian consulted various oracles to gain confirmation of his subsequent power. Experts in the use of the works of Virgil as a means of divination (*sortes virgilianae*) interpreted a passage from the *Aeneid* as referring to him (*Aen.* 6.808–12). He got a similar response by some means from the Temple of Jupiter at Nicephorium (*Script. Hist. Aug. Hadrian* 2.8: Magie 1979–82; cf. Tacitus, *Annals* 6:12). Christians used the Bible in a similar way as a means of divination. Augustine tells us that he once overheard a child say, '*Tolle, lege*' (pick it up, read it), and assuming this to refer to the Bible, picked it up, opened it at random and found in Romans 13:13–14 a scriptural text which determined the subsequent course of his life (*Confessions* 8:29).

The process of consulting the Sibylline Books, including a description of the fifteen officials involved, the so-called *Quindecimviri*, is described in a text from the third century CE. At a time of military crisis during the reign of the Emperor Aurelian (270–5), the Senate argued that it was time to consult the oracles:

> Come ye pontiffs, pure and cleansed and holy (*puri, mundi, sancti*), attired as is meet and with the spirits sanctified, ascend to the temple, deck the benches with laurel, and with veiled hands unroll the volumes and inquire into the fate of the commonwealth, that fate which is unchanging....

There was a lengthy debate in which senators discussed questions like why a deified emperor should need to consult an oracle at all, and then finally a decree was enacted. They went to the temple, consulted the books, brought forth the verses, purified the city, chanted the hymns, celebrated the Ambarvalia...thus was the sacred ceremony carried out (*Script. Hist. Aug. Aurelian* 18.5–20.8: Magie 1979–82). The advice of the Oracle was taken and the enemy for a time repulsed.

An elaborate example of the interpretation of sacred texts from earlier in the Roman Empire shows that there was a rather more sophisticated side to this interaction between literature and religion at Rome (Feeney 1998). In the year 17 BCE, the Emperor Augustus staged a three-day pageant, known as the *ludi saeculares*, that is to say, games celebrating the end of an era (*saeculum*) or, to put it another way, the inauguration of a new age. The Quindecimviri, among whom was Augustus himself, found scriptural authority for the celebration in the Sibylline Books. It was carried out, like the *ludi saeculares* of 249 BCE, in accordance with the Greek rite (*Achivo ritu*), but transformed into an explicit expression of Roman, Augustan national consciousness. The Greek underworld deities, Pluto and Proserpina, were replaced in the ritual by the more worldly and life-giving deities, Moerae, Ilithyiae and Terra Mater, Greek deities newly introduced to Rome, representing respectively Fate, Childbirth and Earth Mother. Special sacrifices were performed in honour of the supreme Roman god, Jupiter Optimus Maximus, and his consort, Juno Regina, as well as Apollo and Diana, whose Augustan Temple on the Palatine hill had recently been built.

But most significant for our present purposes is the role played by the writings of Virgil, who had died two years earlier during the run-up to the festival. Virgil's *Aeneid* had already become some-thing of a sacred text in Augustan Rome, and Horace's *Carmen Saeculare* contains some outstanding examples of how such a text can be interpreted to expand and elucidate its function, while at the same time giving special authority to the interpreter. The *Carmen* was specially commissioned for the event and sung twice by twin choruses of boys and girls on the last day of the festival. Horace begins by invoking Apollo and Diana, referring to the Sibylline Oracle which authorizes the singing of his *Carmen* at the festival, and drawing attention to the sculpture of Phoebus Apollo's chariot and horses on top of the new Temple of Apollo on the Palatine. He works through the Greek deities honoured at the festival, explain-ing their roles for a Roman audience, and proposing a selection of Latin names for them. Then he draws attention to passages in the Sibylline Oracles and the *Aeneid*, confirming or highlighting what had by now become recognized as prophecies fulfilled by Augustus. The comparison between the future emperor and Hercules in Anchises' prophecy is another frequent topic exploited by both Virgil and Horace. The question of whether Augustus was a man, a hero, a demi-god (like Hercules) or actually a god was frequently debated during his lifetime, and in another poem, Horace seems to spell out explicitly what Virgil had done more cryptically. The question that runs through Virgil's elaborate treatment of the Hercules stories in Book 8 of the *Aeneid*, is taken up at the beginning of Horace's Ode 1:12: *Quem virum aut heroa...quem deum...?* 'What man or hero or god...?' (*Odes* 1:12). Virgil, clearly intending readers to identify Hercules as the emperor, makes it clear that Hercules was divine, the subject of an ancient cult at Rome. Horace ends on the same note, with a vision of his hero shaking Mount Olympus when he returns there on his chariot, and hurling lightning bolts at his enemies.

A final example of the interpretation of religious texts in ancient Rome illustrates a phenomenon to which we have referred more than once in this chapter, namely plurality of meaning. Ovid's *Fasti*, the first half of which was written in Rome before he was exiled in 8 CE, is much more than a poetic version of the state calendars inscribed on arches and other public monuments and known as *fasti consulares, fasti triumphales* and the like (Feeney 1998: 1237). It is more a commentary on such sacred calendars (its full title is *Libri Fastorum* 'Books about the Fasti') and consists of elaborate, innovative explanations of Roman religious rites and practices. In particular, he introduces Greek astronomical and astrological material not found in any earlier *Fasti*. What is most interesting is the way in which, by putting forward many conflicting explanations for the same practice, he gives himself the opportunity to enrich the poem with inspiring and nostalgic allusions to Rome's past, as well as carefully selected references to contemporary political, literary and philosophical issues. Not unlike Jewish Midrash, Ovid's aim is to interpret the ancient traditions in a way that gives them a contemporary appeal and a meaningful social and political function. In other words, reading Ovid's *Fasti*, one learns more about the society in which he lived than about Roman religious traditions – rather as one learns from Jewish interpretations of the Bible more about the world of the Talmud than about the world of the Hebrew Bible.

Before moving on to rabbinic and patristic interpretation, mention must be made of the interpretation of the Avesta in Zoroastrian tradition. The interpreters of the Avesta, known as the *Magi* in Greek, were experts in the ancient and arcane language in which the words of their founder, Zoroaster, were believed to have been handed down orally since his lifetime *c.*1000 BCE. The power of the Magi, from whose name the words magic and magician are derived, resided partly in their ability to recite and interpret the Avesta, but also in their unique expertise in the interpretation of dreams, astrology and other esoteric matters. Plato refers to 'the theology of Zoroaster' (*mageia Zoroastrou*) (*Alcibiades* 1.122A) and Cicero writes of their immense power in Persia (*On Divination* 1:91). Their reputation and influence can also be seen in the presence of the Persian loanword *raz* (mystery, secret) in Aramaic and post-biblical Hebrew (Dan. 2:28f.; 4:6).

Their *Zands* (interpretations) of the ancient Avestan texts date back to early times. They probably existed in various vernaculars until under the Sassanians they were replaced by an official Pahlavi (Middle Persian) Zand. This became the authorized commentary on the Avesta and was frequently combined with it in editions known as the Zand-Avesta. In some cases, like the well-known work known as the *Bundahishn* 'Creation', the original Avestan text has been lost and its Zand is all that survives. The Avestan language in its original oral form was for the most part unknown to all but the Magi, and interpreting it, especially in the bizarre and difficult Pahlavi script in which it was eventually written down, required immense knowledge and skill. The resulting Zands are vast works of scholarship, which incorporate translations and commentaries accumulated over many years, and often contain, like the Jewish Talmud and Midrash, conflicting opinions and minority views.

In the Jewish tradition from around 200 BCE it was, to a very large extent, beliefs about scripture and exegetical method that determined the boundaries between the various forms of Judaism, Pharisees, Sadducees, Essenes and later Christians. Thus the Pharisees accepted that alongside the written Torah there existed a body of equally authoritative material known as the oral Torah, much of it consisting of biblical exegeses designed to bridge the gap between ancient scripture and contemporary developments in religion. The Sadducees, in contrast, considered the written Torah alone to be authoritative, claiming for themselves the ability to explain the plain meaning of the text. For example, they denied that the resurrection of the dead could be found anywhere in the text of the Torah and totally rejected what they considered to be the new-fangled methods and principles of exegesis used by the Pharisees and others to find it there. This ultra-conservative stance, however, on the part of the religious establishment at Jerusalem was quite exceptional and had little effect on Judaism elsewhere. Almost all of the surviving Jewish literature from the period, whether written by Greek-speaking Jews of Alexandria, the Qumran community, the early Christians or the rabbinic sages, is characterized both by the passionate belief that sacred scripture must speak to the present and by the enthusiastic adoption of Hellenistic exegetical methods to realize this. As Philo put it: the literal meaning of the text, written for a situation quite different from the present, has nothing to say, and allegorical and other methods have to be used to discover its inspired 'non-literal meaning'. In Paul's words, 'the letter killeth, the spirit maketh alive' (2 Cor. 3:6). In a much-quoted passage from the Mishnah, 'Greater weight is given to the words of the scribes [i.e. the interpretation of the Law], than to the words of the Law itself' (MSanh. 11:3).

The rabbinic literature contains references to sets of exegetical rules, methods or principles known as *middot*. The 'Seven Middot of Hillel' and the thirty-two middot of Rabbi Jose the Galilean are mentioned more than once, while according to Rabbi Ishmael, whose suspicion of far-fetched interpretations has already been mentioned (p. 149), there was a set of thirteen middot by which the Torah was to be interpreted. These middot include such principles as *qal wa-homer*, that is, inference from a minor case to a major one (if X is the case, how much more is Y?), *gezerah shawah*, inference by analogy, and *binyan ab*, deduction from the fact that two or more texts contain the same term, as well as a variety of lexical devices like etymology, paronomasia, gematria and notarikon (see p. 126–8). The traditions about these collections of exegetical principles probably reflect concerns within the Palestinian community in the second century CE when decisions on the canon of Hebrew scripture, as well as on how it should be interpreted, were taken as part of the policy of consolidation and self-definition. As we have seen, a parallel process was going on at the same time in the Church where Christian authorities like Marcion and Irenaeus were making similar pronouncements on scripture and methods of interpretation. But most of the principles of rabbinic exegesis, derived from the Hellenistic models discussed earlier, were universally familiar a century or more before that.

Some widespread principles of rabbinic exegesis are not included in any of these lists. One of the most conspicuous absences is the principle known as *al tiqre* 'do not pronounce (a word as X, but as Y)'. This depended on the fact that the Hebrew script was basically consonantal, and before the invention of a system of pointing by which the vowels were represented, the same string of consonants could be pronounced in more than one way, each with different meaning: DBR could be *dabar* (word), *dober* (speaker), *deber* (plague), *debir* (inner sanctuary), etc. In most contexts there is no doubt which is meant, but in some there is doubt and in every case it would be possible for an exegete to say *al tiqre dabar* here, read *deber* instead. A good example appears in an interpretation of Exodus 32:16: 'Do not read *harut* ("engraved") but *herut* ("freedom") because you will find no free person except those who occupy themselves with the study of the Law' (MA bothh 9:2; Sarna 1991: 206). Whether the omission of this method from all three lists of middot was due to suspicion of this particular method in some circles, perhaps on the grounds that it allowed too much freedom to the interpreter, cannot be proved. But it is remarkable that it is absent from all three lists, and we may surmise that in some contexts, perhaps connected with the invention of pointing, it was considered at least controversial, like allegorization.

The resulting interpretation of scripture, based on these exegetical principles, was known to the rabbis as *derash* as opposed to *peshat*, the plain meaning of the text, and the verse-by-verse commentaries on scripture which incorporated *derash* were known collectively as Midrash. The earliest examples of midrashic literature come from the third century CE and comprise commentaries on four of the five books of Moses. These four works, though written in Hebrew, are known by Aramaic titles: *Mekhilta* on Exodus, *Sifra* on Leviticus, *Sifre* on Numbers and *Sifre* on Deuteronomy. As they contain predominantly legal material, they are described as *halakhic* as opposed to the *haggadic* commentaries on the whole of the Torah, Psalms and other books which are predominantly homiletical. Rules of exegesis were more strictly controlled in the case of legally binding halakhah than in haggadic interpretations which abound in anecdotes, legends and theological speculation.

The Qumran community, who like the first Christians believed they were living in the last days, applied to scripture another type of exegetical principle quite unlike any of the rabbinic methods of interpretation (Brooke 1985). For them every text was approached with the expectation that it would refer to some aspect of the history or current eschatological experience of the community. Their readings of the Law and the Prophets were dominated by the twin convictions that the end of the world was near, and that they alone of all contemporary Jewish sects, especially those controlling the Temple at Jerusalem, knew the truth and could prepare themselves properly for the day of judgement. A remarkable example is their interpretation of passages, which were originally prophecies of judgement, but in their new Qumran context have become prophecies of hope and salvation. An Amos passage foretells the fall of Samaria in 722 BCE and the exile of the citizens to Syria and beyond. At Qumran the text is interpreted as follows:

> I will exile the tabernacle of your king and the bases of your statues from my tent to Damascus' (*Amos* 5:26–7) – the Books of the Law are the tabernacle of the king, as God said, I will raise up the tabernacle of David when it is fallen (Amos 9:11); the king is the congregation, and the bases of the statues are the Books of the Prophets whom Israel despised. The star is the Interpreter of the Law and shall come to Damascus, as it is written, A star shall come out of Judah and a sceptre shall rise out of Israel (Num. 24:17). The Sceptre is the Prince of the whole congregation and when he comes, he shall smite all the sons of Seth (Num. 24:17).
> (Damascus Document 7)

They knew the word midrash, but seem to have avoided it in favour of their own special term, *pesher*, a word unknown in rabbinic

Hebrew and probably related to Aramaic words for interpreting dreams and visions (e.g. Dan. 2:4, 5; Targum Gen. 40:5, 16; 41:11–13). The pesher literature found at Qumran includes both commentaries on selected passages or anthologies and commentaries on continuous texts such as Isaiah, Hosea and Psalms. One of the best known, as one of the first of the Dead Sea Scrolls to be published, is Pesher Habakkuk which interprets the words of the prophet as violent invective against the sect's chief enemies, the Romans (Chaldaeans1:6–16) and the Jerusalem priesthood (2:5–17):

> Woe to him who causes his neighbours to drink, pouring out his wrath – interpreted this concerns the Wicked Priest who pursued the Teacher of Righteousness to the house of his exile that he might confuse him with his venomous fury. And at the time appointed for rest, for the Day of Atonement, he appeared before them to confuse them and cause them to stumble on the Day of Fasting, their Sabbath of repose.
>
> (Commentary on Habakkuk 11)

The reference to 'feasts' in particular provides the interpreter with an opportunity to point to one of the community's main objections to the Jerusalem hierarchy – their erroneous calendar which rendered invalid feasts and fast days observed in the Temple.

The early Christians also applied other principles in addition to the rabbinic ones just referred to. For Christian interpreters the life, death and resurrection of Christ gave new meaning to the Law and the Prophets. The old texts were now fulfilled, that is to say, taking the Greek word *pleroo* at face value, 'filled' with new meaning. Just as the text in its literal sense often meant little to Philo and a richer spiritual meaning had to be found by means of allegory or some other exegetical method, so the early Christian writers sought to find Christ in every text. Isaiah 7:14, for example, refers to his birth, 9:1 to his arrival in Galilee, 53:4 to his healing miracles, 53:5–6 to his suffering, 53:9 to his death and burial and 33:10 to his resurrection. Isaiah was a particular favourite, but this exegetical process was by no means confined to Isaiah and the other prophets: the whole of scripture was now fulfilled, that is, filled with new meaning. Christ himself is presented as the model when, in the Sermon on the Mount, he says he has come to fulfil the Law and the

Prophets, and then proceeds to 'give new meaning' to some of the Ten Commandments.

As the Christian authorities grew in power and confidence, and especially after Christianity had become the state religion under Constantine in the fourth century, the perceived fact that the text of scripture could mean more or less anything the interpreter wanted it to mean, no longer posed a significant threat to authority, but provided the Church with a formidable armoury which could be used to expose and reject the errors of any heretical minority. The identification of Wisdom in Proverbs 8:22 with Christ provides a good example of how the process worked. Does it or does it not mean 'The Lord created me...'? According to orthodox doctrine, expressed by the state Church's creeds formulated in the fourth and fifth centuries, Christ was not created, he was not part of creation, but 'eternally begotten of the Father'. It was argued therefore that the Hebrew verb used here is the same as that used of the birth of Cain in Gen. 4, and, for doctrinal reasons, must be taken in that sense. The Church authorities represented by such leading figures as Irenaeus, Tertullian, Augustine, Calvin, and many others made sure that this interpretation was enshrined in the Latin Vulgate (*Dominus possedit me*) and accepted by the whole Roman Church. The verb also appears in a number of cosmological contexts with the meaning 'create' (e.g. Gen. 14), and that is how it was translated in the ancient Greek, Syriac and Aramaic versions of Proverbs 8:22, as well as most modern versions. Anyone who adopted such an interpretation, however, including the whole of Arian Christianity and the Jews, was branded by the Church as a heretic.

Patristic exegesis found Christian doctrine in every part of Hebrew scripture. Jerome said that Isaiah was more evangelist than prophet because 'he described all the mysteries of Christ and the Church so clearly that you would think he is composing a history of what had already happened rather than prophesying about what is to come' (Sawyer 1996). In some cases he is referring to the plain meaning of the text, e.g. 'to us a child is born...he was wounded for our transgressions' (53). Elsewhere he resorts to allegorical or symbolic meanings just like those he criticizes in others, e.g. 'the government shall be upon his shoulder' (9:6) refers to Christ carrying the cross with the inscription 'King of the Jews' on it, and the winepress in Isaiah 63 is the Cross. Scriptural authority could be found for virtually every Christian doctrine and practice from the virgin birth (Judg. 6:37–8; Isa. 7:14; Jer. 31:22; Ezek. 44:2) and the Trinity (Gen. 18:2; Isa. 6:3) to the eucharist (Gen. 14:18; Isa.

55:1f.), the sign of the cross (Isa. 66:18; Ezek. 9:4) and the institution of bishops and deacons (Isa. 60:17 LXX).

Such methods of exegesis continued in use in the Church, virtually unchallenged down to the seventeenth-century. Historical criticism, aided by archaeological discoveries, introduced new concerns into biblical scholarship, unknown to the ancient world. But one of the most striking features of recent scholarship has been the way in which current disenchantment with questions of date, source, historicity, authorial intention and an 'original meaning', and preoccupation instead with larger literary units (including whole books), intertextuality, the plurality of meaning and reader response have brought the world of late-twentieth-century scholarship and the world of late antiquity much closer than had previously been thought possible. Like Philo of Alexandria, Origen, Ovid and the other ancient interpreters we have been considering, modern writers appreciate that texts have many meanings, not just one, least of all a single, original meaning (McKnight 1985: 56–8, 96–7). Allegorical interpretations are being taken seriously (Young 1997). The final form of the text is being given priority again, whether under the title of canonical criticism (Childs 1979: 69–83; Coats and Long 1977), redaction-criticism (Perrin 1970) or some more sophisticated literary theory (Handelman 1982; Conrad 1991). Current interest in reception history and the *Wirkungs-geschichte* (impact-history) of sacred texts similarly switches attention away from the original literary forms and sources to their final canonical form and how they have been handled and interpreted by the various religious communities that hold them to be sacred (Beuken, Freyne and Weiler 1991). Franz Rosenzweig, ahead of his time, cleverly suggested that the symbol R of pentateuchal criticism should stand for *Rabbenu*, that is, *mosheh rabbenu* 'Moses our teacher', as much author of the Pentateuch as any putative *Redactor* (Buber and Rosenzweig 1994).

11

CONCLUSION

In this final chapter we shall try to draw together some general conclusions on the nature, origin and function of sacred languages and texts, relating, where appropriate, aspects of the situation in the first Christian centuries to modern developments. The first and probably the most obvious theme running through our study is simply the central importance of language in the history of religions. Basic to virtually all the cases we have discussed is a belief in the power of words. Common to many traditions, as we have seen, are stories about creation by the word. In these the creator is depicted as issuing commands which are instantly obeyed. God said, 'Let there be light' and there was light (Gen. 1:3). The Egyptians had a similar tradition about their creator God Ptah (*ANET* 5). The rabbis noticed a correspondence between the 'Ten Words of Creation' in the Genesis story and the 'Ten Commandments' given at Sinai, while the first Christians believed the words of Jesus had a divine creator's authority: 'He said to the sea, "Peace, be still!" and the wind ceased and there was a great calm' (Mark 4:39).

We noted a connection between naming and creating in many traditions. Simply knowing someone's name and being able to address or summon a person by name implies having power over him or her. This means that knowing the name of a deity, and so being able to invoke a deity by a personal name, has particular significance. To heighten the sense of awe surrounding the deity there may be strict rules on the circumstances in which a divine name like that of Israel's God, Yahweh, may be used, as well as cautionary tales about what happens if the rules are broken. All kinds of euphemisms were devised to avoid pronouncing the name of God corresponding to 'Heaven forbid!' and 'Thank Goodness!'. Some Christians have surrounded the name of Jesus with a similar taboo and avoided pronouncing it except in the context of the liturgy, where the pronunciation of the name is accompanied by a bow of the head – a tradition claiming Pauline authority (Philipp. 2:10). Greek and Roman writers also drew a distinction between deities known by personal names, whether mythological (Zeus, Aphrodite, Poseidon) or personifications of human attributes (Virtue, Fortune, Peace), who could be represented in art, invoked and worshipped, and *ho theos* 'the god' or other philosophical notions of the gods, who had a less personal and more transcendent character or function. Conversely, when Yahweh chooses to reveal his name to Moses (Exod. 3) he is seen as a peculiarly personal deity who has graciously entered into a special relationship with his people.

To know the meaning of someone's name often adds another ingredient to this recurring feature of religious tradition. Fascination with words and meanings, popular etymologies and word-games of all kinds are found among virtually all language-users, ancient and modern, and have had a particularly interesting role to play in sacred languages and sacred texts. We looked at examples from ancient Greek epic, classical philosophy and Roman comedy as well as from the biblical and rabbinic literature. The degree to which such language activities are taken seriously varies considerably from one context to the next. In some cases the purpose is homiletical: the four letters of the name ADAM in Greek are interpreted as representing the four cardinal points of the compass (*Arktos* 'north', *Dusis* 'west', *Anatole* 'east', *Mesembria* 'south'). This makes the point that Adam stands for all humanity 'fulfilling by his name east and west and south and north' (Sib. 3:24–26; *OTP*: 1, 362; 2 Enoch 30:13; *OTP*: 1, 152). Some of the numerical explanations of names (gematria) are polemical like the number of the beast (666) in Revelation which, in both Latin and Hebrew, can be calculated to point to the Emperor Nero (Rev. 13:18). Other candidates incidentally include, in various languages, the Pope, Martin Luther, John Knox, Napoleon and Hitler, and a recent discussion of gematria points out that in English there are over 1,000 words with the same total (Crystal 1998: 80–3). In some contexts, however, the significance of names or letters was clearly very great: for example, in the traditional system for using the twenty-two letters of the Hebrew alphabet as numerals, the notation for fifteen and sixteen had to be adjusted to avoid using for secular purposes combinations of letters associated with the sacred tetragrammaton (*tet/waw* and *tet/zayin* instead of *yod/he* and *yod/waw*).

It matters a great deal which words are used. Rituals are not valid if they are not accompanied by the correct words, in the correct language and with the correct pronunciation. Only texts written in a language officially approved by the institution are permitted to be used at public worship, and change to new terminology or modern versions is very slow and in some contexts virtually unthinkable. This leads us on to a second recurring theme: the extraordinary conservatism of religious communities and institutions, discussed at length in Chapter 3 in relation to Judaism, but characteristic to a greater or lesser degree of virtually all the religious traditions we have been considering. The retention of ancient biblical Hebrew as the language in which the Bible had to be read and studied, as well as the language of the liturgy, is one example, unquestioned until modern times. The success of the painstaking efforts of the Masoretes, scribes specially trained in the official policy and regulations of the Jewish authorities, to preserve the Hebrew text of scripture exactly as they received it was spectacularly confirmed by the discovery of biblical manuscripts at Qumran in 1947. These were a thousand years older than the extant mediaeval Masoretic manuscripts which were virtually all we had before then, and yet there are almost no major divergences between them. The Samaritans have continued to use the Old Hebrew script, obsolete everywhere else since before the Babylonian exile, until modern times. Ancient Phoenician survived in the liturgy of some north African communities long after it had died out as a spoken language. The Magi likewise sought to preserve what they believed to be the words of the founder of their religion Zoroaster, without writing them down, in the original Avestan language known only from the Avesta for a thousand years at least. The guild of priests responsible for the preservation and management of the Sibylline Books, which played such a significant role in Roman state religion right down to imperial times, had to be experts in Greek as no translations were permitted till well into the second century CE. Hymns associated with some of the Roman festivals continued to be sung in varieties of ancient Latin until they were unintelligible to everyone, including the priests.

The reasons for this widespread and well-established phenomenon are not very hard to identify and need not detain us here. On the one hand, language is an expression of a worshipping community's identity, and those responsible for preserving or controlling that identity use the traditional forms of language and ritual to do this. Priests may also use their own exclusive expertise in an ancient sacred language to maintain their dominant role in the community. The Magi, for example, acquired a hostile reputation in some quarters, not always unjustified, for using their special powers for their own political ends. On the other hand, the continuing pressure of influential minority groups, like the 1661 Prayerbook Society which was set up in recent years to oppose the use of new Alternative Service Books in the Anglican church, and Latin Mass fanatics in Catholicism who insist on retaining Latin, proves how reluctant religious people can be to change the language they use in worship. They are moved by the familiar sounds of the traditional language, even if they do not always know what it means, and argue for its superior beauty or mystical power. In other words, unintelligibility is sometimes associated with sacredness, and translation with modernization and secularization.

The cultural influence and universal appeal of much of the language of *King James' Authorized Version of the Bible* (1611) as well as the 1661 Prayerbook, outside the Church in English literature and the arts as well as inside it, have also played a role in raising it to the level of a 'sacred language' on a par with Latin in traditional Catholicism and Hebrew in Judaism. Proof that the language of the *Authorized Version* transcends normal mundane and historical categories in popular belief can readily be found in the frequently quoted comment by an enthusiastic opponent of new translations: 'If the *Authorized Version of the Bible* was good enough for St Paul, it's good enough for me'. The survival of thou/thee-forms in modern translations of the 'Lord's Prayer' and the 'Hail Mary' is another illustration of the power of popular tradition to withstand reforming tendencies.

A powerful antidote to the linguistic conservatism common to so many religious traditions has a much longer and more successful history particularly in Christianity. From the very beginning communication was given the highest priority among Christian leaders and preachers. There seems to have been no interest in creating or adopting a special sacred language, and little effort to preserve either the 'sacred words' of Jesus or the words of 'sacred scripture' in their original language. It was the content of the Gospel that mattered, apparently, rather than its linguistic form, 'the spirit rather than the letter', as Paul said in a different context. Within a couple of centuries the words of Jesus were available in Greek, Latin, Syriac, Coptic and probably other languages as well. By then there existed Jewish versions of the Hebrew scripture in Greek and probably Syriac, and these were taken over and monopolized by the Church as Christian scripture. But in the next few centuries enormous expense and scholarly effort were devoted to the task of translating Christian scripture, including the words of Jesus and the Hebrew Bible, into virtually every language in the Roman Empire and beyond. Christian scholars invented new scripts for some languages such as Armenian, Georgian, Gothic and later the Slavonic languages, which previously had had none.

The contrast with Jewish tradition was at first very striking. Despite the Bible translation efforts of those first centuries BCE and CE, and the accompanying existence of a considerable body of Jewish literature in Greek and some in Aramaic, Jewish belief in the priority of ancient Hebrew as the only sacred language survived virtually unchallenged; while for Christians there was rarely any interest in the original Hebrew or Aramaic or even Greek of the original writers. With the political establishment of the Church at Rome in the fourth century, however, and the ecumenical councils of the fifth, the old hierarchical conservatism resurfaced. The various regional authorities, anxious to define and control Church beliefs and practices, gave their official blessing to certain translations of scripture which then became authoritative 'sacred texts' in their own right and in the same way in which Hebrew scripture had always been understood. The influence of Jerome's Latin Vulgate, soon to be known as *Biblia Sacra Latina*, upon western Christendom in general, and European languages and literatures in particular, is only one example of this process. The same happened to the ancient Greek, Syriac, Armenian, Gothic, Ge'ez and other versions, some of which are still used in contemporary Christian liturgies. We have already mentioned *King James' Authorized Version* as another example of the same process whereby a particular version of scripture assumes the status of sacred text, and then defiantly resists any modernizing alternative for centuries.

The missionary zeal of the first Christian centuries, however, as expressed in Bible translation, revived dramatically in the late Middle Ages thanks to the efforts of John Wycliffe (*c.*1329–84), Martin Luther (1483–1546) and others. Since then down to modern times no expense has been spared on translating the Bible into the vernacular. The British and Foreign Bible Society, founded in 1804, and the immensely influential Summer Institute of Linguistics, which began its research and training programmes in the States in 1934 and is now active in over fifty countries, are powerful testimonies to the continuing commitment of Christian scholars and missionaries to providing minority peoples throughout the world with the Bible in their own language (Bendor-Samuel 1994: 4405–10). The number of different English versions of the Bible published this century alone, some more experimental than others, some with a seal of approval from one or more of the major Christian institutions, some without, is another indication of the same evangelical concern to ensure that scripture is read and correctly understood by as many people as possible. An important issue addressed in most of the new versions concerns inclusive language, that is to say, non-gender-specific language designed to 'include' women in a way that was either left to interpreters ('*man* here includes women... *he* in this context means she as well as he...'), or deliberately avoided as in some of the older patriarchal translations. 'God created man in his own image' is the best known example, in which despite unmistakeable indications in the context that 'man' here (Hebrew *adam*) is a collective noun like the words translated 'beasts', 'fish', 'birds', 'cattle' and so on, and is most accurately translated 'human beings'. The fact that it takes a plural verb ('and let them have dominion...') and explicitly includes both male and female, has been resisted for centuries by translators, commentators and theologians eager to find scriptural authority for their doctrines. The *New Revised Standard Version* is one of the most radical attempts to redress the balance, substituting 'humankind' for 'man' (with an apologetic footnote), and inclusive 'they' for 'he', 'people' for 'a man' and the like throughout the Bible. The NRSV translators did not go as far as Phyllis Trible in her brilliant suggestion that *adam* in Genesis 2 might be translated 'earth creature', made of *adamah* 'earth' and not gender-specific until verse 23 when the words *ish* 'man' and *isha* 'woman' are first used.

By contrast there are only two official English versions of the Hebrew Bible and converts to Judaism have to learn Hebrew. They also have to know some Aramaic, since several popular Jewish prayers, notably the 'Kaddish' in the Daily Prayerbook and the 'Kol Nidre' in the Yom Kippur service, are still printed and recited in the ancient Jewish vernacular. Orthodox reluctance to encourage the use of English in the liturgy, even alongside the Hebrew text, can be seen in the fact that the English translation facing the Hebrew text in the prayerbook most frequently used in British synagogues is still an antiquated nineteenth-century version, and the publication of a more up-to-date version has constantly been delayed.

Our final general observation on the interaction between language and religion in antiquity, as we have observed it throughout this study, concerns what we might nowadays refer to as globalization. From as early as the eighth century, Greek and Phoenician traders and explorers had established influential colonies in Italy, Gaul, Spain and North Africa. The Greeks got their script from the Phoenicians, and the Romans got theirs, via the Etruscans, from the Greeks. In the East, under Darius the Great (522–486 BCE), a new type of powerful and highly effective central government characterized by a 'benevolent imperialism' (Ghirshman 1954: 152) was established, which in effect linked Persia with the Mediterranean world in a new and disciplined communications network. The celebrated 'Royal Road' described by Herodotus, which ran from Susa, the Persian capital, to Sardis in Asia Minor, was its most impressive element.

The Persians are credited with inventing the first imperial postal service which was taken over and developed by Alexander the Great and his successors. The Greeks borrowed from Persian one of their words for 'postman, courier' (*angaros*). In ancient Greece, there obviously existed means of *ad hoc* communication by messenger, travelling by road or by sea, or by beacon as in Clytemnestra's beautiful description of the coming of the news of the fall of Troy to Mycenae in Aeschylus' *Agamemnon* (lines 282–316). Similarly, in the Roman Republic there is plenty of evidence for a network of communication by messenger (Latin *tabellarius*) available to those who could afford it. But it was Augustus who first attempted to establish a real postal service for official communications throughout the Empire, dependent on lines of posting stations (*mansiones*), maintained and defended at local expense, and on the local requisitioning of personnel, vehicles and animals. The abuse of this system, complaints and unrest on the part of the local communities involved, and attempts to shift the burden of its upkeep on to state finances, are recurring issues in the literature, but its efficiency and its unifying influence are striking characteristics of the Roman Empire.

By the time of Christ, it was assumed that most people throughout the world from Spain to Persia, even businessmen with only a modest education, knew Greek as well as their own vernacular. By then, too, there were native Greek speakers living in Greek-style cities all over the world. Under the Roman emperors this situation continued for a century or so. Latin replaced Greek as the lingua franca only in the West, where the Greeks had not settled in such strength and their language had never taken such a hold. The second century actually witnessed serious attempts under Hadrian and his successors to restore or maintain the dominance of Greek in the Empire – in literary and intellectual circles at least. By then the flourishing book trade was an important feature of the Roman Empire, and this, combined with a strong centralized educational policy in schools as well as the army and the civil service, resulted in a degree of widespread cultural uniformity which the world had not seen before. The same style of Latin handwriting was then in use in Upper Egypt and Northern England. Books written in Rome were being read in Gaul or North Africa within weeks of their publication.

What this all means is that, even without specific intervention from central government, developments in one part of the world were inevitably open to influences from another. We noted two extremely important examples of this phenomenon as they affect sacred language and literature. The first concerns the possible impact of the Antonines' literary activities in the second century CE on Judaism, Christianity and Zoroastrianism. The collection, editing and canonization of the Greek classics coincided precisely with the first efforts of these three religious traditions to define their canons of scripture. Three Greek versions of scripture were produced in the second century. It was in the second century that the first serious attempts were made to define the canon of scripture in Judaism and Christianity. Decisions on the Hebrew canon, which were to become binding for all time, were taken at Yavneh at the beginning of the century. Marcion's unsuccessful efforts to dissociate Christian scripture from Jewish came soon after, and the earliest official list of New Testament writings, the Muratorian Canon, is probably to be dated to the latter part of the same century. Both Rabbi Meir's collection of rabbinic sayings and then the Mishnah itself, Rabbi Judah's official canon of oral Torah, come from that period, as do the earliest attempts by the Magi to write down the sayings of their prophet Zoroaster in the Avesta. There were clearly other factors involved in this process, but the suggestion that religious leaders and scholars were aware of contemporary developments, in imperial Rome as well as in other parts of the world, and influenced by them, cannot be lightly dismissed.

While these second-century editorial activities on the part of rabbis, church fathers, Magi and others may have lacked decisiveness and lasting authority, the decisions of the fourth and fifth centuries show nothing of that temporary nature. The great ecumenical councils of the Church, held at Nicaea, Constantinople,

Chalcedon and Ephesus, sought to determine the character of Christian doctrine, practice and organization for all time, and because of the global power of the Church at the time went a long way towards achieving this. Theological issues and terminology were clarified. Creeds were formulated. Texts were canonized. The 'orthodox' Christianity of the West defined itself at these councils over and against other varieties of Christianity and other religious traditions, theologically, liturgically, linguistically, and the effect of this was that the other traditions took steps at the same time to define themselves over and against orthodox Christianity. It was then that the Eastern Churches completed their own versions of scripture in Syriac, Armenian, Georgian, Coptic, Ge'ez and Gothic, and defined the content and order of their canons – each expressing their theological and liturgical identity. These Christian traditions have remained distinct and separate ever since, even when worshipping in the same building as in the case of the Church of the Holy Sepulchre in Jerusalem, divided by language as much as by practice and belief. It was then, too, that the Talmud, the foundation document of all subsequent varieties of Judaism, was completed, as well as the immensely difficult task of writing down and editing the Zand-Avesta under the aegis of the Zoroastrian establishment in Persia.

Armenia had been the first nation to embrace Christianity as the established religion as early as the third century. Now, Christianity was the official religion of other states as well, including the Roman Empire. A sense of national identity combined with Christianity to produce powerful political forces in many parts of the world. Latin, the official language of the Roman Empire, was dominant in the West, but the dominance of Greek began to be eroded by the state-supported vernaculars adopted by Church leaders in the East, including Syriac, Ge'ez and Coptic. The success of Christianity posed a challenge to other religions too and, as we saw, led to measures to consolidate Jewish and Zoroastrian traditions as well. We end as we began with the picture of a world unified or dominated by the great ecumenical councils, on the eve of the Islamic conquests, and poised to expand beyond its classical frontiers to include the continents of Africa and Asia.

BIBLIOGRAPHY

Ackroyd, P.R. (1968) *Exile and Restoration. A Study of the Hebrew Thought of the Sixth Century*, London: SCM Press

Ackroyd, P.R. and Evans, C.E. (eds) (1970) *Cambridge History of the Bible*, vol. 1, Cambridge: Cambridge University Press

Aeschylus, English translation by H.W. Smith (1922), 2 vols, Cambridge, MA: Loeb Classical Library

Alter, R. (1992) *The World of Biblical Literature*, London: SPCK

Alter, R. and Kermode, F. (1987) *The Literary Guide to the Bible*, London: Collins

Andersen, F.I. and Forbes, D. (1992) *Vocabulary of the Old Testament*, Chicago: Loyola University Press

Anderson, L. (1993) 'Haunting the margins of history: Toni Morrison's *Beloved*' in J.G. Davies and I. Wollaston (eds) *The Sociology of Sacred Texts*, Sheffield: Sheffield Academic Press, pp. 156–65.

Apuleius, *Metamorphoses (The Golden Ass)*, English translation by J.A. Hanson (1989), Cambridge, MA: Loeb Classical Library

Aristotle, *Rhetorica*, English translation by H. Rackham (1937), Cambridge, MA: Loeb Classical Library

Asher, R.E. (ed.) (1994) *Encyclopedia of Language and Linguistics*, 10 vols, Oxford: Pergamon Press

Augustine, *City of God*, English translation by G. McCracken *et al.* (1965–81), 7 vols, Cambridge, MA: Loeb Classical Library

Augustine, *Confessions*, English translation by W. Watts (1912), 2 vols, Cambridge, MA: Loeb Classical Library

Augustine, *De Doctrina Christiana*, English translation by R.B.H. Green (1995), Oxford: Oxford University Press

Bal, M. (ed.) (1989) *Anti-Covenant. Counter-Reading Women's Lives in the Bible*, Sheffield: Sheffield Academic Press

Balas, D.L. and Bingham, D.J. (1998) 'Patristic exegesis of the books of the Bible' in W. Farmer (ed.) *International Catholic Bible Commentary*, pp. 64–115, Collegeville, Minnesota: St John's Abbey Press

Barker, M. (1988) *The Lost Prophet. The Book of Enoch and its Influence on Christianity*, London: SPCK

Barr, J. (1983) *Holy Scripture: Canon, Authority, Criticism*, Philadelphia: Westminster Press

Barr, J. (1977) *Fundamentalism*, London: SCM Press

Barr, J. (1968) *Comparative Philology and the Text of the Old Testament*, Oxford: Clarendon Press

Barr, J. (1961) *The Semantics of Biblical Language*, Oxford: Oxford University Press

Beard, M. and North, J. (eds) (1990) *Pagan Priests. Religion and Power in the Ancient World*, London: Duckworth

Beckwith, R. (1985) *The Old Testament Canon of the New Testament Church*, London: SPCK

Bendor-Samuel, J. (1994) 'Summer Institute of Linguistics' in R.E. Asher (ed.) *Encyclopedia of Language and Linguistics*, 8: 4405–10, Oxford: Pergamon Press

Beuken, W., Freyne, S. and Weiler, A. (eds) (1991) *The Bible and its Readers*, London: SCM Press

Biblia Patristica. Index des Citations et Allusions Bibliques dans la Littérature Patristique (1975–7), J. Allenbach *et al.* (eds), 2 vols, Paris: Centre national de la recherche scientifique.

Biblia Sacra iuxta Vulgatam versionem (1975), 2nd edn, R. Weber, 2 vols, Stuttgart

Blanc, M. (1994) 'Societal bilingualism' in R.E. Asher (ed.) *Encyclopedia of Language and Linguistics*, 1: 355, Oxford: Pergamon Press

Blau, L. (1903) 'Lilith' in *Jewish Encyclopedia*, 8: 87f., New York: Funk & Wagnall

Blenkinsopp, J. (1989) *Ezra–Nehemiah*, London: SCM Press

Boman, T. (1960) *Hebrew Thought Compared with Greek*, London: SCM Press

Bori, P.C. (1994) *From Hermeneutics to Ethical Consensus Among Cultures*, Atlanta: Scholars Press

Bourdieu, P. (1992) *Language and Symbolic Power*, Cambridge: Polity Press

Bowman, A.K. and Woolf, G. (eds) (1994) *Literacy and Power in the Ancient World*, Cambridge: Cambridge University Press

Boyarin, D. (1994a) *Intertextuality and the Reading of Midrash*, Bloomington: Indiana University Press

Boyarin, D. (1994b) *A Radical Jew. Paul and the Problem of Identity*, Berkeley: University of California Press

Boyce, M. (1984) *Textual Sources for the Study of Zoroastrianism*, Manchester: Manchester University Press

Bremmer, J.N. and Martinez, F.G. (eds) (1992) *Sacred History and Sacred Texts in Early Judaism*, Kampen: Kok Pharos

Brenneman, J.E. (1997) *Canons in Conflict. Negotiating Texts in True and False Prophecy*, Oxford: Oxford University Press

Brock, S.P. (1994) 'Greek and Syriac in Late Antique Syria' in A.K. Bowman, and G. Woolf (eds) *Literacy and Power in the Ancient World*, pp. 149–61, Cambridge: Cambridge University Press

Brooke, G.J. (1985) *Exegesis at Qumran. 4Q Florilegium in its Jewish Context*, Sheffield: Sheffield Academic Press

Brown, P. (1997) *The Rise of Western Christendom. Triumph and Diversity AD 200–1000*, Oxford: Blackwell

Brown, P. (1971) *The World of Late Antiquity. From Marcus Aurelius to Muhammad*, London: Thames & Hudson

Brown, R.E. (1970) *The Gospel According to John*, New York: Doubleday

Brown, R.E., Fitzmyer, J.A. and Murphy, R.E. (eds) (1990) *The New Jerome Biblical Commentary*, London: Geoffrey Chapman/Mowbray

Bryer, A. (1991) 'The Pontic Greeks before the Diaspora', *Journal of Refugee Studies* 4(4): 315–34

Buber, M. and Rosenzweig, F.R. (1994) *Scripture and Translation*, Bloomington: Indiana University Press

Butler, J. (1997) *Excitable Speech. A Politics of the Performative*, London: Routledge

Caesar, Julius, *Gallic War*, English translation by H.J. Edwards (1986), Cambridge, MA: Loeb Classical Library

Camp, C. and Fontaine, C.R. (1993) *Women, War and Metaphor. Language and Society in the Study of the Hebrew Bible*, Atlanta: Fortress Press

Carroll, R. and Prickett, S. (eds) (1997) *The Bible. Authorized King James Version*, Oxford: Oxford University Press

Cary, M. (1980) *A History of Rome Down to the Age of Constantine*, Basingstoke: Macmillan Press

Castelli, R.E. (1991) *Imitating Paul. A Discourse of Power*, Louisville, KY: Westminster/John Knox Press

Catullus, English translation by F.W. Cornish, revised G.P. Goold (1987), Cambridge, MA: Loeb Classical Library

Charles, R.H. (1913) *The Apocrypha and Pseudepigrapha of the Old Testament*, 2 vols, Oxford: Oxford University Press

Charlesworth, J.H. (ed.) (1983–85) *The Old Testament Pseudepigrapha*, 2 vols, London: Darton, Longman & Todd Ltd

Childs, B.S. (1979) *Introduction to the Old Testament as Scripture*, Philadelphia: Fortress Press

Chilton, B. (1982) *The Glory of Israel. The Theology and Provenience of the Isaiah Targum*, Sheffield: Sheffield Academic Press

Christ, H. (1977) *Blutvergiessen im Alten Testament. Der Gewaltsame Tod des Menschen untersucht am hebräischen Wort dam*, Basel: Reinhardt

Cicero, *De Oratore*, English translation by E.W. Sutton and H. Rackham (1942), Cambridge, MA: Loeb Classical Library

Cicero, *De Senectute. De Amicitia. De Divinatione*, English translation by W.A. Falconer (1979), Cambridge, MA: Loeb Classical Library

Cicero, *In Pisonem*, English translation by N.H. Watts (1931), Cambridge, MA: Loeb Classical Library

Clement of Alexandria, *Anti-Nicene Fathers*, vol. 2, Grand Rapids: Eerdman, reprinted 1983

Clement of Rome, the Epistles of, and the Epistles of Ignatius of Antioch, English translation by J.A. Kleist (1946), Westminster, MD: The Newman Bookshop

Clements, R.E. (1980) *Isaiah and the Deliverance of Jerusalem*, London: SCM Press

Clines, D.J.A. (ed.) (1993) *Dictionary of Classical Hebrew*, Sheffield: Sheffield Academic Press

Coats, G.W. and Long, B.O. (eds) (1977) *Canon and Authority. Essays in Old Testament Religion and Theology*, Philadelphia: Fortress Press

Coggins, R.J. and Houlden, J.L. (eds) (1990) *Dictionary of Biblical Interpretation*, London: SCM Press

Cohen, J. (1989) *'Be Fertile and Increase, Fill the Earth and Master It.' The Ancient and Mediaeval Career of a Biblical Text*, Newhaven: Yale University Press

Collins, J.J. (1983), 'Sibylline Oracles. A new translation and introduction' in J.H. Charlesworth (ed.) (1983) *The Old Testament Pseudepigrapha*, 1: 317–472, London: Darton, Longman & Todd

Conrad, E.W. (1991) *Reading Isaiah*, Minneapolis: Fortress Press

Coulmas, F. (1992) *Language and Economy*, Oxford: Blackwell

Crim, K.R. (ed.) (1976) *Interpreter's Dictionary of the Bible, Supplementary Volume*, Atlanta: Abingdon Press

Crystal, D. (1998) *Language Play*, Harmondsworth: Penguin

Dalman, G. (1922) *Jesus/Jeschua*, Leipzig: Hinrichs

Danby, H. (1933) *The Mishnah*, Oxford: Oxford University Press

Daube, D. (1984) *The New Testament and Rabbinic Judaism*, Salem: Ayer & Co.

Davies, J.G. and Wollaston, I. (eds) (1993) *The Sociology of Sacred Texts*, Sheffield: Sheffield Academic Press

Davies, W.D. (1948) *Paul and Rabbinic Judaism*, London: SPCK

De Lange, N. (1976) *Origen and the Jews. Studies in Jewish–Christian Relations in Third Century Palestine*, Cambridge: Cambridge University Press

Derrida, J. (1991) 'Des Tours de Babel', translated by J.F. Graham in *Semeia 54 Post-structuralism as Exegesis*, D. Jobling and S.D. Moore (eds) (1992), pp. 3–34, Atlanta: Scholars Press

Dirksen, P.B. (1990) 'The Old Testament Peshitta' in *Mikra. Text, Translation, Reading and Interpretation of the Hebrew Bible in Ancient Judaism and Early Christianity*, M.J. Mulder and H. Sysling (eds), pp. 255–97, Minneapolis: Fortress Press

Douglas, M. (1999) *Leviticus as Literature*, Oxford: Oxford University Press

Driver, G.R. (1957) *Aramaic Documents of the Fifth Century BC*, Oxford: Oxford University Press

Driver, S.R. (1913) *Introduction to the Literature of the Old Testament*, Edinburgh: T. & T. Clark

Elbogen, I. (1993) *Jewish Liturgy. A Comprehensive History*, translated by R.P. Scheidlin, New York: Jewish Publication Society

Elliott, J.K. (1993) *The Apocryphal New Testament*, Oxford: Clarendon Press

Encyclopedia Judaica (1971–2), 16 vols, Jerusalem: Keter

Eusebius, *Ecclesiastical History*, translated by G.A. Williamson (1965), Harmondsworth: Penguin

Eusebius, *Preparation for the Gospel*, translated by E.H. Gifford (1903), Oxford: Oxford University Press

Evans, C.A. (1989) *To See and Not Perceive. Isaiah 6:9–10 in Early Jewish and Christian Interpretation*, Sheffield: Sheffield Academic Press

Exum, C. (1993) *Fragmented Women. Feminist (Sub)versions of Biblical Narrative*, Sheffield: Sheffield Academic Press

Farmer, W. (ed.) (1998) *International Catholic Bible Commentary*, Collegeville, Minnesota: St John's Abbey Press

Fathers of the Church (1947–), Washington: Catholic University of America Press

Feeney, D. (1998) *Literature and Religion at Rome. Cultures, Contexts and Beliefs*, Cambridge: Cambridge University Press

Fernhout, R. (1994) *Canonical Texts: Bearers of Absolute Authority. Bible, Koran, Veda, Tipitaka. A Phenomenological Study*, Amsterdam/Atlanta, GA: Rodopi

Fish, S. (1980) *Is there a Text in the Class? The Authority of Interpretive Communities*, London: Harvard University Press

Fishbane, M. (1985) *Biblical Interpretation in Ancient Israel*, Oxford: Oxford University Press

Fishwick, D. (1964) 'On the origin of the ROTAS-SATOR square', *Harvard Theological Review* 57: 39–53

Fitzmyer, J.A. (1979) *A Wandering Aramaean: Collected Aramaic Essays*, Missoula: Fortress Press

Fowler, R.M. (1991) *Let the Reader Understand: Reader Response Criticism and the Gospel of Mark*, Minneapolis: Augsburg Fortress

Freedman, D.N. (ed.) *ABD*.

Frend, W.H.C. (1984) *The Rise of Christianity*, Philadelphia: Fortress Press

Frye, N. (1982) *The Great Code. The Bible and Literature*, Orlando: Harcourt Brace

Gabel, J.B., Wheeler, C.B. and York, A.D. (1996) *The Bible as Literature. An Introduction*, 3rd edn, Oxford: Oxford University Press

Gager, J.G. (1983) *The Origins of Anti-Semitism. Attitudes Toward Judaism in Christian and Pagan Antiquity*, Oxford: Oxford University Press

Gamble, H.Y. (1995) *Books and Readers in the Early Church. A History of Early Christian Texts*, Newhaven: Yale University Press

Garcia, Martinez, F. (ed.), translated by W.G.E. Watson (1994) *The Dead Sea Scrolls Translated: The Qumran Texts in English*, Leiden: E.J.Brill

Garrison, R. (1997) *The Graeco-Roman Context of Early Christian Literature*, Sheffield: Sheffield Academic Press

Gellner, E. (1957) 'Is belief really necessary?' in *Hibbert Journal*, 56, pp. 31–41, reprinted in I.C. Jarvie and J. Agassi (eds) (1974) *The Devil in Modern Philosophy*, London: Routledge, pp. 52–63

Gerhardsson, B. (1964) *Tradition and Transmission in Early Christianity*, Lund: Gleerup

Gesenius, W. (1910) *Hebrew Grammar*, E. Kautzsch (ed.), 2nd English edn by A.E. Cowley, Oxford: Clarendon Press

Ghirshman, R. (1954) *Iran. From the Earliest Times to the Islamic Conquest*, Harmondsworth: Penguin

Ginzberg, L. (ed.) (1954) *Legends of the Jews*, 7 vols, 10th edn, New York: Jewish Publication Society (one-volume edn, Philadelphia, 1975)

Goodman, M. (1994) 'Texts, scribes and power in Roman Judaea' in A.K. Bowman and G. Woolf (eds) *Literacy and Power in the Ancient World*, pp. 109–25, Cambridge: Cambridge University Press

Goodman, M. (1987) *The Ruling Class of Judaea. The Origins of the Jewish Revolt against Rome* AD 66–70, Cambridge: Cambridge University Press

Gordon, R. (1990) 'From the republic to principate: priesthood, religion and ideology' in M. Beard and J. North (eds) *Pagan Priests. Religion and Power in the Ancient World*, London: Duckworth pp. 179–98

Grant, M. (1994) *The Antonines. The Roman Empire in Transition*, London: Routledge

Handelman, S.A. (1982) *Slayers of Moses. The Emergence of Rabbinic Interpretation in Modern Literary Theory*, New York: State University of New York Press

Harden, D. (1971) *The Phoenicians*, Harmondsworth: Penguin

Harrington, D.J. (1996) *Wisdom Texts from Qumran*, London: Routledge

Harris, W.V. (1989) *Ancient Literacy*, London: Harvard University Press

Hayman, P. (1989) 'Was God a magician? Sefer Yetzirah and Jewish magic' in *Journal of Semitic Studies* 40: 225–37

Hengel, M. (1989) *The 'Hellenization' of Judaea in the First Century after Christ*, London: SCM Press

Hennecke, E., Schneemelcher, W. and Wilson, R.McL. (eds) (1963–5) (eds), *New Testament Apocrypha*, 2 vols, London: Lutterworth

Hill, D. (1967) *Greek Words with Hebrew Meanings*, Cambridge: Cambridge University Press

Hirsch, E.D. (1976) *The Aims of Interpretation*, Chicago: University of Chicago Press

Homer, *The Iliad* (1924), English translation by A.T. Murray, 2 vols, Cambridge, MA: Loeb Classical Library

Homer, *The Odyssey* (1919), English translation by A.T. Murray, 2 vols, Cambridge, MA: Loeb Classical Library

Horace, *The Odes and Epodes* (1916), English translation by C.E. Bennett, Cambridge, MA: Loeb Classical Library

Hornblower, S. and Spawforth, A. (eds) (1996) *Oxford Classical Dictionary*, 3rd edn, Oxford: Oxford University Press

Horst, P.W. van der (1994) *Hellenism – Judaism and Christianity. Essays on their Interaction*, Kampen: Kok Pharos

Horst, P.W. van der (1991) *Ancient Jewish Epitaphs. An Introductory Survey of a Millennium of Jewish Funerary Epigraphy (300 BCE–700 CE)*, Kampen: Kok Pharos

Irenaeus, English translation by J.P. Smith (1952), London: Longman

Irenaeus, *Isidori Hispalensis Episcopi Etymologiarum Sive Originum Libri XX*, W.M. Lindsay (ed.) (1911), Oxford: Oxford University Press

Iser, W. (1974) *The Implied Reader*, Baltimore: Johns Hopkins University Press

James, M.R. (1950) *The Apocryphal New Testament*, Oxford: Oxford Unversity Press

Jastrow, M. (1903) *A Dictionary of the Targumim, the Talmud Babli and Yerushalmi, and the Midrashic Literature*, Philadelphia and New York: Judaica Press, reprinted 1950

Jeffreys, D.L. (ed.) (1992) *A Dictionary of Biblical Tradition in English Literature*, Grand Rapids: Wm B. Eerdmans Publishing Co.

Jewish Encyclopedia (1903), 10 vols, New York: Funk & Wagnall

Josephus, English translation by H.St. and J. Thackeray, R. Marcus, A. Wikgren and L.H. Feldman (1926–65), Cambridge, MA: Loeb Classical Library

Juvenal and Persius, English translation by G.G. Ramsay (1918), Cambridge, MA: Loeb Classical Library

Kee, H.C. (1980) *The Origins of Christianity. Sources and Documents*, London: SPCK

Kelber, W.H. (1997) *The Oral and the Written Gospel. The Hermeneutics of Speaking and Writing in the Synoptic Tradition, Mark and Paul*, Bloomington: Indiana University Press

Kelly, J.N.D. (1975) *Jerome. His Life, Writings and Controversies*, London: Duckworth

Kerrigan, J. (1952) *St Cyril of Alexandria. Interpreter of the Old Testament*, Rome: Pontifical Biblical Institute

Krauss, S. (1898) *Griechische und lateinische Lehnwörter im Talmud, Midrasch und Targum, I*, Hildesheim: Olms

Kugel, J.L. (1997) *The Bible As It Was*, London: Harvard University Press

Kutscher, E.Y. (1982) *A History of the Hebrew Language*, Leiden: E.J. Brill

Lane Fox, R. (1994) 'Literacy and power in early Christianity' in A.K. Bowman and G. Woolf (eds) *Literacy and Power in the Ancient World*, pp. 126–48, Cambridge: Cambridge University Press

Lauterbach, J. (1970) 'The naming of children' in *Studies in Jewish Law, Custom and Folk-Lore*, New York: Ktav, pp. 30–74.

Levenson, J.D. (1993) *The Hebrew Bible, the Old Testament and Historical Criticism. Jews and Christians in Biblical Study*, Louisville, KY: Westminster/John Knox Press

Loewe, R. (1990) 'Jewish exegesis' in R.J. Coggins and J.L. Houlden (eds) *Dictionary of Biblical Interpretation*, pp. 345–54, London: SCM Press

Longenecker, R.N. (1975) *Biblical Exegesis in the Apostolic Period*, Grand Rapids: Wm B. Eerdmans Publishing Co.

McKane, W. (1989) *Selected Christian Hebraists*, Cambridge: Cambridge University Press

McKane, W. (1970) *Proverbs*, London: SCM Press

McKnight, E.V. (1985) *The Bible and the Reader. An Introduction to Literary Criticism*, Philadelphia: Fortress Press

MacMullen, R. (1984) *Christianizing the Roman Empire AD 100–401*, Newhaven: Yale University Press

Magie, D. (translated) (1979–82) *Scriptores Historiae Augustae*, 3 vols, Cambridge, MA: Loeb Classical Library

Malamat, A. (1973) 'The Aramaeans' in D.J. Wiseman (ed.) *Peoples of Old Testament Times*, Oxford Clarendon Press

Midrash on Psalms, English translation by W.G. Braude, 2 vols, Newhaven: Yale University Press

Midrash Rabbah (1939), H. Freedman and M. Simon (eds), 10 vols, London: Soncino

Millard, A. (1995a) 'The knowledge of writing in Iron Age Palestine', *Tyndale Bulletin*, (46)2: 207–16

Millard, A. (1995b) 'Latin in first century Palestine' in *Solving Riddles and Untying Knots. Biblical, Epigraphic and Semitic Studies in Honor of Jonas C. Greenfield*, Z. Zevit, S. Gitin and M. Sokoloff (eds), pp. 451–8, Winona Lake IN: Eisenbrauns

Millard, A. (1982) 'In praise of ancient scribes', *Biblical Archaeologist*, Summer, 143–53

Miller, F. (1993) *The Roman Near East 31 BC–AD 33*, Cambridge, MA: Harvard University Press

Mitchell, A.C. (1997) 'Greet the friends in my name: New Testament evidence for the Greco-Roman *topos* on friendship' in *Greco-Roman Perspectives on Friendship*, John T. Fitzgerald (ed.), Atlanta: Scholars Press

Moeller, W.O. (1973) *The Mithraic Origin and Meanings of the ROTAS-SATOR Square*, Leiden: E.J. Brill

Montefiore, C.G. and Loewe, H. (eds) (1963) *A Rabbinic Anthology*, New York: Schocken

Morley, J. (1988) *All Desires Known*, London: Collins

Moscati, S. (ed.) (1964) *An Introduction to the Comparative Grammar of the Semitic Languages*, Wiesbaden: Otto Harrassowitz

Muraoka, T. (1994) 'Bible translation: the ancient versions' in R. E. Asher (ed.) *Encyclopedia of Language and Linguistics*, vol. 1, pp. 349–51, Oxford: Pergamon Press

Neusner, J. (1994) *Introduction to Rabbinic Literature,* New York: Doubleday

Nicene and Post-Nicene Fathers, Series 1, Augustine and Chrysostom, 14 vols (1886–9); Series 2, Cappadocians and others, 14 vols (1890–1900), reprinted Peabody, MA, 1994

Niditch, S. (1996) *Oral Word and Written Word. Ancient Israelite Literature*, Louisville, KY: Westminster /John Knox Press

Perrin, N. (1970) *What is Redaction Criticism?* London: SPCK

Pesikta Rabbati, English translation by W.G. Braude (1968), Newhaven: Yale University Press

Philo, with an English translation by F.H. Coulson and G.H. Whitaker (1954), Cambridge, MA: Loeb Classical Library

Plato, *Charmides, Alcibiades*, with an English translation by W.R.M. Lamb (1927), Cambridge, MA: Loeb Classical Library

Plato, *Cratylus, Parmenides*, with an English translation by H.N. Fowler (1926), Cambridge, MA: Loeb Classical Library

Plato, *Euthyphro, Apology, Crito, Phaedo, Phaedrus*, English translation by H.N. Fowler (1914), Cambridge, MA: Loeb Classical Library.

Plautus, *Amphitryo, Bacchides*, English translation by P. Nixon (1916), Cambridge, MA: Loeb Classical Library

Plautus, *The Little Carthaginian (Poenulus)*, English translation by P. Nixon (1932), Cambridge, MA: Loeb Classical Library

Plinius Secundus, Caius, *Natural History*, English translation by H. Rackman (1938), London: Heineman, Loeb Classical Library

Polzin, R. (1993) *Moses and the Deuteronomist. A Literary Study of the Deuteronomistic History, Part 1. Deuteronomy, Joshua and Judges*, New York: Seabury Press

Polzin, R. (1980) *Moses and the Deuteronomist. A Literary Study of the Deuteronomistic Source*, New York: Seabury Press

The Postmodern Bible, The Bible and Culture Collective (1995), Newhaven: Yale University Press

Pritchard, J.B. (ed.) (1969a) *Ancient Near Eastern Texts Relating to the Old Testament*, New Jersey: Princeton University Press

Pritchard, J.B. (ed.) (1969b) *Ancient Near Eastern Pictures Relating to the Old Testament*, New Jersey: Princeton University Press

Quintilian, *Institutio Oratoria*, English translation by H.E. Butler, 4 vols (1979–86), Cambridge, MA: Loeb Classical Library

Rabinowitz, I. (1993) *A Witness Forever. Ancient Israel's Perception of Literature and the Resultant Hebrew Bible*, Bethesda, Maryland: CDL Press

Ray, J. (1994) 'Literacy and language in Egypt in the Late and Persian Periods' in A.K. Bowman and G. Woolf (eds) *Literacy and Power in the Ancient World*, pp. 51–66, Cambridge: Cambridge University Press

Roberts, C.H. (1970) 'Books in the Graeco-Roman World and in the New Testament' in P.R. Ackroyd and C.E. Evans (eds) *Cambridge History of the Bible*, 1: 48–66, Cambridge: Cambridge University Press

Rogerson, J. and Davies, P.R. (1989) *The Old Testament World*, Cambridge: Cambridge University Press

Roux, G. (1966) *Ancient Iraq*, Harmondsworth: Penguin

Rowland, C.C. (1985) *Christian Origins. An Account of the Setting and Character of the Most Important Messianic Sect of Judaism*, London: SPCK

Saenz-Badillos, A. (1993) *A History of the Hebrew Language*, translated by J. Elwolde, Cambridge: Cambridge University Press

Samarin, W.J. (1972) *Tongues of Men and Angels. The Religious Language of Pentecostalism*, New York and London: Macmillan

Sampson, G. (1985) *Writing Systems. A Linguistic Introduction*, London: Hutchinson

Sanders, E.P. (1985) *Jesus and Judaism*, London: SCM Press

Sarna, N.M. (1991) *Exodus*, Philadelphia: Jewish Publication Society

Sasson, J.M. (1976) 'Wordplay in the Old Testament' in K.R. Crim (ed.) *Interpreter's Dictionary of the Bible, Supplementary Volume*, pp. 968–70, Atlanta: Abingdon Press

Sawyer, D.F. (1993) *Midrash Aleph Bet*, Atlanta, GA: Scholars Press

Sawyer, J.F.A. (ed.) (1997) *Reading Leviticus. A Conversation with Mary Douglas*, Sheffield: Sheffield Academic Press

Sawyer, J.F.A. (1996) *The Fifth Gospel. Isaiah in the History of Christianity*, Cambridge: Cambridge University Press

Sawyer, J.F.A. (1990a) 'The "original meaning of the text" and other legitimate subjects for semantic description', *Continuing Questions in Old Testament Method and Theology*, revised M. Vervenne (ed.), pp. 63–70, 210–12, Leuven: J. Peeters

Sawyer, J.F.A. (1990b) 'yš' in J. Botterweck and H. Ringgren (eds) *Theological Dictionary of the Old Testament*, translated by D. Green, 5: 441–63, Grand Rapids: Wm B. Eerdmans Publishing Co.

Sawyer, J.F.A. (1989) 'Daughter of Zion and servant of the Lord in Isaiah. A comparison' *J. Stud of the OT* 44: 89–107

Sawyer, J.F.A. (1986) 'The role of Jewish Studies in biblical semantics' in *Scripta signa vocis*, H.L.J. Vanstiphout (ed.), pp. 201–8, Gromingen: Egbert Forsten

Sawyer, J.F.A. (1973) 'Hebrew terms for the resurrection of the dead', *Vetus Testamentum* 23: 218–34

Sawyer, J.F.A. (1972) *Semantics in Biblical Research*, London: SCM Press

Sawyer, J.F.A. (1967) 'Root-meanings in Hebrew', *Journal of Semitic Studies* 12: 37–50

Scholem, G. (1965) *Jewish Gnosticism, Merkabah Mysticism and Talmudic Tradition*, New York: Jewish Theological Summary of America

Schuerer, E. (1979–87) *The History of the Jewish People in the Age of Jesus Christ (175 BC–AD 135)*, revised edn by G.Vermes, F. Millar and M. Black, 4 vols, Edinburgh: T. & T. Clark

Schultens, A. (1761) *Hebrew Origins or the most ancient nature and character of the Hebrew Language recovered from the interior of Arabia (Arabiae penetralibus revocata)*, Leiden: Luchtman

Schwartz, H. (1998) *Reimagining the Bible. The Story-Telling of the Rabbis*, Oxford: Oxford University Press

Septuaginta (1931–), Göttingen: Vandenhoeck & Rupprecht

Sherwood, Y. (1996) *The Prostitute and the Prophet. Hosea's Marriage in Literary Theoretical Perspective*, Sheffield: Sheffield Academic Press

Sifre Deuteronomy, English translation by R. Hammer (1986), Newhaven: Yale University Press

Singer, S. (1892) *Authorized Daily Prayer Book*, revised edn by J.H. Hertz, London: Eyre & Spottiswoode

Smith, W. Cantwell (1993) *What is Scripture? A Comparative Approach*, London: SCM Press

Staniforth, M. (ed.) (1968) *Early Christian Writings*, Harmondsworth: Penguin

Strack, H.L. (1931) *Introduction to the Talmud and Midrash*, New York: Jewish Publication Society

Suetonius, with an English translation by J.C. Rolfe (1924), Cambridge, MA: Loeb Classical Library

Tacitus, *Annals*, English translation by J. Jackson (1986), Cambridge, MA: Loeb Classical Library

Talmon, S. (ed.) (1991) *Jewish Civilisation in the Hellenistic-Roman Period*, Sheffield: Sheffield Academic Press

Tompkins, J.P. (ed.) (1980) *Reader Response Criticism: From Formalism to Post-Structuralism*, Baltimore: Johns Hopkins

Trachtenberg, J. (1939) *Jewish Magic and Superstition*, New York: Meridian Books

Trevett, C. (1996) *Montanism. Gender, Authority and the New Prophecy*, Cambridge: Cambridge University Press

Trible, P. (1984) *Texts of Terror. Literary Feminist Readings of Biblical Narrative*, Philadelphia: Fortress Press

Turcan, R. (1996) *The Cults of the Roman Empire*, English translation, Oxford: Blackwell

Ullendorff, E. (1968) *Ethiopia and the Bible*, London: British Academy

Vermes, G. (1997) *The Complete Dead Sea Scrolls in English*, Harmondsworth: Penguin

Vermes, G. (1973) *Jesus the Jew. A Historian's Reading of the Gospels*, London: Collins

Vermes, G. (1970) 'Bible and Midrash: early Old Testament exegesis' in P.R. Ackroyd and C.E. Evans (eds) *Cambridge History of the Bible*, 1: 199–231, Cambridge: Cambridge University Press

Virgil, with an English translation by H.R. Fairclough (1986), vol. 1, *Eclogues, Georgics, Aeneid, Books 1–6*, Cambridge, MA: Loeb Classical Library

Vroom, H.M. and Gort, J.D. (eds) (1997) *Holy Scriptures in Judaism, Christianity and Islam. Hermeneutics, Values and Society*, Amsterdam: Rodopi

Warmington, B. (1964) *Carthage*, London: Penguin

Watson, F. (ed.) (1993) *The Open Text. New Directions for Biblical Studies?*, London: SCM Press

Weinfeld, M. (1992) 'Deuteronomy' in *ABD* 1: 165–80

Weitzman, M. (1994) 'Judaism' in R. E. Asher (ed.) *Encyclopedia of Language and Linguistics*, 4: 1827–31, Oxford: Pergamon Press

Whybray, R.N. (1965) *Wisdom in Proverbs. The Concept of Wisdom in Proverbs 1–9*, London: SCM Press

Widengren, G. (1973) 'The Persians' in D.J. Wiseman (ed.) *Peoples of Old Testament Times*, Oxford: Clarendon Press

Wiles, M.F. (1970) 'Origen as biblical scholar' in P.R. Ackroyd and C.E. Evans (eds) *Cambridge History of the Bible*, 1: 454–88, Cambridge: Cambridge University Press

Williams, C.G. (1981) *Tongues of the Spirit. A Study of Pentecostal Glossolalia and Related Phenomena*, Cardiff: University of Wales

Wiseman, D.J. (ed.) (1973) *Peoples of Old Testament Times*, Oxford: Clarendon Press

Woolf, G. (1994) 'Power and the spread of writing in the west' in A.K. Bowman and G. Woolf (eds) *Literacy and Power in the Ancient World*, pp. 84–98, Cambridge: Cambridge University Press

Ya'ari, A. (1958) *Studies in Hebrew Booklore* (in Hebrew), Jerusalem: Kirjal-Stephen

Yadin, Y. (1971) *Bar-Kokhba. The Rediscovery of the Legendary Hero of the Last Jewish Revolt against Imperial Rome*, London: Weidenfeld & Nicolson

Young, F. (1997) *Biblical Exegesis and the Formation of Christian Culture*, Cambridge: Cambridge University Press

INDEX

Aboth, Sayings of the Fathers 68–9, 97–8
abracadabra 124
abstract terms 91–3, 120–1
acronyms, *see* notarikon
acrostic 125, 144
Adam 37, 122, 163 167
Aeschylus 113, 145, 148, 167–8
Aesop 143
Afro-Asiatic 11, 16
aggadah 158
Akiba, Rabbi 4, 30, 57, 60, 62, 65–7, 104, 111, 122–3, 125, 150–1
al tiqre 157
Alexander the Great 12, 32, 80, 167
Alexandria 5, 8, 18, 34, 45, 62, 66, 82, 88, 147–50, 156
allegory 148–51, 157, 160–1
alphabet 48–50, 53, 80, 109, 125–6, 144, 163
Amenemope, Sayings of 101
Amos 103, 146, 158
amulets 123–4
anachronisms 49, 97
angels 25–6, 37, 41, 104–5, 119, 121
ankh-sign 16
Antioch 45, 149

Apuleius 31, 122
Aquila 83, 90, 121
Arad 49
Aramaic 12–15, 23, 27, 35–7, 42, 47, 51–2, 54, 70–2, 79–82, 83–6, 122
Arianism 160
Aristarchus of Samothrace 148–9
Aristophanes 145
Aristotle 18, 33, 45–6, 131, 139, 145
Armenia, Armenian 11, 17, 22, 55, 57, 88, 170
Arnobius 149
Arval brothers 24, 38, 83
Ashoka 14
Assyrian 15, 47, 80
atbash 127–8
Athens 45, 129, 147, 152
Atticus 61
Augustine 14, 20, 79, 138, 141, 152, 160
Augustus 21, 35, 38, 46, 61, 102, 113, 153–4, 168
Avesta, Avestan 17, 23–4, 39–40, 47–8, 55–6, 74–5, 155–6, 164, 169–70

Babel, Tower of 26, 31, 85
Babylonian Talmud, *see* Bavli

Bacchus 41
Bar Kokhba 59
Baraita 68
barbarian 4, 13, 30, 33
Barr, J. 91, 116
bat qol 107, 151
Bavli 70
Ben Zoma, Simon 131, 151
Biblical languages 1, 113, 116
Biblical studies 1–3, 5–6
bilingualism 8–9, 21, 25, 43, 79, 131
binyan ab 157
blasphemy 121
book trade, book manufacture 8, 44, 56–7, 61, 77, 109–10, 168; books, distrust of 46–8
borrowing, see loanwords
Boyarin, D. 2
British and Foreign Bible Society 166–7
Brown , P. 2

Caesarea 46, 62, 69, 73, 147
Cairo Geniza 63, 110
calligraphy 48
calque, see semantic borrowing
canon 5, 56, 59–60, 66, 110
canonization 59–75, 168–9
carmen saeculare 38, 154
Cato the Censor 21, 129
cautionary tales 25, 64, 111
Celsus 46, 69–70
Celtic 17, 19, 39
Christian names 117–19
Church Latin 22, 37
Church of the Holy Sepulchre 169
Cicero 21, 37, 46, 61, 79. 131, 139–40, 155
Clement of Alexandria 150
Clement of Rome 38, 71–2, 86, 147

codex 56, 74
Codex Vaticanus 74
commentary 68–70, 78, 148, 154–6
comparative linguistics 115
conservatism 8, 25–6, 28, 164–6
Constantine 16, 22, 39, 55, 69–70, 75, 119, 160
Constantinople 86
Coptic 16, 22, 34, 87–8
copying 8, 28, 61, 145
covenant 53–4, 135
creation 26, 105, 109, 119, 125–6, 149, 155, 160, 162
cult-text 5
cuneiform 15, 47, 49–50

Dahood, M. 116
Daniel 81, 100, 103
Daube, D. 1
David 53, 98, 108
Davies, W.D. 1
de Mille, Cecil B. 53
Dead Sea Scrolls 2, 6–7, 26, 30, 52, 56–8, 62, 66, 72, 121, 158–9, 164
Deborah 136–7
Decalogue see Ten Commandments
deferential language 131–2
Delphi 35, 106–7, 136, 152
Demosthenes 130–1, 139–40
denunciations 138–41
derash 157–8
Deuteronomy 54, 134–5
Dio Cassius 46, 60
Dionysus 41
disciples 41, 72, 144–7
divination 152
divine inspiration 8, 102, 106–9
divine name 25, 119, 126–7, 162–3 see also tetragrammaton
Douglas, M. 3, 134

Driver, G.R. 116
druids 7, 19, 47

Ecclesiastes 47, 64–5, 98, 101, 110
Ecclesiasticus 31, 52, 54, 63, 66,
    79, 101, 106, 121, 130
education 3, 18, 20, 24, 32, 54, 77,
    101, 168
Egyptian 16, 49, 87–8, 118
Elamite 11, 17
Elephantine papyri 51
Eliezer ben Hyrcanus, Rabbi 106–
    7, 151
Elijah 107–8, 151
Enoch 62–3, 66–7, 71, 94–5, 100,
    102–3
Ephesus 46, 73
Ephphetha 83, 123
Ephrem the Syrian 87
Essenes 55, 156
Esther 52, 56, 64–5, 118
Ethiopic 15–16, 34, 67, 88
Etruscan 19, 139
etymology 8, 114–17, 119, 157,
    163
euphemism 162–3
Eusebius 60, 62, 83, 87, 100
Excitable Speech 137
Execration Texts 140
exegetai 152
Ezekiel 64, 110–11, 145
Ezra 98, 109–10

Fasti 59, 154–5
fescennini 139
finger of God 52
Five Books of Moses 48–9, 51, 145
Frumentius 88–9
fulfilment 74, 84, 159–60
fundamentalism 109

Galatia 17,19, 73

Galen 46, 63, 100
Galilaeans 31, 84, 139
Garshuni 87
Gathas 39–40, 75
Gaulish 19, 55
Ge'ez 16, 34, 88, 90
gematria 8, 48, 126–7, 157, 163
gender 113–14, 136–8, 167
Genesis Apocryphon 27
German 20, 93–4
Gezer calendar 50
gezerah shawah 157
globalization 167–7
glossolalia 8, 24, 40–3, 107
gnostics 59, 73, 124, 149
Goodman, M. 1
Gospel 73, 99
Goths, Gothic 20, 22, 55, 57, 88–
    9, 94
graffiti 44, 50, 144–5
Greek 10, 17–22, 31–5, 37–9, 82–
    6, 89–95, 147–8, 168–70
Greek Bible 66, 71–4

Habakkuk 145, 159
Hadrian 22, 32, 46, 60, 62–3, 77,
    83, 152, 168
halakhah 158
Ham, Hamitic languages 10–11,
    16
Hamito-Semitic, see Afro-Asiatic
Hanina ben Teradion 106
Hebrew 11–13, 17–18, 23, 26–30,
    39, 89–94, 157, 166
Hebrew mind 7, 91–3
Heraclitus 145
hermenutical rules 148–9, 156–8
Hermes 79, 112
Herodotus 18, 145, 167
Hesiod 18, 34 148
Hexapla 90–1, 147–8
Hezekiah 49–50, 145

hieroglyphics 4, 16, 49–50
Hillel 98, 148–9, 156
Hippocratic corpus 60, 63
Hittite 17, 139
Homer 5, 18, 34, 46, 61, 63–4, 112–13, 145, 148, 151
Horace 46, 61, 129, 139, 154
Hosea 146, 159
hymns 5, 37–40, 49, 59, 63–4 , 75, 83, 87, 164

imitation, see mimesis
incantation 37, 123–4
inclusive language 167
Indo-European 16–17, 90–2
interpretation 8, 40–2, 79, 143–61
intertextuality 74, 161
ipsissima verba 76, 79, 83–6, 99, 143–4, 151, 161, 165
Irenaeus 151, 157, 160
Isaiah 41, 53, 56, 72, 83, 103–4, 107, 117, 122, 130, 140–2, 144–6, 159–61
Ishmael, Rabbi 156–7
Isidore of Seville 79
Isis 16, 21, 35, 87

Jamnia see Yavneh
Japheth 10–11, 83
Jeremiah 41, 53, 103, 127–8, 130, 145
Jerome 38, 85, 90, 109, 143, 151, 160, 166
Jerusalem 10, 84–5, 145
Jerusalem Bible 115–16
Jerusalem Talmud see Yerushalmi
Jesus 25, 64, 72–3, 76–7, 83–6, 99, 103, 107, 122–3, 129, 144, 146, 159–60, 163, 165
Jewish studies 1, 5
Job, Book of 59, 97
Job, Targums of 27, 36, 81

John Chrysostom 141, 149, 151
Josephus 32–3, 62, 64, 148
Joshua 52
Jubilees, Book of 63–4, 66–7, 94–5
Judah the Prince , Rabbi 32, 67–9, 73, 169
Judas Maccabaeus 52
Julius Caesar 21, 47, 131
Justin Martyr 73, 86, 141
Juvenal 33

ketib 57–8
King James Authorized Version of the Bible 24, 94, 165
koine Greek 9, 18, 33, 79

language learning 54
language science 38, 114–16
language skill 130–1
Latin 13–14, 18–22, 37–9, 55, 165, 170
Law and the Prophets. the 52, 73, 159–60
Leviticus 54, 111, 133
libraries 8, 44–6, 51, 60–1, 85–6, 145
Lilith 122
linguistic vulnerability 137–8, 142
lips 108, 130, 141
literacy 5, 25, 44–58, 144–5
literal interpretation 148–50
loanwords 39, 68, 93–4, 155, 167
Luther, Martin 59, 93–4, 166
Lycaonian 10, 17

Maccabees, Books of 4, 51–2
Maecenas 61
magi 39–40, 46–7, 75, 77, 136, 155–6, 164–5, 169
magic 16, 122–6, 155
mamona 83
Mandaean 15

maranatha 37, 122
Marcion 59–60, 62, 73–4, 157, 169
Marcus Aurelius 46, 69
martyrdom 104, 106, 122
masoretes 30, 48, 57–8, 164
Massada 63
meditation 3, 42–3
megillah 56
Meir, Rabbi 60, 67, 131, 151, 169
memory, *see also* mnemonic 144
Mesrop 17, 55, 88–9
middot, *see* hermeneutical rules
Midrash 70, 78, 96, 150–1, 157–9
Miller, F. 1
  mimesis 61, 101, 132
Mishnah 27, 55, 62–3, 67–70, 97, 169
missionaries 8, 85, 166–7
Mithraism 35, 125
mnemonic 24, 60
Montanism 108, 136, 138
Mordecai 118
Moses 48–9, 52, 83, 97, 102–7, 117–18, 122, 130, 134, 148–9, 161
Muratorian fragment 62, 71, 169
mystery religion 4, 16, 31, 35, 152
mysticism 16, 48, 111

Nabataean 12, 15,
Nag Hammadi 2, 16
nationalism 8, 25, 29, 56, 65, 146
Nehemiah 28, 51, 81
New English Bible 115–16
New Revised Standard Version 167
Noah 10–11, 31
notarikon 128, 157
number of the beast 126

oracle 21, 31, 35, 49, 61, 152–4

Oral Torah 55, 67–9, 97, 104, 143–4, 156
orality 7, 46–8, 55, 68–70, 74–5, 80, 143–7
Origen 46, 85, 90–1, 109, 111, 147–8, 150–1, 161
original words, *see* ipsissima verba
Orpheus 100, 103
Orphic Hymns 5, 35, 63
Ovid 154–5, 161

Pahlavi 17, 40, 47, 57, 75, 155
Palmyra 15, 22
Papias 83
parables 54, 143, 147–8
parrhesia 129–30
Paul 17, 38, 40–1, 44–5, 47, 71, 73, 86, 102, 118, 129, 132–3, 136, 147–8, 150, 156, 165
Pella 45
Pentecost 11–12, 31, 40–1, 85
Pergamum 45–6, 147
Persian 17, 22, 39–40, 47, 155, 167
persuasion 131
peshat 157–8
pesher 158–9
Peshitta 2, 15, 82, 86, 151
Pharisees 65, 156
Philo 32, 41, 55, 87, 108, 148, 150, 156, 161
Phoenician 13, 24, 164
Phrygian 11, 17
Plato 18, 46–7, 112, 145, 148–9, 155
Plautus 34, 113
Pliny the Elder 38–9
plurality of meaning 150–2, 161
Plutarch 46, 62
pointing 57, 157
polemical language 58, 139–42, 163

Pompeii 38, 124–5
Porphyry 69–70
postal service 167–8
power of language 130–1, 137–8, 162–6, *see also* power of names, naming
power of names, naming 119–23, 162–3
prayer 28, 36–7, 42–3, 132, 142, 165, 167
Prayerbook Society 165
preaching 59, 130–1, 140, 165
preliterary stage 143–7
priests 25–6, 39–40, 47–8, 55, 77, 96, 120, 136, 145, 150, 155, 159, 164–5
prophecy, prophets 40–2, 53, 97–8, 102–7, 134, 136, 144–5, 152
Prophets, the 63–4, 6, 145–6
proverbs 54, 129, 148
Proverbs, Book of 130–1
Psalms 42, 53, 74, 98–9, 108, 116, 133, 145
pseudepigrapha 99–100
pseudolanguage 42–3
pseudonymity 8, 61–2, 99–102
Ptolemy 46, 63
Punic 13–14, 34, 39, 119
Pythagorean literature 5, 61, 100

Q 73–4
qal wa-homer 156–7
qere 57–8
Quintilian 101, 131, 139
Qumran, *see* Dead Sea Scrolls

rabbis 54–5, 136, 146–7, 151, 169
reception history 2, 74, 143, 161
register 131–2
Revised Standard Version 132
rhetoric 130–1
Rome 10, 37, 45–6, 73, 86, 152–5

root-meaning 116–17, *see also* etymology
Rosenzweig, F. 161
Rosetta Stone 16
ROTAS-SATOR square 124–5
runic 20

Sabaean 15
sacred language 4–5, 26–30, 90, 163, 165
sacred texts 48, 68–9, 78, 110, 151–2, 161, 163–5
Sadducees 65–6, 156
Salii 37
Samaria 49, 146
Samaritan 14–15, 29–30, 146, 164
Samson 118
Sanders, E.P. 1
Sanhedrin 98
Sappho 18, 145
Sassanids 39–40, 74–5, 155
Saul 41
Sayings of the Fathers, *see* Aboth
schools 8, 44, 49, 168
scribes 48, 53–4, 57–8, 80, 101, 104, 144–5, 164
scrolls 56, 105–6, 109–10, 145
semantic borrowing 39, 92–4
semantic range 92–4
Semitic languages 10–11, 90–2, 113
Sennacherib 12
Septuagint, (LXX) 2, 24, 30, 71–4, 82–3, 90–3, 98, 151
Sheba, Queen of 15
Sheffield 116
Shem 10–11
Sibylline Oracles , Sibylline Books 21, 31, 35, 59, 61, 76, 102–3, 126–7, 153–4, 164
silence 131
Siloam inscription 49

Sinai 31, 52, 69, 76, 97, 104–6
Sirach, *see* Ecclesiasticus
Socrates 112–13
Solomon 50–1, 53, 83, 98, 101, 144–5
Song of Songs 4, 64–5, 98, 111, 150–1
Sophocles 18, 145
sortes vergilianae 152
speaking in tongues, *see* glossolalia
stammer 130
state religion 39–40, 69–70, 75, 160, 170
study of the Torah 11
style 131–6
Summer Institute of Linguistics 166–7
Swedenborg, Emanuel 59
Syriac 15, 55, 57, 82, 87

Tacitus 20, 152
talitha kumi 37, 83
Talmud 14, 19, 55–7, 70, 96, 143–4, 150–1, 169
TaNaK 52
Targum 36, 54, 70–1, 80–2
Tatian 86
Tel Dan 49
Tel Deir Alla 50
Temple at Jerusalem 28, 53, 57, 61, 77, 109–10, 132, 145–6, 158–9
Temple of Jupiter 61, 152
Temple of Saturn 45
Temple Scroll 66
Ten Commandments 53, 135–6, 162
Tertullian 38, 86, 108, 138, 149, 151
tetragrammaton 58, 119–24, 163
Texts of Terror 137
teyqu 108

Theodore of Mopsuestia 104, 149
theophoric names 118–19
Theophrastus 131
Thomas, Gospel of 72–3, 102
Thucydides 18, 60, 145
tongue 24, 26, 40–3, 104, 129–30, 140
Torah 48–58, 63, 96–7, 102, 105–6, 114, 121, 156
Tosefta 68–9
translation 76, 95, 165–7
Trible, P. 167

Ugaritic 12, 116
Ulfilas 20, 55, 88–9, 94
unintelligibility 24, 37–8, 40–3

Vandals 20
vassal-treaties 53–4
verbal inspiration 108–9
Vermes, G. 1
vernacular 10, 32, 39, 72, 86–9, 155, 168, 170
Virgil 35, 46, 59, 61, 79, 152, 154
vocabulary 91–3, 115–17
Vulgate 166

Wirkungsgeschichte 2
Wisdom 160
Wisdom of Jesus ben Sira, *see* Ecclesiasticus
Wisdom of Solomon 61–2, 71, 87, 98, 101
word of God, word of the Lord 103, 106, 108, 162
word-games 125, 163
writing 44, 47–50, 53–5, 88–90, 145
Writings, the 52–3, 63–4, 66
Wycliffe, John 166

xenoglossy 42

Xenophon 18

Yavneh 59–60, 67, 169
Yerushalmi 70
Yochanan ben Zakkai, Rabban 110,
 125

Zand 40, 75, 155
Zarathustra, *see* Zoroaster
Zoroaster 39, 83, 103, 164,
 169
Zoroastrianism 17, 23, 34,
 39–40, 74–5, 77, 155–6